HOW TO EXPERIENCE BEAUTY AND NEW LIFE
IN DEAD AND DARK PLACES

MISTIE HOUSE

FOREWORD BY KIM WITCHER

Emergence

Copyright © 2021 by Mistie House

All rights reserved. No part of this publication may be reproduced, distributed, or transmitted in any form or by any means, including photocopying, recording, or other electronic or mechanical methods, without the prior written permission of the publisher, except in the case of brief quotations embodied in critical reviews and certain other noncommercial uses permitted by copyright law.

Unless otherwise noted, Scripture quotations are taken from the Holy Bible, New International Version®, NIV® Copyright ©1973, 1978, 1984, 2011 by Biblica, Inc.® Used by permission. All rights reserved worldwide.

Scriptures marked TPT are from The Passion Translation®. Copyright © 2017 by BroadStreet Publishing® Group, LLC. Used by permission. All rights reserved. thePassionTranslation.com

Scriptures marked AMP are from the Amplified Bible (AMP) Copyright © 2015 by The Lockman Foundation, La Habra, CA 90631. All rights reserved.

Scriptures marked ESV are from the English Standard Version (ESV) The Holy Bible, English Standard Version. ESV® Text Edition: 2016. Copyright © 2001 by Crossway Bibles, a publishing ministry of Good News Publishers.

Scriptures marked NLT are from the New Living Translation (NLT) Holy Bible, New Living Translation, copyright © 1996, 2004, 2015 by Tyndale House Foundation. Used by permission of Tyndale House Publishers, Inc., Carol Stream, Illinois 60188. All rights reserved.

Scriptures marked NLV are from the New Life Version (NLV) Copyright © 1969, 2003 by Barbour Publishing, Inc.

Scriptures marked VOICE are from The Voice (VOICE) The Voice Bible Copyright © 2012 Thomas Nelson, Inc. The Voice™ translation © 2012 Ecclesia Bible Society All rights reserved.

Scriptures marked MSG are from The Message (MSG) Copyright © 1993, 2002, 2018 by Eugene H. Peterson

Scriptures marked NKJV are from the New King James Version (NKJV) Scripture taken from the New King James Version®. Copyright © 1982 by Thomas Nelson. Used by permission. All rights reserved.

Distributed globally by Boss Media
New York | Los Angeles | London | Sydney

Author Photo by: www.BritNicolePhotography.com

Paperback ISBN: 978-1-63337-475-1
E-book ISBN: 978-1-63337-476-8
Library of Congress Control Number: 2021901972

Manufactured and printed in the United States of America

What Readers Are Saying About Emergence

Mistie House's *Emergence* is a wonderful read that will keep you glued to your seat as you find yourself immersed in the author's life's story—the good, the bad, and the ugly. You'll find yourself quickly bonding with Mistie as she takes you into her plights, tossing etiquette and embarrassment aside to show you how to turn the consequences of bad choices into victories. Although fairytales aren't realistic for most of us, *Emergence* delivers in giving much-needed hope that through Christ Jesus, we all can live a happily ever-after.

Sherrie Clark
Best-Selling and Award-Winning Author, Ghostwriter, Editor, and Publisher CEO, Storehouse Media Group
Communication Strategist and Speaker

"No doubt, Mistie House penned *Emergence* in the secret place, knowing firsthand the extravagant love of King Jesus. The One who rolls up His sleeves and chases after His Bride to free her from the enemy's lies . . . lies that leave her identity marred, lured into the illusion that the mirror has the power to define her beauty. Mistie's creative interlacing of a classic fairytale, scriptures, and her personal struggles all link to a redemptive love story. This book will awaken many hopeless hearts to their True Love—Jesus, where they too will discover how to mirror His face."

Reba Russell
Author, Executive Director and Pastor, Total Freedom Ministries

"In a time where women of all ages are bombarded with images and voices telling them who they should be and what they should want, Mistie reaches in and reveals what we were all made to long for . . . love. True love is not found in a fairytale; it is found in Jesus. *EMERGENCE* masterfully weaves together a well-known fairytale, her own story, and God's Word, and invites you to discover your story through the love of Jesus."

Tommy and Lana Spencer
Youth Pastors at The Church at Bushland

"Mistie has done an incredible job at weaving the truth of God's love and mercy into her own story. She is open and honest making herself vulnerable which is one of the greatest and bravest decisions we can make. She shares her journey with all its ups and downs, broken moments, and hope filled ones so that we can know the truth . . . no one is beyond the reach of God. He is always there ready to take us as we are, and heal us in order to give us a new life filled with hope for tomorrow. Thank you, Mistie, for having the courage to share your beautiful story. This will be a blessing to all especially those who feel they are beyond the reach and unworthy of God's grace and love."

Sarah Schurman
Sit Still My Daughter Ministry, Creator of
Sit Still My Daughter Magazine

Mistie's testimony in *Emergence* is powerful and creative. Her message strengthens the heart with the truth that a beautiful identity in Jesus is no fairy tale—it's real life! Mistie compassionately ministers through her storytelling and prayers. As you journey through this book, you will have an opportunity to discover transformation in your own life. What a gift!

Kim Witcher
Executive Pastor, Trinity Fellowship Church

What Readers Are Saying About Emergence	III
Dedication	VI
Foreword	VII
Introduction	VIII

SECTION I   THE FALL — 1
- Chapter 1   In the Beginning and Once Upon a Time — 3
- Chapter 2   The Lie and the Apple — 15

SECTION II   THE FALL OF THE NEXT GENERATION — 29
- Chapter 3   A New Found Paradise Slipping Away — 31
- Chapter 4   The Wages of Sin — 45
- Chapter 5   On Our Own — 61

SECTION III   THE RISE OF FREEDOM — 81
- Chapter 6   On My Own — 83
- Chapter 7   The Wishing Well — 95
- Chapter 8   My Gift from God — 109
- Chapter 9   Mirror, Mirror — 127
- Chapter 10   War with the Wind — 149
- Chapter 11   Deep in the Dark Forest — 169
- Chapter 12   Polished for Purpose — 181
- Chapter 13   Every Sheep Needs a Shepherd — 193
- Chapter 14   Bring Me Her Heart — 209

SECTION IV   PARADISE RESTORED — 227
- Chapter 15   The Father's Princess — 229
- Chapter 16   Heigh Ho! Let's Go! — 251
- Chapter 17   The Sleeping Death — 265
- Chapter 18   The One, The Only — 283
- Chapter 19   White as Snow — 301
- Chapter 20   Someday Our Prince Will Come — 327

A Royal Invitation	345
Acknowledgments: Rooted in Love and Gratitude	347
Let There Be Light	349
About The Author	351
Notes	352

Dedication

This book is dedicated to all those who have been longing, wishing, and dreaming for true love;

To all of those who have gone searching for love in all the wrong places, only to find rejection, abandonment, emptiness, and devastation;

To all those who have had their dreams stolen, their hearts broken, and their lives turned upside down;

To all those who have felt betrayed, enslaved, forgotten, or mistaken;

To all those who are lost, looking for answers, relief, freedom; and hope.

Look no further.

This book is also dedicated to my husband Chris (my miraculous gift from God), my precious daughters, and my amazing parents.

Above all, I dedicate this work to God, who has done and continues to do miraculous works in me, through me, and for me.

Foreword

The Bible tells us that we conquer the accuser by the blood of the Lamb and the powerful word of our testimony. Sharing the personal testimony of what Jesus has done in our own lives has immense power to defeat the enemy.

A testimony is much more than fact telling of a personal story. A testimony acknowledges and magnifies the transformational work of Jesus in our lives. A testimony honors Jesus for all of the miraculous, beautiful outcomes that can only be attributed to Him. These victorious outcomes give value to the challenging aspects of our experiences.

Jesus truly does make all things work together for the good of those who love Him and have been called according to His purpose. Mistie's testimony of her emergence is a beautiful example of how Jesus does just this! I highly respect Mistie's courageous vulnerability to share her testimony of emergence from a place of defeat into a place of brilliant victory. I have seen the beautiful evidence of a victorious life in Mistie throughout the years I have known her as a member of our church. She no longer shies back, but instead shines forward with beauty and grace as she leads other women into knowing their value and significance.

Mistie desires for you to also experience life with an awakened heart and an understanding of the truth of your beautiful identity in Jesus Christ! It is endearing to me that our Father God spoke to Mistie's heart through the symbolism of a classic fairy tale. Mistie's creative application and ministry throughout this book offer opportunity to identify with the characters and experience our own emergence with our King Jesus. Unlocking greater power in your testimony lies ahead as you apply the truths found in these pages!

Kim Witcher
Executive Pastor, Trinity Fellowship Church, Amarillo, Texas

Introduction

I recently had a dream of being broken down on the side of the road. I cried out and called for help. I then saw a man in the distance walking toward me. He came over to my car and began repairing it with his bare hands. He didn't have a single tool with him. After he finished, he got into the driver's seat and invited me to jump in the passenger side. Then he drove me safely back home.

The man was Jesus!

This is my story of how I found myself lost, stranded, broken down, and empty from the choices I made to venture out alone and go my own way. However, Jesus came to me in my time of need and brokenness as I cried out and called on Him for help. He came to my rescue and repaired my broken heart. Then He turned me around, navigating the way, leading me on a beautiful and miraculous journey safely back home with Him.

Jesus wants to do the same for you.

The purpose of this writing is not simply to share *my story*; my purpose is to share *my discovery*. I'm writing this book in hope that those who read it will also discover the path to their true love, identity, and purpose in Christ alone. There are many paths in life; inevitably, there are only two paths that matter. One path leads to life and the other to death.

I have traveled the wrong path that leads toward death and destruction, but I am here to say that it is never too late to stop and change your direction. I am now on the path that leads to life. That path is Jesus, and in Him, I am experiencing the abundant life I was created to live as I walk with Him daily, and our relationship grows. I can walk in freedom, knowing that the road ahead leads to good things because that is what His Word promises us.

> *"For I know the plans I have for you,"* declares the Lord, *"plans to prosper you and not to harm you, plans to give you hope and a future" (Jeremiah 29:11 NIV).*

My prayer is that throughout embarking upon this journey alongside me, you will evaluate your own life and determine which path you are on. It is my prayer that you would call on Him and allow Him to help repair your brokenness, fill your emptiness, and navigate the way to a full and blessed life.

On this journey, we'll travel through my life's ups and downs, revealing who I've met and what I've found. Along the way, I'll expose the consequences of my sin as I bit the apple and detoured from the path of life, and how those choices sought to steal, kill, and destroy my future. However, I will also reveal the outcome of grace and share how choosing to follow and obey God leads to freedom.

Throughout this journey, we'll look at the Word of God and how the stories throughout Scripture parallel with our own as followers of Jesus. In particular, we'll look at the fall of man in the Garden of Eden and the life of Christ, as well as explore the classic tale of *Snow White*.

Emergence is a call to bring to light and reveal that which is hidden and concealed, exposing the enemy's lies and revealing God's truth. As you set out on this hopeful journey, you'll discover through powerful revelations of God's Word that not only are there two paths we must choose between, but also that there are two opposing forces at work in the lives of all of God's children.

This writing is meant to demonstrate how life, in all its beauty and sorrow, has intention and, if correctly positioned, can result in a life of salvation, redemption, transformation, and resurrection. Peace, joy, and abounding love can be yours, not just for a lifetime, but for all eternity.

The promise of abundant life can be reclaimed for all those who choose to receive it.

> *"The thief comes only to steal and kill and destroy; I have come that they may have life, and have it to the full" (John 10:10 NIV).*

SECTION I

CHAPTER ONE

In The Beginning and Once Upon a Time

The story of *Snow White and the Seven Dwarfs* has always struck an enchanting chord with me. Perhaps it is because I find that I share much in common with this princess's delicious fairytale.[1] Perhaps you do too.

How so?

Follow me through this allegory as I weave three cords together—the classic tale of *Snow White*, biblical stories including Adam and Eve, and my own creative narrative.

Let's find out if your story somehow magically entwines with mine.

Dear beloved, you are a brilliant work of art designed by the Maker Himself. Come in close and hear what the Lord of all creation has to say to you, His greatest masterpiece.

In the beginning and once upon a time . . . God created the heavens and the earth. He formed mankind perfectly to walk and talk with Him in the Garden of Eden. He desired intimacy and union with His children then, and He desires the same with you and me today. His love for His creation is far beyond anything we could ever understand. God is working to draw us nearer to His heart. He wants us to discover His love so He may reveal our true identity and purpose for existing as we receive Him into our lives.

Emergence

For we are His workmanship [His own master work, a work of art], created in Christ Jesus [reborn from above—spiritually transformed, renewed, ready to be used] for good works, which God prepared [for us] beforehand [taking paths which He set], so that we would walk in them [living the good life which He prearranged and made ready for us] (Ephesians 2:10 AMP).

To set the scene of this wild adventure you and I are about to set out upon, I first want to take you on a short back road and visit the lives of the people I grew up around and the environment I grew up in. So, picture yourself jumping in whatever luxury vehicle, sporty coupe, classic hot rod, or royal carriage that makes you most comfortable. Buckle your seat belts, crank up the tunes, put on your shades, or draw your horses for you carriage, and let's get rolling!

I was just a small-town girl, which is a huge overstatement.

I grew up in a small community rather than a town, in the middle of nowhere in Oklahoma. So imagine spectacular sunsets in the evenings, grassy fields sprinkled with flowers, and rustic dirt roads. The only neighbors we had within miles were my precious grandparents. They were farmers and the hardest working people I have ever known. I admired them so much. Some of my most precious childhood memories were captured in their wonderful two-story white house trimmed with floral accents and bordered with elm trees. We'll get to some of those memories in a bit.

My grandma was the cutest little lady with soft gray hair that curled just right. She was full-blooded Italian, but you would never know it. Her parents never taught her to speak Italian because they didn't want her to have broken speech, which saddens me. It would have been nice to have learned the language from her.

She was the kindest person in the world, gentle, soft-spoken, modest, and loved the Lord. So much of my Christian upbringing is attributed to her. I absolutely adored her, and spending time at her house was always a treat. One reason for this was that she had a sweet tooth just like I did. So, we were always getting into the sugar. We would make delicious chocolate pudding or my all-time favorite— her famous caramel meringue pie. During the holidays, her enclosed front porch would be lined with an assortment of homemade cookies, candies, fudge, puddings, and meringue pies. It was like something

In The Beginning and Once Upon a Time

out of *Willy Wonka's Chocolate Factory*. It was so tempting to dive right in. Many times, I nearly reached down to pull off all of the fluffy meringue peaks one by one and make them mysteriously disappear.

I might have a slight obsession for marshmallow-like substances. Often times, I would get in to trouble for sneaking into the pantry and eating entire jars of marshmallow cream my mom intended to use for baking. Also, I might have gotten caught roasting marshmallows on our electric stove top. And I had no problem eating meringue raw and actually preferred it that way.

One of my favorite treats to make at Grandma's famous factory was ice cream shakes. She had several different bottles of flavoring to choose from, such as butter pecan, cherry, maple, and butterscotch. Once we finally worked up our sugary vice, we would hop into the green bomb (which was her huge olive-green car), and drive out to deliver a shake to Grandpa while he worked in the field. The whipped cream and sprinkles topping were when she would let me sit on her lap and drive the bouncy green bomb once we were safely in the field. The cherry on top of this adventure was when Grandpa let me ride on his lap and drive the tractor. They did this for all their many kids and grandkids. They were the best, and we were a blessed family.

I used to help my parents and grandparents tend to the farm. I fed chickens, plucked chickens, (not a fond memory), fed ducks, cows, pigs, and sheep. I helped my grandma cook, clean, garden, and occasionally can vegetables, jellies, and jams.

I helped my grandpa mow the large acreage. Once, I even buried the riding mower nearly halfway up to its neck in sand. I feared my grandpa was going to ring my own neck, and bury me with it, but he never even raised his voice. He was gentle, kind, and understanding throughout the entire process as he and my loving mom helped me dig it out. When we finished, we took it over to his shop where he had me blow it off with his air hose. He was great at teaching lessons and telling old stories.

Oh the shop! It had this amazing smell of oil, gasoline, and grease. My siblings and I loved to pretend there. For fun, we would often play shop. We would pull up on our bikes, ring the bell for service, and rummage through Grandpa's stuff, borrowing that same air hose, his tools, old gloves, cans of oil, and anything else we deemed useful to give our bikes a tune up. In all honesty, we probably borrowed a little too frequently. He probably always wondered how he went through a can of oil so quickly. Shhh, don't tell!

My grandparents were truly special people.

My parents were the coolest parents growing up. They were young, adventurous, and fun. Mom was stunning and looked the part of an Italian beauty with long, dark hair, olive skin, a slender figure, and beautiful blue-gray eyes. She was also very creative and could make something out of nothing. She was great at making Halloween costumes. My favorite was when she made my sister a Strawberry Shortcake outfit with a cute little strawberry bonnet and skirt, and she made me an adorable gray bunny costume with white ears made out of pipe cleaners. She even gave me a carrot to complete the look. It was so cute and eventually was passed down to my younger brother.

Mom had a great imagination. Sometimes she would plan themed-dinner nights. My top favorite was Chinese night. We would go to the grocery store and buy an assortment of canned Chinese foods, frozen eggrolls, and fortune cookies. We didn't have any Chinese restaurants nearby, so we had to take what we could get and make the best of it. Then we would go home and surround our coffee table with pillows on the living room floor and wait for Dad to come home to surprise him. We would all dine together cross-legged on the floor with chopsticks in hand and pretend we were in another place. The food was terrible, but the experience was truly magical and unforgettable. When growing up in little places, you learn to pretend a lot.

My mom also loved music. When dad was working, we would often blast the stereo and dance around the house. Our home was just like a scene from the movie *Mermaids*, where the mother, played by Cher, and the daughters would sing, dance, and have the time of their lives while acting like complete dorks together. This was our crazy Italian family. And it was awesome! I grew up listening to all kinds of music (pop, rock, country, and Christian). You name it, we sang it, from Cher, Roxette, The Cranberries, and Whitney Houston, to Ace of Base, Point of Grace, Michael Jackson, and Alan Jackson. We sang Garth Brooks's anthems, belted out Mariah Carey's ballads, and danced to Paula Abdul's latest hits. We worshiped faithfully to gospel hymns and sweated religiously to jock jams. Music, singing, and dancing, have *always* held a special place in our hearts. I can't remember a time without it.

In The Beginning and Once Upon a Time

My dad was a lot of fun as well when he was home and not working. In addition to being an outdoorsman who loved to fish, hunt, and camp, he was also a black belt in Taekwondo and even instructed classes for a while. I loved being able to spout off that my dad was a black belt—talk about bragging rights. That was the best. He taught my sister and me a self-defense demonstration that we got to perform in front of the community. We wore our tiny karate uniforms with our little white belts and we got to publicly kick our dad's rear. It was amazing.

Dad was also very talented. He was a great country singer, and he and his band performed gigs all over the region. They had a CD and T-shirts, and they performed at our local dances. I was so proud to watch him sing on stage. I would eagerly wait until intermission with the hopes of getting to dance with my handsome daddy, who also happened to be a great dancer and entertainer. He lit up on stage like a shining star.

My siblings were also a lot of fun . . . most of the time. Siblings have their moments.

My older sister was the guardian and was the mature one who loved to sit and listen to the adult conversations rather than run around and play. She was very responsible and always looked out for us. If anyone tried to mess with us, she had our backs, and trust me, you did *not* want to get on her bad side. While in the fifth grade, I cried in the gym locker room because I was told that someone had said something mean about me. My sister, a year and a half older, found out about it. She marched straight up to the round, bald offender with a crazy temper and told that man off to his face. Of course, he blew up and followed after her charging into the girls' locker room denying what was said. I was hunched down against the wall hugging my knees while the two of them went at it, yelling back and forth. It was terrifying. My sister was my hero in that moment. However, looking back, the funny thing about it was that my sister was so quick to jump on anyone who bullied us around. I later discovered the reason for this was because as the oldest, she felt that was *her* job.

My younger sister was the entertainer. When she was around five years old, nearly every day she dressed up in a fancy mauve dress that she had worn in our cousin's wedding when she was their flower girl. She was always off by herself and singing opera at the top of her lungs. We always teased her that she was adopted because she was the only one of us kids with dark hair. Don't get me wrong; she was beautiful.

We just liked to tell her we didn't know where she came from to get under her skin.

She was four years younger than me and drove me crazy at the time. I found it extremely annoying how she always wanted to be involved in whatever I was doing.

My cousin, who was my age, came to stay with us one summer. We were really close and loved hanging out together. One day we drove our minivan to our mailbox to get the mail. Since I was only around thirteen, this was a big deal since it was about a half-mile away. Driving the minivan and cranking up the music was, sadly, the "cool" thing to do. Of course, my little rug rat sister wanted to tag along with us. We told her no, locked her out of the van, and took off down the desolate country road. While we were out, we zoomed off toward the mailbox and also grabbed my grandparents' mail for them. Unbeknown to us, my little sister, had walked over to their house. So when we were inside dropping off their mail, she snuck over to the back of the van and climbed up onto the bumper.

My cousin and I finished chatting with Grandma and hopped back into our ride and headed home, completely unaware of the mischievous cargo that had attached herself to the rear of the car. Despite my sister's attempt to hang on for dear life, she went tumbling off at the first minor bump we hit. We didn't realize what had just occurred and happily went on our way. However, my happiness was quickly altered once I arrived home and heard from my mother. She had just received a phone call from Grandma explaining what had happened. My poor little sister was now lying on my grandparents' couch with scrapes, bruises, and a minor concussion. Needless to say, this turned out *not* to be my "coolest" moment.

My little brother was the protector. He was the youngest and such a little cutie with blonde hair and big blue eyes. Because he was six years younger than me, I took care of him as a baby. He had a little silky-white pillow that he carried around with him everywhere. I would sneak into his room in the morning and peer through the railing of his crib while he slept on that pillow, waiting for him to wake up so that we could play. When he got a little older, he would dress up in one of our old Taekwon-do uniforms and pretend to fight off all the bad guys. He was so protective of his sisters as well as our grandma, walking her home through "the woods," as we called it, to make sure she got home safely.

In The Beginning and Once Upon a Time

The woods were awesome, consisting of rows of huge trees between our house and our grandparents' home. When our cousins came over, we would make super-cool forts to hide out in while playing "war." It was pretty exhilarating. We had the best time hiding out and constructing memories in those woods.

My little brother also had quite the little temper. When he got mad, he would overheat to boiling in an instant. At that point you had better run because it took a lot to cool him back down. Each of us watched from the window when one day, my dad literally took him outside and sat on him in the snow until he agreed to calm down and chill out. This little boy from "the woods" was cute and cuddly, but beware; he could go a little savage on you at any given moment.

As for me, I was the creative dreamer. I was the second-oldest and middle child and basically my older sister's sidekick. When we were little, we wore matching outfits. In college, everyone thought we were twins, except she had long and curly dark strawberry-blonde hair with green eyes, and I had long and straight ash-blonde hair with blue eyes. As children, we always wore our hair in cute pigtails and looked like little country bumpkins, except my pigtails stuck straight out because of my thin, fine hair.

If you met me today, you might never guess I grew up on a farm, but I promise you, those country roots still run deep.

I loved drawing cartoon characters as a kid and was attracted to anything artsy or creative. This must explain why I loved holidays and decorating so much. I would marvel at the warmth and excitement of Halloween and the wonder and beauty of Christmas. Making crafts and yummy treats was so magical to me. One of my favorite memories was when my mom got us green glowsticks for trick-or-treating. These were the thick green ones that shone brightly all night. There was just something about that bright green light that said Halloween to me. I think it reminded me of Frankenstein. I loved it. I would go trick-or-treating over to our grandparents' house and get bags filled with homemade goodies and best of all, my grandma's giant cherry popcorn balls!

Christmas time was magnificent. I could hardly wait to turn on the Christmas carols and pull out all of the wonderful decorations. I loved to crawl underneath the Christmas tree and look up at all of the colorful twinkling lights as they reflected off of each shimmering ornament. There was nothing quite as remarkable to me as the joy and excitement of the holidays.

Emergence

The older I got, however, the more exciting something else became for me—boys! I was *so* boy crazy. I will never forget how embarrassed I was when my kindergarten teacher addressed the class about kissing behind the building during recess. In fourth grade, I had *two* boyfriends at the *same* time. One day, we were riding the school bus, and I had one boy on each side of me. The girls in the bus started singing this made-up song, "Oh you can't get to heaven, being a two-timer." This was never a good thing.

This should have spoken to me early on and warned me to change my ways and stay away from boys. Unfortunately, it didn't.

In fact, my obsession with boys led me down a painful path. Nonetheless, this path also began a journey of discovering true love, identity, and purpose in my life.

Sit Tight

We are now going to switch gears and head down the main road. Here is where my story really begins. You might want to make sure your seatbelt is securely fastened because the winding road we're taking might get a little bumpy. At times, you might feel like you're on a roller-coaster ride and get a little carsick. In that case, just roll down the window, and let in some fresh air. *But be sure to hang in there, and remain seated until the end of the ride because I don't want you to miss out on where we're going.* The beauty of this expedition is found both in the journey as well as in the destination.

So hold on. This gutsy pilgrimage is going to be a royal ride to remember. *I promise you, in the end, you'll be glad you got in the carriage with me.*

Born Again

I remember the day I received salvation. I don't remember the date or even how old I was, probably third grade, but I remember the *moment* very well. I was at a Baptist summer church camp called G.A. Camp, which stood for Girls in Action.

As we sang the song, "I have decided to follow Jesus," I felt the pull in my heart to step out and come forward to the altar to receive Him into my life. I walked up front with tears rolling down my cheeks and told someone I wanted to confess that I was a sinner and that I wanted to receive Jesus into my heart as my Lord and Savior. This day marked my spiritual birthday.

I was born again!

> *If you declare with your mouth, "Jesus is Lord," and believe in your heart that God raised him from the dead, you will be saved (Romans 10:9 NIV).*

I have decided to follow Jesus. No turning back. No turning back.

Smaller Isn't Always Simpler

I grew up in a Christian home and church community and with the same kids all throughout attending our small public school where everyone knew each other. Our classes were so small that two grades were combined into one classroom. For instance, first and second graders shared one classroom. When my class was the older of the two, I loved school. I had a lot of friends and did my very best academically.

However, when in one of the lower grades, I didn't enjoy school as much because most of the older girls wouldn't accept me. One girl in particular seemed to have it out for our family, and she had a lot of pull with the other girls and succeeded at turning others against me. So instead, I looked to the boys for friendship and affection. They always seemed to like me a lot and it came easy for me to make friends with them. It was the downside to attending such a small school—not a lot of options.

This was tough on me growing up, and my siblings dealt with this as well. Every other year, I was either on top of the world or at the bottom of the food chain. During those latter years, I felt the sting of rejection. My self-esteem hit bottom as well as my performance at times, as every day for another year of school, I had to face those who didn't care for me. I believe it began to shape my desire to be accepted early on and my tendency to look toward boys to fill that empty space.

During my eighth-grade year, I had been a bubbly and joyful teenage girl. My best friend and I were nicknamed "Giggles 1" and "Giggles 2" because we were continuously laughing and having fun. We were inseparable.

Our school was very active in theater and often put on plays. One day after school, my friend and I decided to go into the auditorium and rummage through some of the costumes backstage. We found some big fancy dresses and just had to try them on. Then we paired them with animal heads to complete the look. The high school kids were having basketball practice, so we headed to the gymnasium and casually strolled in, parading our wild fashion ensembles and waving like we were beauty queens. Everyone stopped and stared, but no one said a word. She and I were goofy like that and didn't care what anyone thought of us. We were bold and fearless. All that mattered is that we were having fun and had smiles on our faces.

I loved basketball. The summer before my ninth-grade year, I practiced all the time, working hard to make one of the starting positions on the team. I had a plan and would do everything I could to make it happen.

Finally, I felt like I knew who I was. My appearance was changing as I morphed from a skinny stick figure to a slightly curvier shape, thanks to the little bit of weight I had gained. Glasses were replaced by contacts, and my teeth had been straightened by the braces I still wore. I had grown in my confidence and felt like I was becoming beautiful, and that I was finally accepted by others on a regular basis.

About this same time, I picked up and swallowed a tiny lie (a rotten seed) based on my experiences of how others treated me. It slowly began to warp my thinking—beauty equals acceptance, and acceptance equals love. Thus, a new obsession was being molded, shaped, and developed—the obsession to strive for (look to) beauty in order to feel loved and valued. This twisted entanglement was secretly tormenting me and holding me captive from becoming who I truly was, yet I was blind to it, new contacts and all.

Despite some tension at home, and my oblivion to recognize the sick seed I had ingested, life had begun looking up . . . up until the day it all came crashing down.

Broken Pieces

My dad was thirty years old when a tragic accident happened. He worked for the county. One day while putting in a cattle guard, some of my dad's coworkers decided to play a trick on him. They pushed over one of the loading ramps in the truck while he was standing near it to scare him. They assumed he was far enough out of the way. Sadly, they

In The Beginning and Once Upon a Time

assumed wrong, and the ramp came crashing down and fell on my dad, breaking his back. Dad lay there, pinned under that ramp in the cold, as light snow fell on his face. He was in pain and frightened, not knowing what the future would hold.

Fortunately, he wasn't paralyzed. Even so, my dad, once completely healthy, strong, and active, now had dropped to fifty-percent disability in a split-second. He was no longer able to continue living life the way he had previously. He lay in the hospital bed we had set up for him in our dining room with weights attached to it for traction. This tragic accident affected all of us. My hero who once taught us Taekwondo would no longer be able to instruct us. Work became much-more difficult for him. He was in and out of the hospital all the time with surgeries and injuries due to the accident. This also put a financial strain on my parent's marriage. My mom was now worried about money and fearful we were going to lose everything we owned.

My dad was doing the best he knew how at the time and given the circumstances. He was dealing with the reality of what had happened to him and that his mentality was shaken as well as his physicality. He was struggling to provide for his family of six at thirty years old, so he began to search for creative ways to make ends meet. He began singing and performing to bring in extra income. I also believe that this only added to the marital tension. My dad was gone a lot and often went alone to dances while my mom stayed behind with us kids.

My mom and dad who were once so much fun and loving were now fighting *all* the time. We would hear them arguing at night from our bedrooms. My mom grew increasingly depressed and shut everyone out for a while. They separated many times, and each time was heartbreaking.

Then the day came during my freshman year, when my dad woke my siblings and me up one morning to say . . . he was leaving for good.

My mom wanted a divorce.

CHAPTER TWO

The Lie and The Apple

The truth is that my mom still loved my dad, but she was done waiting for things to change. She had this idea in her mind that divorce was the only way to get through to him. Therefore, it was necessary to follow through. Granted, she also thought that after two years or so, if he changed during that time, they could possibly get remarried. She thought divorce was the only way to show him that she was serious. There were some who tried to talk her out of this idea, and others who supported it. Either way, she was convinced that divorce was the only option to bring about the change she hoped for. She knew things could not continue as they were for the sake of all our wellbeing. My dad told her plainly that if she divorced him, it was over. But she believed it was only a threat to keep her from pulling the plug on their marriage.

I understand now why she didn't believe the truth of the reality of the situation. I believe it was because she had been deceived in the past and had grown accustomed to hearing embellishments. Honest and open communication had been an issue in their marriage, so it perhaps makes sense as to why she didn't believe the boy who may have cried wolf too many times in his youth. Make no mistake, the enemy (Satan) plays off of our emotions as well as our past experiences to get us to fall for his latest fib. This is just one of many ways in which the enemy deceives us.

Emergence

According to the Merriam-Webster dictionary, *deceive* means to cause to accept as true or valid what is false or invalid.

This is what the enemy does to us all in such times. He comes to deceive, steal, kill, and destroy. He will say and do anything to break apart a marriage (especially a Christian marriage) using his own attractive exaggerations to decorate and beautify his fabricated stories. That is exactly what ended up happening.

My mom filed for divorce.

She believed that ending their marriage was the only way she could possibly save their marriage.

I will never forget the moment when my mom realized that my dad *had* been telling her the truth in this instance. *It was over if she filed for divorce.* He did move on. Now, any and all hope she had of reconciliation was shattered. It was in that moment that she realized her possible dream of reconciliation for the future was never coming true. She realized she had been deceived and lied to and that divorce hadn't solved her problems. Instead, it broke their union, and it broke my poor mother's heart.

Maybe a part of me wanted to believe the lie that divorce was the solution to fix all my parents' problems as well, and in that moment, we all blamed my dad for not making the illusion of reconciliation upon divorce a reality. I think we each secretly thought, believed, and hoped that our mom and dad might get remarried, so divorce in our minds wasn't the end. I guess we all took a bite of that apple after all. Each of us felt its sickening effects. Oh, how our stomachs ached in pain when our eyes were opened, and the truth was digested—it was over.

Now I understand that my dad was *not* the one to blame for this lie that promised delusionary hope. *Satan was.* Although my dad had bitten some apples in the past as well, he was honest and truthful with my mom about the consequences of divorcing him. He begged her not to go through with it. But because lies, secrecy, and sin had already created wedges between them, trust was broken, and the ability to discern truth was clouded. She bought the convincing lie from the enemy and made her choice to follow through, believing that in doing so, this was the *only way* her dream of having a happy future together could still *possibly come true.*

My parents were both Christians who loved the Lord. Even still, they were not immune to the enemy's attacks. None of us are.

The Lie and The Apple

Biting the Apple

Just as the enemy slithered into the Garden of Eden and deceived Eve, I believe he slithered into my mom's thoughts and deceived her as well as us all. This is what he does. He gets us alone and comes to us in our desperate time of need, weakness, brokenness, and vulnerability and offers "his twisted solution" to our problems. He plants a false vision of hope into our thoughts that promises all we desire. It is cruelty at its best. The enemy dangles a beautiful, juicy, ripe apple in front of us that appears promising, yet is filled with rotten deception. With his crafty tongue, he whispers that with one bite, all your dreams and heart's most inner desires will come true. He is so stealthy that he makes us believe it's our own idea. This is how we become victim to his evil plan.

I'm not suggesting in any way that the enemy's lie, nor my mom's decision, was *solely* responsible for the fall of my parents' marriage. There was *much*-more involved than that, and both my parents had a part to play in it. There were many problems, and neither of my parents handled things perfectly. Even though they sought out Christian counseling, they still couldn't work out their differences. I'm in *no way* judging or blaming either of them for that. I love my parents dearly and wish nothing more than to honor them. They both were hurting terribly and dealt with their pain in their own way, pushing one another further and further apart. I'm simply choosing to focus on this one issue—the enemy's deception.

Deception and lies create wedges between us and God as well as our spouse. And where there is space between us, there is wiggle room for the enemy. The closer we lean into God, the more the enemy is pushed out, leaving less room for sin, death, and destruction to operate.

That being said, I do believe the enemy's lie *helped* "encourage" my mom to follow through with the divorce by placing a pretty bow on the idea and embellishing what she could possibly gain through it. In other words, he dressed it up and made it look really good. He disguised it from what it really is—ugly! Divorce is ugly. There is no denying that truth. It is *never* pretty. Regardless of whether or not it *was* or *is* necessary; it is *always* painful.

I don't wish to focus on my parents' failures or mistakes in an attempt to make them look bad; rather, I wish to share a bit of their story as a testimony to help others see the enemy's tactics used to hurt God's children in times of pain and desperation. My parents are loving people, both of whom just made some misguided decisions in their very young age at a time when they felt trapped in their circumstances.

This is something we all do. But we can all also learn from them.

The focus is on this: recognizing the enemy's schemes. Would she have gone through with the divorce if she had been exposed to truth and had clearly seen the consequences of her actions? Perhaps, ultimately or eventually, but we'll never know for sure. That moment in time has passed, and that decision was made.

Regardless, we do know that deception is trickery, and she was tricked into taking a bite of that rotten apple which I believe *helped* lead to the fall of their marriage. The enemy promised her goodness, and what he delivered was brokenness.

The Fall

Now the serpent was more crafty than any of the wild animals the Lord God had made. He said to the woman, "Did God really say, 'You must not eat from any tree in the garden'?"

The woman said to the serpent, "We may eat fruit from the trees in the garden, but God did say, 'You must not eat fruit from the tree that is in the middle of the garden, and you must not touch it, or you will die.'"

"You will not certainly die," the serpent said to the woman. "For God knows that when you eat from it your eyes will be opened, and you will be like God, knowing good and evil."

When the woman saw that the fruit of the tree was good for food and pleasing to the eye, and also desirable for gaining wisdom, she took some and ate it. She also gave some to her husband, who was with her, and he ate it" (Genesis 3:1–6 NIV).

As we know from Genesis in the case of Adam and Eve, that one bite led to death.

The enemy desires to separate us from God and invite us to death. When Adam and Eve bit the fruit, they sinned against God. Now banished from the Garden of Eden, they were separated from

The Lie and The Apple

God and given the penalty of death that was passed down upon their descendants. When my mom chose to bite the apple (believe the enemy's lie) and follow through with a divorce, it too led to death and separation that has affected our family.

We all have bitten the apple of some type. Biting the apples the enemy offers us plays out devastatingly in some way.

However, all is not lost. Jesus is greater than our enemy, and He came so that we may have life. He paid the price for our sin, making a way for us to live and never die. He can redeem, rebuild, renew, restore, and deliver us from anything the enemy takes from us. Both of my parents remarried for over twenty-five years. God loves them and gifted them both with another chance of love and happiness. Thank God for second chances!

I have also witnessed this exchange in my own life. That's why I'm writing to you, so that you too may experience the life, freedom, redemption, and resurrection that only God can give.

We all make decisions that lead to destruction and mistakes that cause us pain, and we'll continue to do so. Although both of my parents made some mistakes, they did *many* things right. They're extraordinary, caring people who love the Lord and have taught their children to do the same. They also love us and have taught us to love others. They rooted their children in the love of God. What greater gift could they have bestowed upon us? I am beyond grateful for it and them. They did their job to train up a child in the way they should go. Although at times, my siblings and I have strayed from the path, eventually we would come back to our roots as the proverb teaches.

> *Train up a child in the way he should go, And when he is old he will not depart from it (Proverbs 22:6 NKJV).*

Recognizing the enemy's schemes and attacks can prevent us from heading down a devastating path. Consequently, recognizing God's plans for our lives, learning to discern His voice, and obey His commands leads us upward on a blessed path.

> *In the way of righteousness is life, and in its pathway there is no death (Proverbs 12:28 NKJV).*

Emergence

Who is our Enemy?

The Bible tells us that there is no condemnation for those who are in Christ Jesus (Romans 8:1). If we're saved believers, then we are forgiven for all of our sins, mistakes, and failures. Once we are saved, we remain saved. Our enemy knows this. Although he knows he can no longer rob us of our salvation, he still has the power to rob us of our dreams, peace, joy, freedom, inheritance, purpose, calling, and the blessed life that Christ died for, if we allow him access. So how can we prevent this from happening?

First, we must *recognize that we have an enemy who hates us and wants to destroy us*. Our enemy is Satan. As I began to write about this subject, I pictured the story of *Snow White*. So much symbolism is packed into her story that resembles my own, and maybe yours as well. Therefore, I'm going to analyze and compare Snow White's story to ours using my own personal evaluation. I'll share my thoughts through my own creative interpretation and expression.

In the story, the Evil Queen hates Snow White because she's a beautiful princess, and her beauty surpasses the queen's own. She's very jealous of her and will stop at nothing to destroy her. The queen plots out an evil plan to have Snow White killed.

Our enemy, much like the Evil Queen, also hates us (the children of God) and hates marriage (the sacred covenant established by God) because he knows who we are and is jealous of us. We are sons and daughters of the King of kings and Lord of lords. We are the bride of Christ. We are heirs to the throne. Our enemy is jealous because he has been summoned to death whereas we've been destined for life and glory. He has been cut out of God's royal family and from the covenant God established.

The devil was once the archangel Lucifer who fell from heaven because of pride and idolatry. He wanted to be worshipped above God; therefore, he rebelled against God, was cursed, and banished to Earth. He took a third of the angels, now called demons, with him. He is now the archenemy of God. We, however, are God's creation, made in His image and called to become children of God to reign forever as royalty in the kingdom of heaven. God is drawing us near, inviting us into His presence.

The Lie and The Apple

> *For those who are led by the Spirit of God are the children of God. The Spirit you received does not make you slaves, so that you live in fear again; rather, the Spirit you received brought about your adoption to sonship. And by him we cry, "Abba, Father." The Spirit himself testifies with our spirit that we are God's children. Now if we are children, then we are heirs—heirs of God and co-heirs with Christ, if indeed we share in his sufferings in order that we may also share in his glory (Romans 8: 14–17 NIV).*

Our enemy is defeated but will never stop plotting against us until he is destroyed once and for all. He'll continue to seek to steal, kill, and destroy us. He has been banned from love, which is God Himself; therefore, he is consumed with hate.

Satan wants to take as many unbelievers with him as possible to face doom, and we as Christians are standing in his way. This is why he hates us. We, the Church, bring the gospel of truth to the world, offering life to all who receive it and accept Jesus as their Lord and Savior. In destroying us along with marriage our efforts and our union may be weakened, robbing us and our family of our blessed inheritance, legacy, purpose, and promise. The devil is jealous of the beautiful, intimate relationship and covenant we have with God; consequently, he wants to interfere by getting in the way.

Isolation Is Invitation

When my mother was struggling with depression, in her despair, she isolated herself from everyone. She withdrew to her bedroom and barely came out. I prepared food for her and took it into her room. She wouldn't eat.

We were all very worried about her. Looking back at this time, I can see where the enemy saw an opportunity. This isolation created an invitation for him to come in and whisper his lies to her. No one else was around to help silence them.

In *Snow White and the Seven Dwarfs*, we also see that the Evil Queen waits until Snow White is home alone to make her move.[2] She understands that during this time of isolation, Snow White is the most vulnerable. So the queen carefully plans her attack and creates her disguise. Then when the seven dwarfs go off to work, she slithers her way over to the open window and offers an enticing apple.

Emergence

Snow White isn't even making apple pie at the time. She's making gooseberry pie. But the wicked old lady suggests that apple pie is what the men really like and that she happens to have exactly what Snow White needs. She is so cunning that she tricks Snow White into deviating from what she is working on to try something new and better. Once she has the naive girl's attention, she sneaks in through the open door. Snow White is now falling right into her trap. She urges the beauty to go on and try it, until finally, Snow White takes a bite.

By the time the dwarfs can get to her, it is too late. Snow White has bitten the poisoned apple and fallen into the "Sleeping Death."

Just as the Evil Queen disguised herself and came to Snow White in the absence of others, the serpent disguised himself and came to Eve, and he is still doing this to us.

Although we know that Eve wasn't alone when Satan tempted her, there was no interference from Adam. Eve had engaged in conversation with Satan, and Adam said and did nothing to stop it. He passively stood and watched rather than standing watch, and he too fell into temptation and rebellion and took the bite offered to him.

Why was Eve alone in this battle against Satan? Adam was with her yet did nothing to help silence the enemy. Was he too busy daydreaming about naming all the animals and prioritizing other obligations when he should have been focused on God first and his wife second? When under attack, all the animals and chores can wait. Wake up. Pay attention to what's at stake, and get your priorities in order. Adam should have taken notice to the threat that was being presented. His body was present, but where was his absent mind and words when Eve needed to hear them most?

Ultimately, they both failed to stand guard side by side and back to back to keep watch over the other and protect the covenant of marriage together as one. Again, the focus here is *not* to blame but on recognizing the enemy's tactics in order to overcome the enemy's attacks.

Isolation is the enemy's invitation. He walks around like a roaring lion seeking to devour his prey. When he sees that one is alone in the battle (physically, spiritually, emotionally, or mentally), he pounces.

Be alert and of sober mind. Your enemy the devil prowls around like a roaring lion looking for someone to devour (1 Peter 5:8 NIV).

The Lie and The Apple

We must not isolate ourselves in body, soul, spirit, and mind. This creates an invitation for our enemy to disguise himself and sneak in through an open door or window. When we're alone, we're vulnerable.

We're stronger together. Our enemy recognizes this, and that is why he fights to separate us. We need other Christian people around to help watch our backs, encourage us, speak the truth into our ears, and pray the Word of God over our circumstances. My dad was away working while my mom was left alone to battle despair, and she fell into a battle with the spirit of depression.

She needed the help of her husband and Christian support when no one was around. She was alone, she was in pain, and she was looking for a way out. Meanwhile, the enemy found his way in.

These stories we read in the Bible aren't just told for entertainment purposes. They're lessons. We are to look at them for answers and apply what's taught to our own lives and situations. The Bible was written for us, to expose the enemy and reveal the truth. It was written as a guide for us to live a victorious and eternal life.

I am so thankful that our God loves us so much that He didn't leave us empty-handed or alone to fight off these attacks. He placed the Sword of the Spirit in our hand that unlocks all the secrets to defeating the enemy. He gives us the wisdom, knowledge, and understanding we need to win this unseen battle.

However, knowledge without application is useless…void. We must *apply* this information to our everyday situations. *Then* we will be victorious.

The Bible says that when two or more gather together in His name, He is with us. Not only do we need the influence of other believers around us and the Sword of the Spirit, but we need the presence of God with us. Our Father in heaven is our protector, and we need the Holy Spirit within us to be our guide and shield. The enemy is less likely to mess with us when others are around, and he is *sure* to flee from us when *Daddy* is in town.

For where two or three are gathered together in My name, there I am with them (Mathew 18:20 NLV).

Emergence

The Right Fruit

Jesus offers us the life-giving fruit of the Spirit to feed upon in our time of need and emptiness. If we'll empty ourselves of all our heaviness and weariness before Him, then He'll come alongside us and take up all of the junk that we pick up daily and exchange it for His goodness. We can choose to reach out our hands and take a bite of the life-giving truth He has to offer us as replacement for the enemy's lies.

As we walk alongside Him, He provides us with whatever need we're deficient in, whether it be love, joy, peace, patience, kindness, goodness, faithfulness, gentleness, and self-control. He alone has the perfect fruit fix for every problem. He knows exactly which one to give in our time of desperation if we will choose to depend on Him to be our help and guide.

Our biggest problem may be that we have an eating disorder. We continue to eat the wrong fruit. Rather than being filled with truth, we're being filled with poison and lies. It's time we put down the rotten apples that the enemy has to offer and pick up the ripe fruits of the Spirit that God has to offer. Out of His hands, and out of His garden we are filled with goodness and satisfied with righteousness.

Our Savior takes our emptiness and exchanges it by feeding us with His goodness. The exact opposite is said for our enemy. The enemy feeds off of our emptiness, taking our hopes and dreams from us and exchanges them with empty promises, negative thoughts, and faulty solutions. In many cases, *not all*, it isn't the help of mental evaluations or medical attention that we should be seeking to fix our disorders. Although God gifted psychologists and physicians to *help* heal His people, and I am beyond grateful for them, what we need *most* in our lives is spiritual intervention.

We need to seek out the help of the Holy Spirit to attend to the root cause of most our problems—our lack of His truth and goodness within our hearts. Maybe deep down at the core, in the pit of our hearts, is a bad seed producing sick fruit. We need the help of the Holy Spirit in order to work it out and turn it around.

> *But the Holy Spirit produces this kind of fruit in our lives: love, joy, peace, patience, kindness, goodness, faithfulness, gentleness, and self-control. There is no law against these things! (Galatians 5:22–23 NLT).*

The Lie and The Apple

Leaving Eden

While my parents' divorce was being finalized, my dad would pick us up for visitation weekends. This was one of the hardest things I had yet to experience. We would eagerly anticipate his coming.

When he first showed up, we were full of happiness, and we had a great time together. We'd sing in the car and go bowling. But as our time together began drawing to a close, all of that happiness quickly turned to sadness.

Saying goodbye and parting with our dad was excruciating as we clung to him and wept. I had never seen my dad break down and cry so hard. It was utter devastation. This was the true picture of divorce—*a family ripped apart*.

We were forced to move away from the home we had always known that had been next door to our sweet grandparents. We ended up moving into a tiny town and lived in an even tinier duplex apartment.

My freshman year in high school should have been an exciting time in my life. Rather, it was mostly a time of sorrow, pain, and loss. It felt like everything I had loved and known was taken away, and we were forced to start over. Although my precious mom was doing her best to pick up the pieces and create a new picture for us, we were all shattered.

Anger

Throughout this shifting and transition period, I became very angry and stopped applying myself. My grades dropped slightly, and I just stopped caring for the most part.

That plan I had made before entering the ninth grade of going somewhere ended up with me going nowhere. I gave up. I started walking into basketball practice and taking out my aggression on my teammates, pushing, elbowing, and playing rougher than necessary. I was screaming on the inside and lashing out at the world on the outside.

So much had changed. My coach came to our house to talk to my mother. He offered to pay for my sister's and my basketball shoes because he knew we were struggling financially and in transition. This was such a kind gesture, but at the time, all I felt was shame and embarrassment. I could hardly look at him after that.

Emergence

I had such high hopes for that year; instead, I ended up sitting on the bench watching my team play rather than participating. I can't blame my coach for benching me. I didn't make an effort to learn a single play, and I definitely wasn't a team player.

One day I lashed out at one of my teachers, who happened to be the coach's wife. Since it was spirit week, I dressed up as a little girl. The teacher started making fun of the way I looked.

Jutting my chin forward, I asked her, "Do you know what you look like?"

Astonished and agitated, she responded, "No, tell me."

"You don't want to know," I answered sarcastically.

Wow! Who was this person? Where had that sweet, bubbly spirit gone? I had discovered something about myself, that given the right *ugly* circumstances, I could behave really ugly myself.

This wasn't like me. I wasn't that hateful girl who mouthed off to teachers. It is true that she was unkind first, but I should not have retaliated rudely. I knew better than that; I definitely wasn't raised like that. I was taught to respect my elders and also treat others how you want to be treated. My intake of spiritual fruit was lacking, to say the least, and my heart was completely depleted and deficient. I was a young girl consumed with anger and pain, and I didn't know how to handle it.

Precious one, perhaps you are dealing with anger issues, depression, disappointment, or pain from your past and you don't know how to handle it. I encourage you to pray this mighty prayer.

PRAYER

Jehovah Rapha (The Lord Who Heals),

Help me to lay down all anger, bitterness, resentment, and pride. I need You to soften my heart and help me to forgive those who have let me down. Heal me from the pain of my past—rejection, abandonment, betrayal, or abuse. I bless those who have angered, offended, or hurt me. I know that You love them and died for their sins as well as my own. Therefore, I choose to love and forgive as I have been forgiven. Holy Spirit, I invite You into my current circumstances and I trust You to guide me into all truth, blessings, and abundant life. I bind the spirit of depression and I loose the fruits of Your Spirit to fill me and heal me completely from the inside out. Thank You, Father, for delivering me and setting me free from bondage and captivity.

In Jesus' Name. Amen.

PRAYER OVER YOU

I pray this comforting Scripture over you.

And I pray that he would unveil within you the unlimited riches of his glory and favor until supernatural strength floods your innermost being with his divine might and explosive power.

Then, by constantly using your faith, the life of Christ will be released deep inside you, and the resting place of his love will become the very source and root of your life.

Then you will be empowered to discover what every holy one experiences—the great magnitude of the astonishing love of Christ in all its dimensions. How deeply intimate and far-reaching is his love! How enduring and inclusive it is! Endless love beyond measurement that transcends our understanding—this extravagant love pours into you until you are filled to overflowing with the fullness of God (Ephesians 3:16-19 TPT).

SECTION II

The Fall of The Next Generation

CHAPTER THREE

A New Found Paradise Slipping Away

It wasn't long before my mom started dating. Eventually, she met a nice man. They got engaged quickly, and he became our stepdad. I was happy to see my mom and siblings laugh and smile again, but this new family dynamic was still somewhat difficult for me. Even though he was a fun and good guy, he wasn't my dad.

Their engagement had happened so quickly. I wasn't ready to accept that my dad was gone, and someone else had taken his place.

I missed him terribly.

Throughout this time, my dad had also been dating a sweet lady. They eventually got married as well.

I soon found out we were going to move *again* the summer after my ninth-grade year. This time it was to a new town nearby where our stepdad's job was and a new school—my rival high school. I had attended the same school since kindergarten and grown up with the same people. I had finally begun to love my school, but once again, it was time to leave everything behind and start over. In just over a year's time, we had moved twice. First, I had to say goodbye to my childhood home, my grandparents who lived next door, and most of all—my dad. Then, I had to say goodbye to my school, the kids I had known my whole life and *finally* felt accepted by, and now—my best friend. We left the safety of all we had known and the memories of all we had loved and cherished behind, never to return.

Emergence

Starting over again wasn't easy. At first it was terrifying. This new school was small but still much bigger than my previous school. I knew very few people, and once again, the girls didn't accept me very well. I hadn't grown up with them. Coming from a rival school, I was *an outsider moving in*.

According to sheknows.com, my name Mistie means "misty" and based on the Merriam-Webster dictionary the word *misty* means—obscured by mist, indistinct, vague, confused, and tearful as to blur the eyes or vision. There have been moments of my life when I have felt people have looked at me from a distance and failed to see me clearly, as if a mist or fog were in front of me causing some people to be hesitant to draw near. Once people got close enough to me, though, the mist dissipated, and they were able to see me for who I truly am. Fear and confusion subsided.

The summer I moved into town, girls drove by my house and yelled hateful things out the window at me. They only knew where I was coming from and my name, but they had no idea who I was. They could only see me from a distance heading their way. In their confusion, they grew fearful. Perhaps they felt threatened by me in some way. Either way, I felt *misunderstood* and like an outcast.

Here is one incident in particular that demonstrated this reality. That same summer, I frequently rode my bike downtown where all of the other kids hung out and mingled so I could meet new people and fit in. Two girls wearing sneakers and sporty shorts approached me and invited me to go on a bike ride with them. They appeared to be prepared for an adventure. On the other hand, I was prepared for leisure activities with my strappy sandals and cute denim shorts.

Nevertheless, I accepted their invitation and agreed to join them, feeling flattered that they had invited me, especially since we had never been introduced. I was only familiar with their names and knew that they were popular and athletic.

I assumed they knew I was the new girl in town. I thought this might be a great opportunity to introduce myself to them and begin building friendships.

However, upon beginning our "little adventure," I quickly discovered I was wrong. These girls weren't interested in getting to know me, and they had no intention of befriending me. As soon as I got on my bike, they took off as fast as they could go.

A New Found Paradise Slipping Away

All along, their intention was to humiliate me by leaving me in the dust. I was determined not to let that happen. Despite my condition and appearance, I peddled my heart out and did not allow them to leave me behind. Many times, my feet slipped off the pedals, and I feared I was going to wipe out and eat gravel, but I kept going.

What they didn't anticipate was that I too had some athletic skills and a competitive nature of my own. I was not going to be anyone's victim or prey. Realizing their plan had failed, they eventually gave up trying to ditch me in the dust and headed back to where we began.

They didn't say a single word to me once we arrived back to where we met.

I understood what had just happened. They had invited me only to size up, evaluate, and abandon me. Next time, they better bring a longer measuring stick.

I make jokes about this now, but at the time, it really didn't feel very good. I was searching for acceptance and friendship; instead, I received rejection, manipulation, and near humiliation.

Once again, I had to prove myself. Over and over, I had to show that I was kind, fun, and not a threat; I meant them no harm. And I wasn't out to steal all of their boyfriends. It took a little time, but eventually the girls came around.

I'm so glad that God's invitation is not based upon our performance or His evaluation. There is no cruelty in Him. He is always accepting, loving, and kind, and His invitation is always genuine and sincere. We can always find true and lasting friendship in His welcoming arms. He is not secretly devising a manipulative plan to draw us in, only to turn us away. He loves us now and forever.

If only I would have fully understood this then.

He who loves a pure heart and is kind in his speaking has the king as his friend (Proverbs 22:11 NLV).

For the Lord will not reject his people; he will never forsake his inheritance (Psalm 94:14 NIV).

Although this transition started out rough, it turned out that high school was actually some of the best years of my life. I had a lot of fun and became extremely happy once people finally made the decision to get to know me.

Emergence

Our neighbor even called me "Smiley." I made a lot of friends (even with the two girls on the bikes) and many wonderful memories. I was very involved in many various activities and also became "popular." I became a cheerleader, voted as our class Student Council Representative, cast as the lead role in our three-act play and awarded "Best Actress," selected as a member of the National Honor's Society and Who's Who Among High School Students across America, selected as a Miss BCHS finalist, an All American Cheerleader nominee, as "Friendly Folk," "Funny Folk," and was even voted as Football Homecoming Queen my senior year. It was a glorious adventure and my time to shine.

First Love

Things were going perfectly for me. However, all of the recognition, achievements, and bright lights were pale in comparison to my first love. He was the sunlight to my day.

We met the summer before my sophomore year. He was a grade below me, but we were the same age. I fell head over heels in love with him. He was tall, handsome, and absolutely stunning in my eyes. He was also very sweet and caring. We were a couple throughout all of high school and even after.

When my parents divorced, I was left broken and empty inside. When I met him, I poured everything I had into him. It was like my heart awakened and love began to spring out of it. He made me feel adored, unique, and special. I couldn't get enough of him. He added so much joy and happiness into my life after such a devastating experience. We were the perfect couple. He was the big, strong football player, and I was the sweet and beautiful homecoming queen.

We had plans to get married and honeymoon in Paris. I was so full of dreams and living on the clouds. Life was full of vibrant golden color.

I had found a new paradise.

> *Oh! Give me something refreshing to eat—and quickly! Apricots, raisins—anything. I'm about to faint with love! His left hand cradles my head, and his right arm encircles my waist! (Song of Solomon 2:5–6 MSG).*

A New Found Paradise Slipping Away

Promises and Temptation

I was a junior when I made the decision to be water baptized and the pull on my heart to know God more and to seek after Him continued to grow as I did. Earlier that year, some of my friends had invited me to a Bible study, and I started attending it on a regular basis. My desire was to please and obey God. My parents raised me to have very strong convictions, values, and morals, and I did. Although I knew I wasn't perfect, I always *wanted* to behave perfectly before God even from a very young age.

For me, premarital sex was wrong. I had seen the consequences of this sin in my parents' lives. They got married because they had gotten pregnant during their senior year of high school. As a result, they faced a lot of challenges emotionally and financially, making life harder for them.

I was so passionate about the subject, premarital sex, that I even gave a presentational speech over the topic during my junior year. "We often hear the phrase if it feels good, do it," I told my classmates. "However, this does not warn us of the consequences of choosing these actions."

During a "True Love Waits" campaign at school, we had an opportunity to sign a card promising to abstain from sex until marriage. This promise represented our vow to God to follow His ways and obey His commands.

This decision was a big deal to me. Knowing how passionately in love I was with my boyfriend, I had been struggling with the idea of succumbing to my own flesh and choosing my own will and desires versus choosing to obey God and follow His will and desire for me. Knowing others were already sexually active made waiting even harder. Ultimately, I chose His will. I chose to obey. I chose to make a promise to God and sign the card.

I chose to wait.

> *Oh, let me warn you, sisters in Jerusalem, by the gazelles, yes, by all the wild deer: Don't excite love, don't stir it up, until the time is ripe—and you're ready (Song of Solomon 2:7 MSG).*

Emergence

Misty Eyed

Just months earlier, it was December of my junior year, and I was excitedly preparing for our annual "Hanging of the Green" Christmas Dance. The morning of the dance, my dad arrived unexpectedly on our doorstep with devastating news. He came to tell my siblings and me that our cousin (just a few years younger than me) had experienced a terrible accident while playing basketball at church and had suffered trauma to the brain. He didn't make it and had now gone to be with the Lord.

I spent the majority of that day alone in my bedroom. I had cried so much that my eyes had developed a misty film over them that caused me to barely see.

That evening, I was determined to show up to my dance and put my best foot forward. My sister, the Guardian, helped me get ready. Her college roommate had lent her a long, sparkly navy-blue, off-the-shoulder dress for me to wear. She helped me put on the shimmering gown and then curled and swept my hair back softly to one side.

My date (my first love) arrived on the doorstep with a beautiful flower corsage in hand. My vision was still blurred the entire night, as was the entire experience. My heart wasn't in that place. My boyfriend and I sat off to the side most of the evening and watched as others smiled and danced. But I wasn't smiling, and I wasn't dancing on that day.

More Changes

As I approached graduation, I began to feel like everything was beginning to slip away all over again. I knew this familiar feeling. The life I had grown comfortable in and loved was about to change.

My mom and stepdad, whom I had been primarily living with, moved again in the second half of my senior year. Instead of moving with them this time, I moved in with my dad and stepmom. This decision was nothing against them. I simply didn't want to pick up and start over toward the end of my last year of high school, especially now that things were going so well for me. It was tough being away from them all.

Despite missing my family, I enjoyed living with my dad. It gave me a chance to have him all to myself, and I liked that.

However, as I began to settle in at my dad's house, I realized that this too was only temporary. I would soon graduate and have to leave my home, my school, my parents, and now my first love. I was already missing my mom, my stepdad, and my siblings.

I didn't want to start over again. I was happy living up on the clouds. I didn't want to face the fact that what goes up must eventually come down.

Feeling depressed and angry, I stopped caring all over again. It became harder and harder for me to wake up in the mornings and make it to school on time. The principal had called my house one morning around nine o'clock to see where I was and why I hadn't yet made it to school. I grabbed my car keys, rushed out the door to school, and met him in the hallway with tears in my eyes, apologizing for showing up late. He had taken notice that this ambitious and gregarious girl had started to slack. I was experiencing the early stages of lashing out all over again. I had been down this road before, and I knew where it was headed.

I couldn't allow myself to entirely slip away, so I desperately tried to hold on to everything every moment. The tighter my grip, the more it slipped away.

More Loss—More Mist

One month after my senior graduation, I received the devastating news that one of my classmates, a friend, had died in a car wreck.

Again, we grieved the loss of a friend and the loss of a life taken too soon. Again, I turned to my first love for comfort. He was always there for me. He was able to help keep that sparkle in my eyes when life all around me seemed to lose its luster and clarity.

I didn't want to lose him too.

That summer as I continued to sense everything in my life slipping away I held on tightly to him. I held on so tight to what I desired that I let go of my convictions. My *misty* eyes had become blurred with tears, losing sight of the vision God had for me in the fog of sorrow. I let go of what He desired for me. Nothing else mattered in that moment but my first love and me.

So that same summer after graduation—I lost my virginity.

I Bit the Apple

When I first took a bite of the apple, it tasted good and sweet as all sin does. The sweetness lasts for a time, but it is doomed to end. Of course you don't see the whole story when the temptation is being presented. The sensual apple appears red, juicy and ripe with pleasure. It's enticing to the eyes and alluring to the flesh. Satan flaunts the forbidden fruit in front of our watering mouths, urging us to take a bite and make all of our wildest dreams come true.

My first love was my first dream. He was everything I thought I wanted. He was what I hoped for. I wanted to marry him and spend the rest of my life with him, to have a family together. I wanted to love and be loved by him. He was my beloved. Our love was beautiful and ripe as a vineyard in bloom; however, we didn't tend to our vineyard properly, and little foxes made their way in to ruin the vineyard.

These "foxes" represented the temptation to enter into premarital sex and sin rather than wait on God's perfect timing for love to awaken and bloom according to His perfect plan and desire.

Catch all the foxes, those little foxes, before they ruin the vineyard of love, for the grapevines are blossoming (Song of Solomon 2:15 NLT).

Summer had ended, and it was now time for me to go off to college. The separation from him was torturous. I missed him so much. Every weekend I got the chance, I eagerly made the two-hour drive to come home. My part-time job after classes paid for the gas, which was probably where most of my money went. Every weekend started out joyously and ended in sadness. Saying goodbye was so hard. We kept this up for a while, but the pain of leaving each other hurt both of us. It was just like it was when we had to say bye to our dad at the end of the weekends we had spent together.

My first love was a senior in high school. Each time after we were forced to part, he became miserable and depressed. This was not the way he needed to spend his last year of high school. Therefore, he made the decision to just be friends.

I was heartbroken. This is not what I wanted. I wanted him to fight for me and our future together. Looking back at it now, I can see how this was the best thing for both of us. We needed to take the year off and then see where it picked up after he graduated. In that moment, I didn't look at it from that perspective, though. From my experience with my parents, when a relationship ended, they didn't get back together.

A New Found Paradise Slipping Away

It was over.

Perhaps I hoped that in biting the apple, it would bring us even closer and seal our bond. In reality, the opposite occurred. Sin and ungodliness invite destruction and division, not blessings. Instead, jealousy, fear, insecurity, and eventually separation occurred as a result. These are reasons why sex is reserved for marriage. It is a gift given by God to be enjoyed exclusively within the bounds of marriage. Sex outside of marriage takes two people and temporarily joins them in part as one, but only sex inside of marriage unites them wholly as one. It's a bond that's not meant to be shared with multiple partners; it is intended to be shared with one. Sex within marriage is a special sacred union between a husband and a wife, and only marriage seals the bond.

Sex when unmarried and unbound in legal union, creates an ungodly soul tie to that person and an unhealthy fear of losing them. The reality is that the freedom to walk away and abandon the relationship is always present. This understanding creates conflict and instability within the relationship. Likewise, the relationship is not receiving the Lord's blessings because it isn't operating within God's perfect design.

Having sex before marriage was like taking a bite of our wedding cake before there was even a marriage proposal. Now, bad luck (it's bad luck to "see" the bride before the wedding) had set in to spoil it. Feeding one another this sweet indulgence is meant to come after the ceremony.

Sweet treats have always been my weakness.

Delightful Distractions & Delectable Deviations

Throughout this time, I felt very alone, abandoned, rejected, and unwanted just like I did after my dad left. I stopped going home every weekend and began working more.

This is when I met someone new. I'll call him "Tom."

We worked together, and he was different from anyone I had ever known. Tom had a mysterious, wild side to him, but he was very funny. He always made me laugh and was very charming and intelligent. I appreciated his extreme creativity, something we had in common. Tom helped take my mind off of my broken heart and made me feel very special.

We quickly began dating. Everything we did was new and spontaneous for me. He even took me to see a play for our first date. I was having a really great time with him. Our relationship started moving pretty fast, and I allowed it, even though I knew in my heart I wasn't over my first love and my recent break up. Again, I began to pour myself into someone new in order to fill the empty void and heal the wounds in my soul.

Regardless, I really did care for this boy and enjoyed our time together. We kept getting closer and closer. Eventually, I found myself spending more time over at his apartment than at my own dorm. I disliked my dorm room and had nothing in common with my roommate, so this was a great escape for me.

My new fling and I debated frequently. I shared with him my Christian faith and we argued about our spiritual beliefs and morals. He was a philosophy major at the time and was still studying multiple religions and searching for his faith. I eagerly wanted to help him find it and change him and to help guide him into a relationship with the one true God.

We also argued often about sex. I believed sex was meant for marriage alone. He didn't agree and said he had never met anyone like me. He didn't see anything wrong with having sex outside of marriage. Right here, I should have noted all the dangerous warning signs and drawn a line in the sand of our relationship.

Clearly, we didn't share similar views, even down to the fundamental basics of right and wrong. What is and is not sin and whose opinion was valid ultimately? A true believer is someone who has been born again by the Spirit of God, and their knowledge of good and evil is based upon what God's Holy Spirit and living Word says is truth. Period. Only God's Word is concrete, absolute, and unchanging. An unbeliever's knowledge of good and evil is based upon his own understanding, opinions, or worldly view that could change at any given time.

Despite my recent failure to uphold my promise to God, I still strongly believed that abstinence outside of marriage was what God wanted from His children. Undoubtedly, obeying God was right, and disobeying God was wrong. Even though I didn't always behave as a perfectly obedient child, I still knew the difference and felt His gentle conviction and nudge of correction every time I did something God said was wrong.

Our faith was one of the main differences between us. I didn't share with my new boyfriend for a while that I was no longer a virgin because I didn't want him to think sex was an option with me. My desire was to help bring him closer to God. I also felt a lot of shame and guilt for what I had done, and I didn't want to continue disobeying God. I understood my body was valuable and precious to God and I wished to remain pure and innocent, even though I struggled with temptation and sin.

However, I continued to follow my boyfriend wherever he wanted to take me and walk in dangerous territory, forming a connection with someone who shared opposing beliefs, hoping I could turn him around.

Instead, I began to lose myself and find trouble.

Paul's Final Instructions

And now, dear brothers and sisters, I'd like to give one final word of caution: Watch out for those who cause divisions and offenses among you. When they antagonize you by speaking of things that are contrary to the teachings that you've received, don't be caught in their snare! For people like this are not truly serving the Lord, our Messiah, but are being driven by their own desires for a following. Utilizing their smooth words and well-rehearsed blessings, they seek to deceive the hearts of innocent ones.

I'm so happy when I think of you, because everyone knows the testimony of your deep commitment of faith. So I want you to become scholars of all that is good and beautiful, and stay pure and innocent when it comes to evil (Romans 16:17–19 TPT).

One night, we went to a friend's apartment. They were playing a drinking game. It was a card game, and I didn't know how to play, and I also didn't enjoy alcohol. They talked me into playing anyway, and I had to drink over and over because I was terrible at the game. Of course I didn't *have* to drink. I had the option to say no or discontinue playing the game. I just chose not to. Needless to say, I became intoxicated. We left the party and went back to his place, and once again I was seduced by my flesh and gave into sexual temptation.

I cried afterwards, realizing what I had just done. I was angry with myself for being so weak and foolish. How could I let my guard down so easily? I waited three years before giving into that temptation with my first love and still carried the guilt from it. Now, it had taken only months.

You see, I had discovered in that moment that once you have bitten that apple, it's easier to bite again and again. Despite my will to please and obey God, my flesh was weak.

Struggling with Sin

So the trouble is not with the law, for it is spiritual and good. The trouble is with me, for I am all too human, a slave to sin. I don't really understand myself, for I want to do what is right, but I don't do it. Instead, I do what I hate. But if I know that what I am doing is wrong, this shows that I agree that the law is good. So I am not the one doing wrong; it is sin living in me that does it.

And I know that nothing good lives in me, that is, in my sinful nature. I want to do what is right, but I can't. I want to do what is good, but I don't. I don't want to do what is wrong, but I do it anyway. But if I do what I don't want to do, I am not really the one doing wrong; it is sin living in me that does it.

I have discovered this principle of life—that when I want to do what is right, I inevitably do what is wrong. I love God's law with all my heart. But there is another power within me that is at war with my mind. This power makes me a slave to the sin that is still within me (Romans 7:14–23 NLT).

All of the anger, shame, guilt, fears, and pain I had experienced had made me vulnerable to attack. I let my guard down much easier now. My recent break up had left an empty hole in my heart, and I had yet to fill that void space with God.

This was the open door the enemy had been waiting for. He knew my area of vulnerability. I was emotionally drained and scarred from rejection and abandonment. Instead of seeking help, I only made matters worse.

At the time, I didn't recognize my need to call out to God for help. I was powerless as I kept battling life on my own, seeking to please God yet incapable of following through. I was hurting. Rather than turning to God for comfort, I turned to man over and over again.

A New Found Paradise Slipping Away

I believed the enemy's lie that someone or something could take away my pain and fill my heart with love. I had looked at the enticing apple and saw that it was pleasing to the eye, so I took another bite.

This bite was not juicy and sweet for long.

It quickly turned bitter.

Tom and I continued to date for a while, but I soon discovered that he was not the right one for me, and I ended our relationship.

A Spring of Hope

Meanwhile, spring break was soon approaching. My first love and I had started talking again. School would be ending soon, and in just a few months, he would be graduating. We made plans to see each other over the break. Both of us were excited at the chance to finally be together again soon. My beloved and I were to be reunited. I was up on the clouds again in the hopes that my dream of us as a couple again was soon to come true.

PRAYER

Maybe you are in a situation where you are dealing with loss, devastating change, or struggling with sin, and you feel hopeless. Please remember that God is constant. Although people come and go, and circumstances change, He never changes and neither does His love for you even when we give in to temptation and fall into sin. His grace is always sufficient and His forgiveness is everlasting.

Pray right now, Father, fill me with hope, lead me not into temptation, forgive me and help me turn away from sin, comfort me in times of loss, and remind me of my worth.

Beloved, you have value. Jesus paid a great price for you and I to receive His forgiveness. You are not cheap and as a child of God, your body is a temple of the Holy Spirit. You are set apart from sin and ungodliness to live a holy and sanctified life through the power of His blood. Praise God for His triumphant victory over the enemy and for the redemption He offers His children who believe in Him.

Now, may the God of peace and harmony set you apart, making you completely holy. And may your entire being—spirit, soul, and body—be kept completely flawless in the appearing of our Lord Jesus, the Anointed One (1 Thessalonians 5:23 TPT).

CHAPTER FOUR

The Wages of Sin

While counting down the days to go home, a potential concern came to my attention. Before I could go anywhere, I needed to address it and get an answer either way. I contacted my ex-boyfriend Tom and asked if I could come over to his apartment.

I went into his bathroom and numbingly stared at the two pink lines. I had received my answer…

I was pregnant.

Walking out of the bathroom, I approached him and began weeping in a complete standstill. I had no words to say, just a bottle of conflicting emotions to pour out. We had discussed the possibility of me being pregnant. That is why I took the test at his place. We wanted to find out the result together. After pacing around the room for a minute or so completely astonished at the news, Tom came over and put his arms around me.

Full of compassion and support, he assured me that everything was going to be all right.

Emergence

More Lies, More Apples

A single moment had changed the course of my entire life. Everything I had hoped for was no longer in reach.

Just seasons earlier, I was happily attending prom with my first love. The theme was Shakespeare's *Romeo and Juliet*, one I had helped choose. The romanticism captured by this playwright had always infatuated me. I never would have guessed that in just a short time later, I would have written my own tragic love story, and there was nothing romantic about it. In fantasy, it was beautiful; in reality, it was brutal.

Passionate love had led to my own undoing. I had been warned not to awaken love before its time, yet I had failed to listen and obey. The little foxes I allowed into my garden bed destroyed my beautiful love vineyard.

The enemy had set a snare for me. The moment I bit the apple, *I was trapped.*

I was now a slave to my own sin, bound to its consequences, tortured, tormented, and held captive to its fate. Biting the red apple was like running a red light. You might think you can get away with it once or twice, but eventually, it catches up with you. Sin catches up with us all in one way or the other. Those foxes are sly, sneaky, and swift. Unfortunately, the warning signs were flashing, but I failed to respond and put the brakes on until it was already too late.

The apple promises to give us our greatest desire, but in reality, it takes it from us. My dream of spending my life with my first love was taken from me. It was stolen. My beloved and I were ripped apart before we had a chance to get back together. My eyes were opened, and I realized I had been deceived.

I was tricked.

And I allowed it all to happen.

My first bite of the apple deceived me by promising I could have my greatest desire now without waiting. My second bite deceived me by promising I could bury my pain and find happiness in another person. Every bite was a lie drawing me in for the kill. We don't gain what we want by doing things our own way, in our own timing, and against God's will.

What we truly gain from sin is death. Where we truly end up is in a snare. When our eyes are finally opened and we discover this truth, it is too late—we're trapped.

The Wages of Sin

If only I had known what my sin would *cost* me. If only I had known it would bring death to my dream. If only I had known it would cost me my freedom. If only I had known of the devastation I was to bring upon myself.

The truth is, I should have known. I knew the difference between good and evil. I knew that I was disobeying God, and I chose to sin anyway, just like Adam and Eve. How could I be so naïve? How could I have allowed this to happen?

All sin has consequences. In me was the knowledge of this truth, yet I had not yet learned of the consequences of this truth for myself, until now.

The Bible warns us of this truth in His promises, and God's Spirit within us urges us to stay away. He knows the consequences of sin, and He wants to protect us. That is why He tells us *no*. He loves us so much and wants us to live in freedom, not bondage.

If only I had listened and obeyed God. If only I would have cried out for help before it was too late.

If only.

> *And the* Lord God *commanded the man, "You are free to eat from any tree in the garden; but you must not eat from the tree of the knowledge of good and evil, for when you eat from it you will certainly die" (Genesis 2:16–17 NIV).*

Banishment/Paradise Lost

What now? I had just turned nineteen years old and hadn't even been out of high school for a full year. I was so young, so scared, and so devastated and didn't know what to do. I was still in love with my first love, yet tied to another. I ended up doing what I thought was the right thing and my only option.

I chose to marry the father. I chose to enter back into a relationship that I had ended for very specific reasons.

Letting go of my first love was absolutely shattering. I would go to bed at night only to wake to remember my predicament. I would roll over and weep. A great inconsolable sadness hovered over me. My first love was the one I had dreamed of marrying and having a family with—him, no one else. Him. Why couldn't it have been him?

Emergence

It had always been all about him.

Just when I thought I almost had it all, I lost everything. I didn't even get the chance to talk to him face to face. We didn't get the opportunity to embrace one another and say our final goodbyes. There was no real closure.

It was just over.

When I told my first love what happened over the phone, he asked if Tom forced me. He knew my heart and was shocked at the news. Oh, how it would have been easier if I could have put the blame on another. But the answer was no. The truth was that no one forced me. I made my own decision to bite the apple. Now I was responsible for the death I faced.

We were now forbidden from one another, and just like that, I was exiled out of Paradise. My sin had banished me from my first love. I had been with him for years and knew him so well, yet I was now tied to someone else, someone who wasn't him.

I was leaving my beautiful garden, cast out of my Eden, and heading out into the unknown. But unlike Eve, the Adam of my dreams would not be leaving with me.

> *So the Lord God banished him from the Garden of Eden to work the ground from which he had been taken. After he drove the man out, he placed on the east side of the Garden of Eden cherubim and a flaming sword flashing back and forth to guard the way to the tree of life (Genesis 3:23–24 NIV).*

Naked and Ashamed

My mom knew how torn I was and that I still had feelings for my first love. She also knew that my fiancé and I were not right for one another, that I wasn't ready to get married, and that I was only doing what I thought was the right thing to do.

My fiancé and I knew so little about who we both truly were in the beginning. Then what I had discovered in the end sent me running. I didn't flee because I didn't love him; I fled because I was afraid. When the truth of our relationship was revealed to me, my eyes were opened, and I realized we were not a match made in heaven.

I had enjoyed a great amount of our time together, and he possessed many good and wonderful characteristics and traits. However, we didn't see eye to eye on many important issues, and that fright-

The Wages of Sin

ened me. Most importantly, we didn't share the same spiritual beliefs, nor did we have the same taste in friends. We were two completely different people on different pages. The only page we were both on was that we were both soon to be parents of the same child. We were unequally yoked (two incompatible beings, heading in opposite directions, walking separate spiritual paths).

One night during our engagement, I woke up from a dream that left me distraught. It was a spiritual dream about Tom's salvation and eternal state. I prayed in that moment that he would turn his heart to God and believe and receive Him into his life as Lord.

My mom was right when she told us we should not be getting married. We should have never entered into a forbidden relationship, and we should have never gotten married (2 Corinthians 6:14). Unfortunately, at the time, I didn't yet have the revelation or understanding to know that this type of alliance was forbidden by God. I lacked the wisdom to understand that I was disobeying Him again by marrying someone who was *not yet* sure of His faith and belief in God. Although my mom strongly encouraged us to wait, we were never told by anyone that entering into this type of marriage was biblically wrong. I was ignorant and naïve in my Christian faith and scriptural knowledge.

We were only choosing to get married in an attempt to hide our shame and guilt and cover up our sin, just like Adam and Eve did in the garden. They bit the forbidden fruit, exposing their nakedness, and they hid from God because they were afraid. However, no amount of fig leaves could cover up the truth of what we had done. We were exposed, having disobeyed God, and there was no hiding from our mistake.

I was afraid that God was angry or disappointed with me for my disobedience toward Him, and I wanted to try to make things right, to return to right standing with God, by getting married. Additionally, I was afraid to face this journey alone. Fear had entered into our midst.

> *Then the eyes of both of them were opened, and they realized they were naked; so they sewed fig leaves together and made coverings for themselves. Then the man and his wife heard the sound of the Lord God as he was walking in the garden in the cool of the day, and they hid from the Lord God among the trees of the garden. But the Lord God called to the man, "Where are you?"*

Emergence

He answered, "I heard you in the garden, and I was afraid because I was naked; so I hid."

And he said, "Who told you that you were naked? Have you eaten from the tree that I commanded you not to eat from?" (Genesis 3: 7–11 NIV).

More Promises

The morning of our wedding shower, everything came out into the open between us. I expressed my concerns going into this marriage and also shared with Tom my true feelings. This news hurt him, and I felt terrible about that. This is the boy I had met and wanted to help lead closer to Christ. I never wanted to hurt him or be the cause of any additional pain in his life. I cared for him deeply.

We cried together, and I expressed my fears to him. That was when he promised me that he would *change* and become the person I needed him to be. He promised to give up his old ways of living, his ungodly habits, and those bad connections with others that I was afraid of, all of those issues that caused me to end our relationship in the first place. He promised to take care of me and this baby. He promised that if I married him, he would do this.

He promised.

But through all those promises he made to give up this and that, I never remembered him saying that he would or had given up his life to God. This one important matter should have been clearly discussed before moving any further. But it wasn't. Sadly, I wasn't in a place where I was making sound and wise decisions. I was hurting, lost, confused, scared, ashamed, and in that place where I made quick and rash decisions on my own. I didn't cry out to God and patiently wait and listen for His response.

Instead, I chose to listen to and believe my fiancés promises. In that moment, I chose to put my fears and deepest desires aside and give our marriage and family a chance. This was the sacrifice I was willing to make, to put myself aside and let go of the possibility of being with my first love in order to do what I *thought* was right and best for others. I had experienced what it was like to have a broken family, and I didn't want that for our child. I wanted this child to have a *complete* family. I wanted to give our baby an opportunity to have what I lost.

I had a responsibility to love and care for this child and felt responsible to also give this marriage a chance in order to provide the best life possible for all of us. I felt I owed that to this innocent one growing inside me. I believed that it was achievable for us to all be happy together as a family. I believed this was the right thing to do and I made the choice to follow through with it.

The Gift of Grace

We married on a beautiful summer day. It was a very nice outdoor wedding, and we had an adventurous honeymoon.

I was about four months pregnant, and as soon as the wedding was over, I began to show. Tom and I began getting very excited about bringing a baby into our lives.

We didn't deserve this child. We had disobeyed God, and yet here we were about to receive a miraculous gift. We were actually receiving two gifts. The second was the gift of God's grace. Although it was true we didn't deserve this grace, in God's goodness, He gave it anyway. This is how wonderful and merciful our Father is. Despite our sin, we were allowed to receive these gifts.

In the Garden of Eden, Adam and Eve were banished because they sinned and disobeyed God. This sin caused separation between them and God, and they were forced to leave Eden and forbidden to eat also from the tree of life.

Having now gained the knowledge of good and evil and becoming like God, they were judged. The promise from the deceiver was that they would be like God. This is what tempted them to sin.

However, biting the forbidden fruit opened them up only to the knowledge of good and evil. When they chose to take the bite, they were choosing to attempt to become their own gods over their lives.

> *And the LORD God said, "The man has now become like one of us, knowing good and evil. He must not be allowed to reach out his hand and take also from the tree of life and eat, and live forever" (Genesis 3:22 NIV).*

This is what happens every time we choose to sin and disobey God. We're saying that we are in control of our lives, and God is not. We're attempting to take His place on the throne. We're choosing to be our own God. There is only One God, and we are not Him. He alone is worthy to sit on the throne of our hearts.

When we sin against Him, we're saying that we don't trust His ways and that our ways are best. We were created by God, and we belong to God. He knows us better than we know ourselves, and we are to trust and obey Him. This is what it means to have the fear of God in our lives. We submit our will to Him, and we trust and serve Him out of loving reverence and wonderstruck awe. We don't live to serve or worship ourselves. We were not created to be the god of our lives. We were created in His image, yet we are not Him.

We don't know all, and we don't see all. Therefore, we are to trust the only One who does. Only He knows what is best for us. He created us, not the other way around.

Adam and Eve received God's judgment—the penalty of death, painful toil, and burdensome labor, struggle with evil, and banishment. Satan was also cursed, and the ground was cursed. However, Adam and Eve still received grace in the midst of judgment.

Eve was still allowed to bear children and become a mother. Together, Adam and Eve would multiply the human race. Due to their sin, however, we would all now have to face those same consequences. However, there would eventually be One born from a woman, and He would defeat death and restore life to those who believe and receive Him, giving access once again to the tree of life. That's grace.

> *To Adam he said, "Because you listened to your wife and ate fruit from the tree about which I commanded you, 'You must not eat from it,' Cursed is the ground because of you; through painful toil you will eat food from it all the days of your life. It will produce thorns and thistles for you, and you will eat the plants of the field. By the sweat of your brow you will eat your food until you return to the ground, since from it you were taken; for dust you are and to dust you will return" (Genesis 3:17–19 NIV).*

> *The God of peace will soon crush Satan under your feet. The grace of our Lord Jesus be with you (Romans 16:20 NIV).*

The Wages of Sin

Thorns and Thistles

When my parents moved us next door to my loving grandparents, we built our home on an old maize field that my grandpa used to farm. The land was being used to store hay bales, and the ground had become sandy due to not being cultivated regularly.

We set our house on the property and worked hard planting grass, trees, and shrubs. Despite our attempt to grow new life and green vegetation, there was a problem. Sandburs had spread from the hay bales and consumed the property. These prickly pests were horrible.

We couldn't walk across our lawn without the soles of our shoes being covered with stickers. We would then have to use a tool to scrape them off, but often they would make their way into our home. It was common to hear someone in our family yell from stepping on one of the painful nuisances.

We tried everything to treat our lot and get rid of these weeds. W would go out and pick brown paper bags full of stickers, but we wouldn't even make a dent in the numbers. We would spray, pick, and hoe, but they just kept multiplying. Finally, we burned the field in the hopes that we would get rid of them once and for all. However, our desperate attempt failed once more.

I believe this story represents a spiritual parable of what it might look like if you built your house on the sand rather than on the rock of God's Word.

Jesus often spoke in parables to His disciples. According to the Merriam-Webster dictionary a parable is: a short story that teaches a moral or spiritual lesson, as told by Jesus Christ in the gospels. These illustrative stories, truths, and comparisons are drawn through nature or human life in order to stimulate thinking and awaken spiritual perception. This is how He often speaks to me still, and I pray that He will also use these illustrative stories to speak to you as well throughout the entirety of this book.

I encourage you to invite Jesus (our good Teacher) to reveal to you what He is saying. You can do this by simply asking and praying: "Holy Spirit, what are You saying to me personally throughout this text and Your Word?"

We can try our best to build, sow, and attempt to create life in our lots, but if we choose to build our house on the sand, we will tirelessly struggle to bring forth fruitful life as we labor over thorns and thistles. These thorns and thistles represent the troubles invited into our lot when we choose to walk in sin or when sins are passed down through our generational lines. Some of the culprits responsible for this invitation may be disobedience, rebellion, unbelief in God's Word, and the failure to stand on it, and self-reliance.

It's impossible to remove these troublesome thorns and their painful consequences through our own attempts. By ourselves, we lack the necessary tools and treatment required to eliminate sin and its effects. Therefore, unless properly dealt with, we will continue to track in, carry, and spread the devastation into our homes, families, and the next generation's lot.

Despite our best intentions to sow good seed, troublesome weeds seek sandy spots where they may continue to root, multiply, hitchhike, and eventually choke the life out of the seed sown.

> *Other seed fell among thorns, which grew up and choked the plants, so that they did not bear grain (Mark 4:7 NIV).*

These burdensome sandburs represent the sin of "iniquity" or generational sins that are picked up by parents or grandparents or passed down from them to their children and so on (in the way that Adam and Eve passed their sin on to us). They represent a pattern or cycle of unhealthy, ungodly behavior or tendency to rebel or reject obedience to God's Word rather than stand firmly on it. Sin left untreated in our garden beds prevents the land from receiving God's rain (the blessings poured down from above) over our lot and from bearing fruit. The result is dry ground (hardened hearts), sandy soil where sandburs thrive, and the transference of pain and torment upon the next generation.

None of us are without sin. Therefore, every family has iniquities, even Christian families. If not properly dealt with, cries will continue to be heard as they are tracked into the homes of the descendants. These iniquities can't simply be scraped away; they must be ripped up from the root.

In order to break off iniquities, we must look to God and cry out to Him to remove these painful thorns and thistles from our lives. Then God's Holy fire will consume them once and for all as we turn to Him and refuse to walk in sin any further. Asking God to cover our sin and the sin of our bloodline with the blood of Jesus, and relying on the help

The Wages of Sin

of the Holy Spirit to lead us toward righteousness, are the only tools powerful enough to treat these iniquities. This is how we prevent further transference of pain, and release His blessings of rain.

In the same way that the cross was the only tool and the blood of Jesus was the only treatment powerful enough to rid sin from this evil world inherited from Adam and Eve, Jesus's Spirit is the only solution for breaking off the patterns of generational sin in our families. Only Jesus has the power to conquer sin. We must rely on God and the power of His Word and Spirit to turn us away from sin and to transform our hearts and minds to think and act like Christ.

> *For soil that drinks the rain which often falls on it and produces crops useful to those for whose benefit it is cultivated, receives a blessing from God; but if it persistently produces thorns and thistles, it is worthless and close to being cursed, and it ends up being burned (Hebrews 6:7–8 AMP).*

Building our house on the sand represents living life in our own strength, in our own way, and based on our own desires and beliefs. I want to point out that building on the sand doesn't necessarily mean you don't believe in God and aren't saved. It might just mean that you have stopped believing in His ability and power, that you have stopped trusting Him, relying on His wisdom and knowledge, and that you have stopped standing on His truth. Instead, your focus has shifted away from God and His plan and promises and on to you and yours. As a result, the wavering life you've built through your own power begins to crumble and sink beneath your faltering feet.

By contrast, building our house on the Rock is living life in obedience to God's Word, relying on His strength and provision, and following His direction, plan, and purpose. We're living in faith, trusting Him along the way, and cooperating with God.

Building our homes on the Rock protects us from thorns and thistles. Its solid foundation beneath our feet helps shield and prevent us from walking into unstable, unreliable, and unhealthy situations where life-changing and destructive choices shake us, break us, and mold our lives into the worldly pattern of sandy sin.

God has revealed some of the iniquities of my bloodline and shown how they continued to hitch a ride onto my own life as well as my siblings'. Such iniquities include premarital sex, divorce, anger, bitterness, pride, resentment, rebellion, unforgiveness, isolation, idolatry, depression, fear, worry, distrust, self-reliance, and insecurity, to name a few.

I believe as I moved from place to place in my spiritual walk with God, that for years I was still carrying thorns and thistles with me. I had tried to get rid of them in my own strength but failed. Eventually, God sent His holy fire to come cleanse me and burn away this generational sin at the root once and for all. As a result, I was purified to walk freely without the nuisance of tormenting pain from my past failures and mistakes as well as that of my parents. These particular thorns and thistles would cease to torment me and my descendents. The curse of the ground was removed. My children will no longer inherit thorns and thistles. From here on out, the ground we walk will be blessed because of choosing to obey, stand, and build our home on the Rock of God's Word.

I'm not implying that my children will walk this earth without troubles of their own doing, sin, mistakes, or failures. I'm simply declaring that they will move forward without picking up and carrying on mine. I'm praying now to break off the pull and tendency to lean toward those same destructive patterns of sin carried throughout my bloodline. Instead, they'll receive a push in the upright and opposite direction toward a path of future blessings, not curses. I'm praying that my children will not follow in my sandy footsteps (like mother, like daughter). Rather, they follow in God's (like Father, like Son).

In breaking off this old cycle, I'm collaborating alongside God to write a new decree over my bloodline that carries on a legacy of blessings, yielding fruits of righteousness to be inherited and passed down to the next generation and future generations to come.

> *The seed that fell among the thorns represents those who hear God's word, but all too quickly the message is crowded out by the worries of this life and the lure of wealth, so no fruit is produced. The seed that fell on good soil represents those who truly hear and understand God's word and produce a harvest of thirty, sixty, or even a hundred times as much as had been planted!" (Matthew 13:22–23 NLT).*

The Wages of Sin

The worries of life (financial instability, fear, jealousy, distrust, etc.) have a way of choking out the good seed (the truth of God's Word) that we planted. Troublesome weeds overtake the lot and rob it of its fruit-bearing capability. Even Christians sometimes foolishly build their homes on the sand, failing to stand on God's strength and provision when trouble comes. But it is never too late to start over.

We can wisely invite God into our plans at any time. He can create and design a new project built on fertile ground and a solid Foundation that will weather the storms and stand the test of time.

Unfortunately, this would not take place in my own life until later on down the road.

Build on the Rock

> *"Therefore whoever hears these sayings of Mine, and does them, I will liken him to a wise man who built his house on the rock: and the rain descended, the floods came, and the winds blew and beat on that house; and it did not fall, for it was founded on the rock.*
>
> *"But everyone who hears these sayings of Mine, and does not do them, will be like a foolish man who built his house on the sand: and the rain descended, the floods came, and the winds blew and beat on that house; and it fell. And great was its fall"* (Matthew 7:24–27 NKJV).

"Grace" according to the Baker's Evangelical Dictionary of Biblical Theology is described as the unmerited favor of God toward man. Grace is something we don't deserve or earn, but it's what we receive. We are sinners, yet we've received the precious gift of grace and the bestowal of blessings in exchange for the punishment we deserve. We are allowed to start over and carry on with our lives, in spite of our foolishness, sin, and failures, to build upon the Rock.

Not only will we receive this grace by God when we repent (change our minds and turn away from our sin) and turn toward Him for forgiveness and guidance, but we should also extend grace and forgiveness to others when they hurt, offend, or disappoint us, especially if they're our parents. When we honor our parents, we honor God's desire. We all desire grace and forgiveness, but if we deny it to others, God will deny it to us. So to be set free of our iniquities, we must receive God's Word, apply its truth (do what it says), and extend the gift of grace to others.

Here is a prayer to break off iniquities taken from the book *Ten Steps Toward Christ* by Jimmy Evans: [3]

PRAYER

Father, I recognize this iniquity and repent of my involvement in it. I forgive my parents for anything they have done wrong, and I bless them. I ask for Your forgiveness and receive it. I also break the power of this iniquity off my life in the name of Jesus. I break _____ [name the iniquity(ies)] off my life and all future generations. I renounce it and pray that You will heal me and teach me how to change this area and to walk in obedience to You. I thank You for forgiving me and setting me free in Jesus' Name. Amen.

The Gift of Motherhood

One October day, my husband and I received our precious gift—a beautiful baby girl! She was a shimmer of light that came into our lives. She had beautiful blue eyes, light blonde hair, and was perfectly healthy and the most gorgeous creation I had ever seen.

Although in the beginning, her impending arrival was a surprise to us, she was no surprise to God. She was not a mistake, an accident, or regret. She was an incredible gift. God saw her coming, designed and created her wonderfully, and planned for her arrival. I felt love in a new way when I held her in my arms for the first time.

I had experienced the joy of motherhood. I had experienced the type of love that is both sacrificial and unconditional, the kind that would do anything to protect and provide for your child.

Sacrificial Love

This is the kind of love that God has for His own children. He loves us so much that He was willing to sacrifice everything to save us. That is why He sent His One and only Son to be our Savior. He couldn't bear to see His children sentenced to death. So He made a Way for us. He sent His Son Jesus to die in our place. He bore the penalty of our guilt and shame by dying for our sins on the cross. In doing so, He set us free from eternal death and made a way for us to receive everlasting life.

That is sacrificial love.

> *For God so loved the world that he gave his one and only Son, that whoever believes in him shall not perish but have eternal life (John 3:16 NIV).*

Unconditional Love

His love for us is great and unconditional. We could never disappoint Him enough to lose His love. He is love. He promises to love us forever. He will never leave us nor forsake us. He will not abandon us. No matter our sinfulness, or rebellion, He will always love us. We are His wonderful creation. He's not ashamed of us if we're not ashamed of Him.

He urges us to stay away from sin because He knows how it affects His dear children. He knows that it leads to destruction, pain, and death. He knows that our enemy is always plotting and scheming to set a trap for us. That is why He made a way to redeem us from the fall to save us from eternal damnation. In return, all He asks of us is to love Him with all of our hearts, minds, bodies, and souls, and to love His people.

He doesn't command His children to be perfect. He commands us to love.

> *Jesus replied: "'Love the Lord your God with all your heart and with all your soul and with all your mind.' This is the first and greatest commandment. And the second is like it: 'Love your neighbor as yourself'" (Matthew 22:37--39 NIV).*

God never wanted us to leave the Garden. He never wanted us to lose paradise. He never wanted there to be separation between us and Him. He created us to be together for all eternity. He did, however, give us free will. He wanted us to decide to love and serve Him for ourselves. He didn't force His love upon us. It is up to us to receive His love and receive Him as our Father.

> *Jesus answered, "I am the way and the truth and the life. No one comes to the Father except through me (John 14:6 NIV).*

No matter what you've been through or what you've done, you are worthy of the Father's love and forgiveness. As a born again believer, you don't have to work to cover your sins or make yourself righteous. The cross accomplished that for us. Dear one, instead of walking in shame, guilt, and condemnation, come to the Father and walk in His grace and acceptance. It is the enemy's voice that convinces us to hide from God. But God says, "Where are you?"

Child, step into the light of His redemption. God's not angry or disappointed in you. He's *madly* in love with you.

CHAPTER FIVE

On Our Own

I had heard of these scriptural truths, yet, it took me a long time to *apply* these truths and begin to fully receive this kind of love and to also give it away. As I have said before, *knowledge without application is useless*.

As newlyweds, and also raising a newborn, my husband and I had a lot to learn. We were young and had no clue as to what we were doing. We did our best on our own, but we were in serious need of assistance.

This was a lot for two very young adults to take on by themselves. The stress of a newborn, financial instability, and two people in need of healing and identity, it all took its toll. So much pain and disappointment had been built up inside of me. I overcompensated from this pain by trying to grow up extremely fast and prove myself. I was so ashamed of being a teenage pregnancy statistic. I was still nineteen when I had my daughter. This bothered me a great deal.

I figured that I was the talk of my small town and right at the top of the headlines reading "Homecoming Queen Gets Pregnant Right Out of High School." I felt like such a failure, that all my potential of doing and achieving something magnificent had gone down the drain. Look who I had become instead—a college dropout and screw up. Needless to say, my self-esteem took a nosedive.

Emergence

My assurance only got worse once my husband and I started having marital trouble. I believe we both entered into this marriage with problems and baggage. Our issues didn't go away and were causing a lot of damage physically, mentally, and emotionally.

I didn't know how to properly respond to this damage. Instead, I grew increasingly angry, bitter, and resentful toward my spouse because of the promises that were broken. Secrecy, lies, addictions, and all my greatest fears had entered into our union.

As my husband began to bail on his promise; I began to bail on mine. As he began to welcome in worldly ungodliness without seeing it as a problem, I began to welcome in the idea of escape.

I felt rejected, replaced, ignored, and of no value to him. I didn't feel loved or secure. The thought of living this way until death did us part was intolerable. Step by step, I began to slowly withdraw and walk away in search of love and happiness.

We separated many times in the hope that it would solve our problems. This only masked the pain. Separation was not a real solution for us. It was only a temporary bandage to conceal and hide the wound. The scars were still left underneath, and each time we came back together, our problems were exposed and right there waiting on us. This festering sore kept going from bad to worse.

We so desperately needed godly counsel and support (spiritual ointment) to help us properly work through these issues and heal. Instead, we turned to friends and family, not that most weren't spiritual sources that meant well and provided some wisdom. However, even spirit-filled friends and family members can be pretty biased, tend to take sides, and also react emotionally and defensively rather than productively.

Although we occasionally attended church, we had not found a church to call our home or become members of the body. We needed a strong church home to go to regularly as well as individual time spent with God in the Word in order to get fed spiritually. We needed that nourishment that would help us to grow upright and mature as individuals and as a couple.

We needed a new perspective, one based on truth and grace, not blame.

I went into our marriage with the wrong perspective. I thought, *I'll give it two years and see what happens.*

On Our Own

Without realizing it, I had already set us up for failure by making this inner vow. I had not entered this covenant relationship fully committed before God. I "walked in" with the *hopes* to succeed yet with a backup plan to "walk out" if it didn't. I had picked up this trait through witnessing my parents' divorce.

Even though I hated the idea of divorce, I had seen it as a possibility. Therefore, my "commitment" to this marriage was conditional upon him keeping his promise to change. I was in charge of my life, not God. I was the player, coach, and referee all at the same time. My insistence on being in control automatically limited the possibility of what God was capable of achieving.

What was I thinking? I was thinking like a child. I was a child, a spiritual toddler with the egocentric behavior of a three-year-old. It's all about me.

Likewise, my husband went into this marriage promising that he would change and become the husband I needed him to be. This vow set us up for failure as well and invited unrealistic expectations to be upheld, especially without the work and help of the Holy Spirit in his life.

Within just a few short months of marriage, that promise began to unravel. He wasn't *fully* committed to upholding his commitment made to me and refused to seek outside help.

We both had given it a whirl for a while.

I believe Tom and I both made our share of mistakes and failures. I shouldn't have expected him to become someone he was not at the time and couldn't or wouldn't try to become later on. You shouldn't marry someone in the hopes that they will change into a different or new person. It's an unrealistic expectation, even if they promise. In my opinion, he shouldn't have made promises he didn't fully intend to keep, especially those that were contingent upon marriage in the first place.

Clearly, we were both guilty of breaking commitments and promises. We both failed miserably at meeting the other's needs. I don't feel we were thinking of us as one couple joined by God; we were still thinking of ourselves as separate individuals. Neither of us had yet to grow and mature spiritually. As a result, we responded immaturely and selfishly.

I was secure yet still young in my faith, and he was still in search of his. This unbalanced setup made it near impossible for us to accomplish the will and purposes of God in our lives as individuals and as a couple. One of us had to be willing to abandon his position for the other, especially since we were undoubtedly unequally yoked from the beginning. So, he continued to pull in one direction and I in the other, creating instability, conflict, confusion, and war among us.

True intimacy and harmony were nonexistent within our marriage because we were not spiritually united. Consequently, we were continually at odds with one another, trying to convert the other because we were opposites in our beliefs, morals, and mission. God commands and warns believers to not enter into such alliances for our own protection, as well as that of our children's, and from the temptation of being led astray.

The Temple of the Living God

Don't continue to team up with unbelievers in mismatched alliances, for what partnership is there between righteousness and rebellion? Who could mingle light with darkness? What harmony can there be between Christ and Satan? Or what does a believer have in common with an unbeliever? What friendship does God's temple have with demons? For indeed, we are the temple of the living God, just as God has said: I will make my home in them and walk among them. I will be their God, and they will be my people.

For this reason, "Come out from among them and be separate," says the Lord. "Touch nothing that is unclean, and I will embrace you. I will be a true Father to you, and you will be my beloved sons and daughters," says the Lord Yahweh Almighty (2 Corinthians 6:14–18 TPT).

Living Holy Lives

Beloved ones, with promises like these, and because of our deepest respect and worship of God, we must remove everything from our lives that contaminates body and spirit, and continue to complete the development of holiness within us (2 Corinthians 7:1 TPT).

On Our Own

We married for the wrong reasons. Our greatest problem was never being equally yoked. We chose to get married nonetheless, so here we were forced to deal with this problem. Regrettably, we didn't deal with it well.

Fully expecting a spouse or anyone for that matter to meet all our deepest needs is a setup for failure in any marriage. Only God can meet our deepest needs. Sadly, we never fully invited or expected Him to do so; thus it was our greatest failure.

Yes, deep down I trusted we each wanted the relationship to work. I don't believe either of us was surrounded with the type of influence that "spoke life" over our marriage. We for sure didn't speak life over one another. We retaliated, saying hateful and hurtful things. We each tossed the blame back and forth, refusing to take ownership for our mistakes and failures, just as Adam and Eve did when confronted with their sin in the garden.

In fear of our own nakedness, we shamefully turned on one another. Because out of our own acts of rebellion, we had shamefully turned on God.

> *The man said, "The woman you put here with me—she gave me some fruit from the tree, and I ate it" (Genesis 3:12 NIV).*

> *Then the Lord God said to the woman, "What is this you have done?"*

> *The woman said, "The serpent deceived me, and I ate" (Genesis 3:13 NIV).*

Our marriage was falling apart. The hope of happiness was washing away as the storms came and beat against our house.

Foolishly, we had built it on the sand.

The Bible tells us that woman was created because it was not good for man to be alone. So God created a helper for him.

> *So the man gave names to all the livestock, the birds in the sky and all the wild animals. But for Adam no suitable helper was found. So the Lord God caused the man to fall into a deep sleep; and while he was sleeping, he took one of the man's ribs and then closed up the place with flesh. Then the Lord God made a woman from the rib he had taken out of the man, and he brought her to the man.*

Emergence

The man said, "This is now bone of my bones and flesh of my flesh; she shall be called 'woman,' for she was taken out of man."

That is why a man leaves his father and mother and is united to his wife, and they become one flesh.

Adam and his wife were both naked, and they felt no shame (Genesis 2:20–25 NIV).

Man and wife are meant to be one flesh. Man is to leave his father and mother, and woman is to be his helper. In marriage, the two are meant to become one, to help one another and be united as a couple. They should be naked in front of one another and unashamed.

We were none of these things.

First, we weren't behaving as one. We were divided in so many ways. He would run to his parents and I to mine like little tattletales rather than running to our Heavenly Father. We had not left our parents and didn't cleave to one another. Instead, we were treating one another like enemies rather than joining forces and battling against the real enemy (Satan), who was seeking to destroy our marriage and our family. We were not on one team, fighting *for* one another with one common goal—the victory of our marriage. No. We were fighting *against* one another, each set on winning the argument at hand. (Major Marriage Foul!)

Secondly, we were not behaving like suitable helpers. We were not helping each other heal from our insecurities and weaknesses. Rather, we were pointing out the other's imperfections while refusing to forgive, extend grace, and pray for one another in patience, inviting and allowing the Holy Spirit to work at repairing two very broken vessels.

Third, we were not fully naked in front of the other or naked before God. God created us to be naked and unashamed before Him and our spouse. We were not exposing ourselves with honest and open communication. We did not lay out all of our problems openly and plainly, asking God to shine His light on them. Instead, we remained hidden in the dark before one another in our shame, guilt, and secrecy.

We foolishly crossed the boundary lines of our covenant lot. We each ventured out secretly in our own way—physically, mentally, or emotionally, bringing in dangerous wolves from outside the fence, robbing ourselves of God's blessings and making our lot an unholy and unsafe place. We both disobediently looked back and held onto our past rather than fixing our eyes on Jesus as He led the way forward.

We did not protect our garden.

We were breaking all of the rules, and no time out on separate benches could fix it. We needed God's intervention. We needed a spiritual coach.

We had tried to win on our own, and we were losing badly.

Uninvited Presence

We isolated ourselves from each other. We were like roommates who didn't get along rather than a couple in love. The only companion I had at home was my precious little girl to whom I turned for comfort. I should have turned to God for comfort, our true Companion, the Holy Spirit, and invited Him to reside in our home and rebuild our demolished marriage.

It's worth repeating that isolation is an invitation. Where the Lord's presence isn't, the enemy's presence is sure to come. Unfortunately, as a couple, we just never fully invited God to come into our circumstances.

It wasn't long before I was completely broken down. I was depressed and searching for answers.

My feelings of abandonment intensified. My attempt to fix things and change my husband's heart had failed. I couldn't change him. The more I tried, the further I pushed him away in resentment. He didn't seem to want to change, at least not for me. Rather than turning to God in prayer and allowing God to change his heart and desires, I tried to change it on my own, and I'm no Savior.

I assume he ended up feeling convicted all the time when I should have offered him love, kindness, and forgiveness. Anger, bitterness, fear, and tears had once again become my default setting that was triggered whenever my hurt button was pushed repeatedly. I should have cried out to God when pain came and not lashed out at my spouse. It was ugly.

I did turn to God some for comfort and guidance during this time, but I didn't seek Him long enough for answers or wait for His reply and instruction. It was a one-way conversation.

I grew impatient and listened to my own heart. In a desperate attempt to find relief, I took matters into my own hands by trying to forcefully pry my husband's heart open with a crowbar. We should have put down the destructive tools being used to tear down and rip the other apart. We should have picked up and used the only tool and key that could have unlocked an unwilling heart and built up and brought us back together—God's Word and God's love. When love isn't invited, hate is sure to rear its ugly head.

Yes, it is true that I picked up the Word of God, yet I didn't know how to use it properly. As a result, I didn't apply it effectively. I didn't speak it out loud over our circumstances in faith, believing in hope and trusting that God could bring salvation to our marriage.

There is no way of knowing how things would have played out if these strategies had been applied. But the surrendering of our hands and our thrones, allowing God to use His mighty hands and sit rightfully on His throne, should have been the first resort. I should have asked for Him to work on my husband's heart, beliefs, and issues. I should have been praying for my husband to have God's desires. We should have been praying and asking God to show us how to be married. I should have prayed for patience toward my spouse while God was working on his heart, and for the ability to forgive him in the meantime as He also worked on mine. I should have prayed for the strength and grace to hold on as well as let go. I should have prayed not my will but "Your will be done, Lord."

We should have cried out, called out, and turned to God for everything. We should have been faithful in prayer, patient in affliction, and joyful in hope. We should have allowed God the *opportunity* to repair our broken hearts and marriage. We should have prayed together as a couple. We should have prayed, "God, give me Your heart for my spouse. Help me to love him/her the way You do. Help me to see him/her through Your forgiving eyes. Holy Spirit, come and help us become who You have created us to be, not who we think we are. Help us to help the other become their best self, the person You say they are. Lord, help us to become one flesh."

I should have been praying Acts 26:18 (a powerful Scripture to open our spiritual eyes and turn us around) over my spouse, myself, and our marriage.

> *And you will open their eyes to their true condition, so that they may turn from darkness to the Light and from the power of Satan to the power of God. By placing their faith in me they will receive the total forgiveness of sins and be made holy, taking hold of the inheritance that I give to my children!' (Acts 26:18 TPT).*

We should have done all of these things and more. We should have let go and let God.

On Our Own

We should have built our house on the Rock.

We should have, but we didn't.

Be joyful in hope, patient in affliction, faithful in prayer (Romans 12:12 NIV).

I Bought the Lie—Game Over

After only two short years of marriage, I filed for divorce. I was exhausted from the battle and had lost all hope in my spouse and our marriage, so I threw in the towel and called it quits. Imagine that, . . .my marriage was over after two years. I had spoken death over my marriage from the beginning by suggesting I would give it only two years to work. Its failure should have come as no surprise.

I was so miserable and unhappy that I truly believed divorce was the answer to all my problems. Sound familiar? I wonder where this idea and thought came from.

I was wrong. Divorce may have ended one painful chapter in my life, but it opened up an entire new book of problems. A child had been created and was now caught in the middle of it all. There was no getting out or escaping the sea of trouble that arose after that apple was bitten. I may have been able to walk away, but the soles of my shoes were not yet clean. I was still linked to that decision and its painful consequences until I would one day learn how to break off the destructive cycle.

Divorce was the last thing I ever wanted to happen in my life. I knew how painful it was. I had witnessed this with my parents. Now here I was following in their footsteps, tracking those same thorns and thistles into my own home. I never wanted my child to experience that kind of pain and loss, nor did my parents for me.

However, I believed that our circumstances justified a divorce and still do. It had become an unstable, unhealthy, and unfruitful atmosphere. Circumstances had gotten well out of hand. I had read in my Bible about divorce and when it was acceptable, so I had a lot of questions and concerns about it. I was afraid of letting God down again. I wish I would have reached out more for biblical wisdom, knowledge, understanding, and discernment.

Emergence

Unfortunately, I didn't. I mostly kept my questions and concerns to myself and made my decision. All I knew was that things could not go on as they were. Something *had* to change. We were not living the lives that God had created us to live, and we were not becoming the people we were meant to be. At this point, I didn't know who I was or what I was to become. I had vanished. I was lost. It was a hazardous environment for everyone, especially for our innocent child.

I wonder if this is similar to how my mom must have felt when she too made her decision to divorce.

God could have saved our marriage if we had surrendered it to Him fully and given Him the chance. With God, all things are possible. He is capable of doing anything. However, we have a position to play. Our hearts have to be willing to move and allow Him to work in us. My heart was willing and had let God in, but at the time, I believed my husband's was not. I was unwilling to wait on him to move into position and participate any longer.

We were tied together, and I was unable to move forward and carry the weight of this burden alone while he remained dead weight. I had no strength left in me, and I didn't recognize how to ask God to carry it for me or rely on Him to motivate my spouse. I was ready to get off the bench and enter the game, and begged my husband to do the same, but he refused. My strength was not enough to open his heart. I determined he was comfortable where he was at and would not budge.

Therefore, just as I gave up on my dream to be a starting player in my freshman year of basketball due to a broken heart from my parents' divorce, I again slowly gave up on my husband and on this dream of a happy and successful marriage. My heart was too broken from irreconcilable differences. We were both stuck sitting on that bench while our lives continued to play out rebelliously in front of us because neither of us were willing to compromise our position.

I failed to give up my seat on the throne of playing God in our marriage (unintentionally and unknowingly), and he refused to give up his seat on the bench and play at all. I couldn't accept that outcome one second longer. So I chose to cut our bond of marriage, breaking our burdensome yoke. After all, the two-year clock had run out of time—*game over*. I chose to walk away from our marriage on the day of our two-year wedding anniversary.

On Our Own

Played by the Enemy

On the eve of our anniversary, I accidently left my car unlocked, and thieves stole my stereo that night. I had lived in the country or small towns for most of my life and was used to leaving cars and homes unlocked. Theft hadn't been a real threat so I was lenient toward guarding against invasion.

When I woke up that next morning I remembered it was our anniversary and I was somewhat hopeful and optimistic to celebrate it. Perhaps he had planned something special? Could today be the turning point?

Satan also remembered it was our wedding anniversary. My first encounter with my husband was confronting his anger. He was furious at me for being so careless, sparking yet another dispute between us. Tempers flared up fiery darts, and just like that, my temporary flicker of hope went up in smoke that day for good. This wasn't the turning point in our marriage I had hoped for.

I thought, *If we couldn't even demonstrate feelings of love and affection on this one day, our anniversary, how would we do so in the days to come? Was losing a stereo worth more value to him than me?*

When we thoughtlessly and carelessly leave our marriage and hearts wide open for thieves to come and steal the instrument and weapon of faith and hope that God has given us, we can expect to be robbed of the beautiful song and melody it was intended to play. Our voice is intended to speak life, not death. When we fail to guard and protect the lyrics of our hearts (our words and thoughts intended for good), the enemy takes them, steals them like a thief in the night, and uses them to orchestrate his own appalling musical composition for evil. Remember, Lucifer was the director of music in heaven before he was banished.

We are God's instruments intended for good, but the enemy loves to play with us. He takes our weapons of warfare and protection and uses them against us if we let him. I thoughtlessly allowed the enemy to take away my hope when I carelessly allowed him to steal my voice, my instrument of faith.

> *Be prepared. You're up against far more than you can handle on your own. Take all the help you can get, every weapon God has issued, so that when it's all over but the shouting you'll still be on your feet. Truth, righteousness, peace, faith, and salvation*

are more than words. Learn how to apply them. You'll need them throughout your life. God's Word is an indispensable weapon. In the same way, prayer is essential in this ongoing warfare. Pray hard and long. Pray for your brothers and sisters. Keep your eyes open. Keep each other's spirits up so that no one falls behind or drops out (Ephesians 6:16–18 MSG).

The woeful tune I allowed the enemy to play was anything but merry. Neither was divorce the pretty picture that it appeared to be in my mind. It wasn't my escape to happiness and bliss that I imagined it would be. It was brokenness at its best.

I should have remembered this from my parents' divorce. *A family ripped* apart should have been the familiar picture I saw. However, it wasn't. I pictured myself happily in love again with someone else and my daughter having the happy family she deserved. Just like my mom, I too had been deceived by a lie.

In my time of loneliness, despair, weakness, isolation, and vulnerability, the enemy came into my thoughts and strummed the same poisonous melody into my ears. He suggested, once again, that if I took a bite of this apple, I could have my greatest desire.

He flaunted the idea of being reunited with my first love. This was the familiar picture I saw. I didn't allow myself to focus on a beautiful image of a future with my husband. I began to look backwards and focus on the beauty of the past—an old mental portrait where I appeared happy.

Ultimately, it was my decision to divorce, and I have to take responsibility for all of my decisions. However, like my mother, I believe that the enemy's lie gave me the nudge to follow through with it. If I would have had my eyes set on the reality and true picture of divorce instead of a falsehood, I might not have jumped ship. Likewise, if I would have had my eyes set on God and the reconciliation of our marriage, I would have received the hope and strength I needed to remain in the game and fight for victory, not drop out and succumb to defeat.

Godly perspective, faith, and prayer have the power to change possibilities. Where your eyes venture, your heart follows. It's our enemy's craftiness that leads us to take the plunge and dive into death and destruction. This is what our enemy does. He is very good and experienced at it. He has been deceiving God's people this way since creation. He insinuates and portrays rebellion as cleverness.

On Our Own

This is what I want to make so evidently clear, and it's one of the main reasons for sharing my story with you. It is not because I had some thoughts I needed to get off of my chest or that I wanted to bash an ex-spouse or blame my parents for my problems. Absolutely not! I admire and respect each of my parents for how they have handled all that they have been through in life. They still managed to hold on to their faith in God and lovingly guide and support my siblings and me throughout all our own troubles.

I also feel nothing but forgiveness and grace toward my ex. As you've probably figured out by now, I was quite the mess myself. Blame and judgment is not something I'm licensed to serve. What would be the point in sharing negative thoughts with you? How would that benefit or accomplish anything good in your life? These events occurred years ago. Today we are all very different people, including my ex. I think he is a dedicated father, hard worker, and is still extremely talented. I sincerely wish he and his entire family only God's very best in life.

God can take all our ashes, the pain of our past, and transform them into something beautiful. He can use it to bless, teach, and inspire others if we'll allow Him to. This beauty is what I wish to share with you.

Although it's not easy to open up and share my life with the world, you are worth it to me. The easy thing is to keep it all hidden and buried. But God has done a miraculous work in my life, and that is why I have to share it.

At this point in my story, all hope seemed lost. But I promise, all is not lost. God has breathed new life into me. I'm praying that by pulling my skeletons out of the closet, that light and a new breath of life might also be shed and breathed into you and your troubling circumstances through the power and the wind of His Spirit. I'm pulling from the mistakes, failures, and victories in my life to help you see the ugly, dead side of sin, yet the beautiful side of grace, forgiveness, and resurrection and to reveal the greater battle in all our lives.

I failed to speak life into my marriage, and it died. But God has helped me to see beyond hopelessness through His life-breathing Spirit and His Word. I have experienced His resurrection power when "life" is declared, spoken, and prophesied over the dead, dark, and dry places. That is what I wish you to also see and experience as we travel together throughout this story.

Emergence
The Valley of Dry Bones

The hand of the Lord was on me, and he brought me out by the Spirit of the Lord and set me in the middle of a valley; it was full of bones. He led me back and forth among them, and I saw a great many bones on the floor of the valley, bones that were very dry. He asked me, "Son of man, can these bones live?"

I said, "Sovereign Lord, you alone know."

Then he said to me, "Prophesy to these bones and say to them, 'Dry bones, hear the word of the Lord! This is what the Sovereign Lord says to these bones: I will make breath enter you, and you will come to life. I will attach tendons to you and make flesh come upon you and cover you with skin; I will put breath in you, and you will come to life. Then you will know that I am the Lord.'"

So I prophesied as I was commanded. And as I was prophesying, there was a noise, a rattling sound, and the bones came together, bone to bone. I looked, and tendons and flesh appeared on them and skin covered them, but there was no breath in them.

Then he said to me, "Prophesy to the breath; prophesy, son of man, and say to it, 'This is what the Sovereign Lord says: Come, breath, from the four winds and breathe into these slain, that they may live.'"

So I prophesied as he commanded me, and breath entered them; they came to life and stood up on their feet—a vast army.

Then he said to me: "Son of man, these bones are the people of Israel. They say, 'Our bones are dried up and our hope is gone; we are cut off.' Therefore prophesy and say to them: 'This is what the Sovereign Lord says: My people, I am going to open your graves and bring you up from them; I will bring you back to the land of Israel. Then you, my people, will know that I am the Lord, when I open your graves and bring you up from them. I will put my Spirit in you and you will live, and I will

On Our Own

settle you in your own land. Then you will know that I the Lord have spoken, and I have done it, declares the Lord'" (Ezekiel 37:1–14 NIV).

I want to expose and bring to light the enemy's tactics used to shift our eyes off the true prize and onto the false impressions he makes upon us, thus derailing us from the victorious life God plans for us. Exposure of the enemy's lies can prevent us from becoming his latest victim. I didn't recognize the attack in my parents' life, and I didn't see nor recognize the attack in my own life until it was too late. Satan's lies blind us to the truth. God revealed this knowledge to me sixteen years after my own divorce.

The enemy's lies wreaked havoc in my parents' lives, affecting the next generation, and the enemy's lies wreaked havoc in my own life, affecting the next generation. It all starts with that first rebellious bite of the fruit, the shifting of the eyes to forbidden places. Eve saw that the fruit was pleasing to the eye. And she ate of it.

I walked away from our marriage on the morning of our two-year wedding anniversary. The morning that my dad woke my siblings and me up to say that he was leaving and that my mom wanted a divorce also occurred on the day of their sixteen-year wedding anniversary. There is no question that the enemy hates marriage and comes to steal, kill, and destroy it. Marriage is a covenant relationship between God and His children, and Satan is jealous because he has been cut out of the wedding portrait. His revenge—destroy marriage and destroy the bride of Christ.

My hope is that sharing this knowledge might help to expose the enemy's tactics that were used not only in my own bloodline, but also in the lives of others. In doing so, eyes can be shifted back to the place where they belong. The destructive patterns of sin and rebellion (iniquities) can be prevented from carrying on into the next generation. These destructive patterns can be broken off through awareness and prayer.

We have the power and authority to declare, prophesy, and speak life over our lives, circumstances, families, and children in order to bind the enemy and loose God's resurrection power and victory through the instruments He has given us. First, though, we must see and recognize that there is a real threat in leaving our hearts and mouths wide open for the enemy to come in and steal from us and use for his purposes. This is the purpose of a testimony, to share what you have seen, learned, and discovered to be true about God in your life in order to benefit others.

Emergence

"Truly I tell you, whatever you bind on earth will be bound in heaven, and whatever you loose on earth will be loosed in heaven (Matthew 18:18 NIV).

At a very young age, I had experienced the heartache of having to part with three of the most important men in my life—first my dad, then my first love, and also my first husband. So much had been taken, lost, and stolen.

One thing I have discovered is that people and their commitments are often fleeting and mankind is not very good at keeping promises.

Fortunately, God is!

Even though I walked away from my marriage, gave up on my ex-husband, and I believe we both failed to keep our promises and commitments, God doesn't give up on marriage, walk away from His bride, or fail to keep His promises and commitments to us. After our divorce, my ex told me that if there was one good thing that came out of our marriage, it was that I helped lead him closer to God. I feared that I had failed to direct him to God because I didn't yet see any evidence of change in him. When I made the decision to divorce, I also didn't yet understand that leaving an "unequally yoked marriage" was disobedience (1 Corinthians 7:13–16).

Hearing these words from his mouth comforted me and helped me to believe that perhaps he was changing and that our meeting wasn't a disastrous waste, and our marriage wasn't a complete failure. There was meaning to our meeting. Just because I couldn't see any evidence of change in his actions or behaviors at the time didn't mean none was taking place in his heart. Even more could be taking place right now.

We can't always see the power of the Holy Spirit at work in the lives of others. One thing I did do right was that I prayed many times for him to come to know Christ and to receive Him into his heart as Lord and Savior. If we have prayed and invited Him into those secret and hidden places, then we must trust and believe that He is there knocking at the door and working to be invited in.

Despite our failures and the pain we both put one another through, if out of it all he was turned to God, and I had the privilege of playing even a small part in that, then it was all worth it in the end! Despite my failure to hold on, my decisions to let go, and my inability to warmly demonstrate grace, mercy, forgiveness, and obedience as I should have, I am so thankful that God will never cease to demonstrate His. Although I made the decision to no longer be bound to my ex-spouse, I pray that he has made the decision to forever be bound to Christ. Ultimately, that choice is between him and God, but I believe he has chosen to receive Jesus. I celebrate that victory!

Today, I also pray that the Holy Spirit will continue His work at changing both of our hearts and our minds.

I'm so thankful that God's commitment to love us and never leave us is unshakable, and that His promises are unbreakable. His love never fails even though we often fail to see the wrong we commit, recognize our fault, or desire the willingness to change. He continues to fight for us. He is a God who stays true to His word. That is something the enemy can never take away from us.

Even while Jesus was being crucified for our sins and *His* hurt button pushed repeatedly, He continued to speak words of life over us. Jesus sees us as children and has such compassion toward us, both when we don't know the evil we are doing and even when we do.

Help us, Lord, to be more like You.

While they were nailing Jesus to the cross, he prayed over and over, "Father, forgive them, for they don't know what they're doing."

The soldiers, after they crucified him, gambled over his clothing (Luke 22:34 TPT).

God has made covenant promises with His people to redeem us from all our failures so long as we repent—change our minds and turn our hearts and our eyes back to Him. He holds onto those who have entered into relationship with Him and who love Him. Even though we sometimes walk away from His will for our lives, He never lets us go.

Thank you, Jesus, for your promises to never walk away from us even when we fail You.

Help us, Lord, to take back and reclaim our instrument of faith. This is how the children of God break the recurring cycles of evil—we play our faith instruments LOUD!

Give thanks to the Lord, for he is good. His love endures forever (Psalm 136:1 NIV).

Emergence

Good Comes to Those Who Return to the Lord

"When all these things have come upon you, the good things and the curses which I have told you about, you will remember them in all the nations where the Lord your God has sent you. When you and your children return to the Lord your God and obey Him with all your heart and soul by all I have told you today, then the Lord your God will have you return from where you were held. He will have loving-pity for you. He will gather you again from all the nations where the Lord your God has sent you. Even if you are driven to the ends of the earth, the Lord your God will gather you and bring you back.

"The Lord your God will bring you into the land your fathers lived in and it will be yours. He will bring good to you and make you more in number than your fathers.

"The Lord your God will take away the sin from your heart and from the heart of your children. You will love the Lord your God with all your heart and with all your soul, so you may live. Then the Lord your God will send all these curses upon those who hate you and upon those who made it hard for you.

"You will obey the Lord again, and keep all His Laws which I tell you today. And the Lord your God will bring much good upon all the work you do, and upon your children, and the young of your cattle, and the food of your field. For the Lord will again be happy to bring good to you, just as He was happy with your fathers. But you must obey the Lord your God to keep His Laws which are written in this book of the Law. You must turn to the Lord your God with all your heart and soul (Deuteronomy 30:1-10 NLV).

"For this Law I give you today is not too hard for you, or too far from you. It is not in heaven. You do not need to say, 'Who will go up to heaven for us and bring it down to make us hear it, so we may obey it?' It is not farther than the sea. You do not need to say, 'Who will cross the sea for us and bring it to us to make us hear it, so we may obey it?' (Deuteronomy 30:11-13 NLV).

On Our Own

"'For here's what I'm going to do: I'm going to take you out of these countries, gather you from all over, and bring you back to your own land. I'll pour pure water over you and scrub you clean. I'll give you a new heart, put a new spirit in you. I'll remove the stone heart from your body and replace it with a heart that's God-willed, not self-willed. I'll put my Spirit in you and make it possible for you to do what I tell you and live by my commands. You'll once again live in the land I gave your ancestors. You'll be my people! I'll be your God!'" (Ezekiel 36:26–28 MSG).

If you don't yet believe His promises are true, keep reading. I'll prove them to you.

God is good!

PRAYER

Lord,

Forgive me for doing things on my own. I surrender to You and invite Your presence to come. Open my spiritual eyes to recognize the enemy's attacks and tactics to derail me and my loved ones off course. Help me to see where he schemes to cause deception, division, distraction, and deviation. Set my feet on the path of life, light, righteousness, holiness, and truth. Open my ears and give me supernatural wisdom, knowledge, understanding, and discernment to hear Your voice. Open my mouth to speak life and truth. Give me a new heavenly perspective that shifts possibilities. I declare *life* over the dry bones of my life, marriage, parenting, relationships, and finances and welcome a new breath of Your Spirit to enter into my circumstances and resurrect the dead places. Thank You for Your power to restore and revive.

In Jesus' Name. Amen.

SECTION III

The Rise of Freedom

CHAPTER SIX

On My Own

I'll never forget the day I realized I was on my own. I had just dropped my daughter off at her father's house (our former home). It was time for his visitation. Tom kept the house because there was no way I could afford it by myself. From my perspective, nearly everything appeared to remain the same on his end; meanwhile, everything on my end had been turned upside down. I was the one who had moved out of our home, moved away from our town, and was struggling to move on from despair. I had been putting in job applications around town that day, and I was tired and needed a place to rest for a little while before heading back to my parent's house where I had been staying.

I had nowhere to go for rest and no one to turn to for comfort after saying goodbye to my daughter and the familiar life I had known. I ended up pulling into a McDonald's. Sitting inside at a little table hidden away in a corner, tears streamed down my cheeks as I looked at the empty seat in front of me. I had never felt so alone and needed much more than a Happy Meal to make me "Smiley" again.

With no home to call my own and no daughter with me full time, I felt I had nothing, no one, and no place to go. I felt like I was nobody.

I was on my own.

Eventually, I moved into town and started staying with my very gracious cousin and his family. The ninety-minute drive back and forth to my parents' home to put in applications had become too difficult. I found a job as a billing clerk in a doctor's office and started saving up so that my daughter and I could move into our own apartment. I then bought a bed and secured the first month's rent, but just a week before the move-in date, I received some distressing news.

I was being let go from my job that I had only been at for about three months.

This could not be happening! We were just about to move into our apartment. I had spent most of my savings securing and preparing for that place. I had been working overtime trying my best to get my employer's company caught up financially. The environment was extremely stressful and provided little on-the-job training, leaving me overwhelmed and exhausted, all while I was still going through a divorce. The problem was that they were so far behind on their billing and needed someone with experience to come in and get them caught up quickly. I had no previous experience in that field, and they didn't have the time to train me in that department. So they had to let me go. Knowing I had no billing experience, I'm not sure why they chose to hire me in the first place.

I was now at an all-time low. To make matters even worse, I had to call my former mother-in-law to come pick me up from the job I just got fired from because my car wouldn't start. I broke down hysterically right in front of her. This was the ultimate feeling of humiliation and terror at the same time. I wanted to pull myself together and prove before her how strong I had become on my own now. But I couldn't lie or fake it.

I was an absolute wreck in that crushing moment. She knew it. Although I gathered she didn't take pleasure in seeing me that way (we had maintained a friendly and civil relationship), I knew it wouldn't be long before my ex-husband would know it as well. Perfect!

All I could do over and over was ask, "What am I going to do now?"

Desperate Times & Desperate Measures of Faith

I chose to trust God and move into my apartment as planned. However, as a single mom, I was in a desperate situation and needed to find a job ASAP. Thankfully, I didn't have to wait long and was quickly hired as a part-time bank teller. Although I had been hoping for a full-time position, I took hold of it nonetheless. After all, beggars can't be choosers. I trusted God would provide.

On My Own

I didn't realize this at the time, but losing my job was actually a blessing in disguise. I was miserable at my old job. It was a terrible environment for me, and I needed to be in a place where I was surrounded by love, support, and kindness. I can see now how God picked me up out of that awful place and moved me into a better place. At the time though, none of it made any sense to me. It all made sense to God. I never went without. I always had just enough to get by. Despite the heart-rending transition, He provided for all of our needs.

I will never forget the first Christmas we had in our little apartment. We were celebrating it early because my daughter would be spending the holiday with her dad that year. I put up a five-foot tree in the corner and decorated it beautifully. The two of us listened to Christmas music, sang carols, and unwrapped her presents. Most of her toys came from one of those dollar stores that year, but she didn't notice. She loved them anyway.

When my ex–mother-in-law picked up my daughter to deliver her to her dad for me, she had kindly given me a wrapped present that I had been waiting to open on Christmas Day. It was the only gift I had under the tree for me.

Later that week, the roads were a little slippery. I didn't have the courage to travel alone to my parents' house for Christmas Day, so I decided to stay home instead.

I opened up my lone present, and inside was an empty photo album. Whether it was a sign of the true picture of my life at the time or a sign of starting over, it was indeed a reflection of how I appeared in that moment. *Empty.*

That was the loneliest Christmas I had ever had. I was away from my daughter, away from my family, and alone in that empty apartment. That cold winter year, I cried my very first Christmas tear.

Even though the tinsel didn't sparkle and shine as bright as it once had, there was still a glimmer of hope peering deep beneath the surface. A twinkle of light still flickered inside. Although I couldn't see it or feel it in that moment, it was always there within me.

I was *never* really on my own.

Emergence

Dancing Around the Idea of True Love

I loved my new job and kept advancing to higher positions as well as to full-time. I also worked with great people, many of whom were Christians. It was a very encouraging and rewarding environment to work in. I made many friends, and my confidence began to rise as I continued to flourish in my new position as teller supervisor.

However, I still felt that something was missing. I *longed* for a husband. I still hoped for and wanted a complete (whole) family. I wanted a companion to help me raise my daughter. Although it was true that I was never really on my own, I still felt lonely.

I thought that after I divorced, everything would fall into place just as I had imagined. I knew that starting over would be hard, but I never thought finding love would be.

In my dreams, my first love would come chasing after me, and we would finally be together. I believed all of my dreams would come true. After all, that was the lie I had been fed.

That was not the way things happened.

After my first love graduated, he went off to college. I was still married at the time. He began pursuing a career in law enforcement. By the time that I was divorced and had become available, he had joined the training academy and become unavailable. We wouldn't be able to talk for months.

When his training was finally completed, he went into the field right away. We now lived in separate states, had different schedules, and were miles and miles apart. We tried our best to keep in touch, but once again, our relationship was out of reach. Timing just wasn't on our side. In my heart, I held onto the possibility of someday being reunited with my first love.

I continued to hold on to my original dream.

In the meantime, I began settling into my new life. I went out with my friends occasionally on the weekends. We started going to clubs. I loved dancing, and it was a lot of fun to hang out with the girls. Eventually, I was going less to have fun with my friends and more to meet a guy. I started craving the excitement and the attention I was receiving from them.

On My Own

I didn't know where else to meet anyone. Internet dating was a little scary to me, and the guys at church were shy. I knew that the clubs were not the best places to be searching for future-husband material, but I didn't know where else to look. So, in desperation, I kept going.

I ended up meeting someone who seemed sweet, and a relationship seemed very promising in the beginning. He even brought my daughter a stuffed animal when he met her for the first time. We had been dating for about a month, and I began to fall for him pretty quickly.

However, the longer we were together I began to feel that something wasn't quite right. The more I got to know him, the more I began questioning our relationship. I had started having quiet time with the Lord and journaling about everything that was going on in my life. In fact, my journaling had become more of me speaking to God and writing down my prayers and petitions.

I began opening up to God and telling Him what I felt and expressing my concerns. I wrote a lot about my relationships and my hopes and dreams for me and my little girl. I poured my heart out to Him and sought His guidance. One day, I told God about my concerns and feelings about the relationship I was in. I asked Him to show me and let me know whether this man wasn't the right one for me. Then I wrote this prayer request down in my journal.

The very next day, I received a phone call from my boyfriend. He invited me to meet him at a bar. When I arrived, he broke up with me as all of his friends watched from a distance.

In that moment, I felt humiliated.

I was still damaged from my divorce and sorrowful at how things were turning out with my first love. Therefore, unknowingly in an attempt to self-medicate, I rebounded badly with dating. I had experienced a sad case of infatuation with my now ex-boyfriend. It always begins with optimism and ends with regret. Unfortunately, this wouldn't be the last time I fell for the wrong man.

I had a few more toads to go through before my prince would come.

I Cried Out

I continued down this path of looking for the perfect love in all the wrong places. After each attempt I ended up lonelier than before. I was broken and looking for something or someone to fix me—a man.

Emergence

If I poured myself into one, I thought he would pour back. So, I desperately searched for that one man to fill me. Everything I tried to put in just kept leaking out. My heart was cracking from the drought.

Eventually, I couldn't take it any longer. I finally fell to my knees and cried out to God for help! Sitting on the floor of my tiny living room and crying my eyes out, I confessed to God that I was a shattered mess, and that I couldn't do this anymore on my own. My way wasn't working.

For just a moment, I want to flashback to a story from my high school days. When I played basketball and ran track my freshman year, I began having growing pains and getting cramps in my calves frequently. One day in basketball practice when it was particularly troublesome, I noticed that every time I jumped up to rebound the ball, my calves would cramp up, and I would fall down to the floor in pain. I finally became so upset that I walked off the court and sat down on the floor. I benched myself. My coach came over to me and asked what was wrong. I explained the problem, and he told me I was deficient in potassium and needed to eat bananas.

That should fix it.

Rebounding in my troubled relationships felt a lot the same, except it wasn't my calf muscles that were deficient and experiencing spasms; it was my heart. I had been jumping up with all my might to reach up and grab hold of something that I thought could sustain and fill me, only to come crashing down in pain.

I had finally become so upset in my painful relationships that I walked off the court and took a seat. Just like I did back then, I benched myself for my own good. God took notice of my humility, remorse, and desperation and came to me in that moment. I explained to Him the problem, and I confessed that what I thought I wanted wasn't what I needed. I asked God to bring me the husband He wanted me to have. I made the decision to quit calling my own plays and surrendered control to Him. In doing so, I invited Him into my dream and stepped off the throne. I allowed Him to coach me.

Just like in my dream where Jesus met me when I was broken down on the side of the road after having gone my own way, I was lost, alone, empty, and stranded. I had been calling out to men for help when I should have been calling out to Jesus. Only His hands could repair and fix my brokenness and lead me safely back home.

Finally, I had made the right call.

On My Own

He Responded

One day a friend handed me a piece of paper that someone had given to her. She explained that she believed it was meant for me. This one piece of paper changed my life. It gave me an entirely new perspective. It spoke to me and encouraged me. It gave me instruction, direction, and hope. I had called out to God in desperation, and He heard my cry of surrender. This letter was His response and solution to my prayers. When I reached out to Him, He reached out to me and placed this letter in my hand. I call it "My Love Letter from God."

At the time, I didn't know who wrote it or where it came from. It had no title or author to go with it. I just knew in my heart that it was given to me by God, and that was enough for me.

It said,

Everyone longs to give themselves completely to someone,

To have a deep soul relationship with another,

To be loved thoroughly and exclusively...

But God says to a Christian,

No, not until you are satisfied, fulfilled, and content

With being loved by Me alone,

With giving yourself totally and unreservedly to Me,

With having an intensely personal and unique relationship with

Me alone,

Discovering that only in me is your satisfaction to be found,

Will you be capable of the perfect human relationship

That I have planned for you.

You will never be united with another until you are united with Me

Exclusive of anyone or anything else,

Emergence

Exclusive of any other desire or longings.

I want you to stop planning,

Stop wishing,

And allow Me

To give you the most thrilling plan existing—

One that you cannot imagine.

I want you to have the best.

Please allow Me to bring it to you.

You just keep watching Me, expecting the greatest things.

Keep experiencing the satisfaction that I am.

Keep listening and learning the things I tell you.

You just wait.

That's all.

Don't be anxious.

Don't worry.

Don't look around at the things others have gotten or

That I have given them.

Don't look at the things you think you want.

You just keep looking off and away up to me,

Or you'll miss what I want to show you.

And then, when you're ready,

I'll surprise you with a Love far more wonderful than any you would dream of.

On My Own

You see, until you are ready and

Until that one I have for you is ready (I am working even at this moment to have both of you

Ready at the same time),

Until you are both satisfied exclusively with me

And the life I prepared for you,

You won't be able to experience the Love that

Exemplifies your relationship with Me,

And this is the perfect Love.

And dear one, I want you to have this most wonderful Love.

I want you to see in the flesh a picture of your relationship with me,

And to enjoy materially and concretely

The everlasting union of beauty, perfection, and Love.

That I offer you with Myself.

Know that I love you utterly.

I am God.

Believe it and be satisfied.

"Be Satisfied with Me" Attributed to St. Anthony of Padua

This letter *changed* everything. It opened my eyes to see clearly; it opened my ears to hear His voice, and it opened my heart to receive His love in a new way. It exposed me to truth. *It gave me hope and a promise.*

Emergence

As a result, I turned away from my old way of doing things (acts of rebellion), and I turned to Him and His way of doing things (acts of obedience). In turn, it directed me to Him. It pointed me toward the path of life.

A remarkable thing about all of this is that God reached out to me while I was still lost. Even though I had veered away from His will, He kept following me. He didn't leave and wait for me to find my way back to Him; He continued to come after me.

I didn't intentionally stray away from God's plan and purposes for my life. I hadn't stopped long enough to consider that was what had been happening. Sin blinds us.

I still loved God and desired to please Him. I was simply spiritually immature and doing everything in my own power to experience the love I was aching to find. I never meant to hurt Him or take His place. However, I did choose to ignore His voice at times and not to trust and obey Him. In doing so, I veered down a dangerous path and eventually, lost my way and was captured.

Nevertheless, Jesus came looking for me. He didn't have to do that. He chose to do that. I rebelliously ignored His instruction. He could have left me alone and in the dark, stranded on the side of the road somewhere in the wilderness. Instead, He chose to chase after me, rescue me, and lead me back to the path of life. His love letter was my road map *home* to the glorious place He was leading me to.

You see, not only does God pursue us when we pursue Him, but He also chooses to pursue those who belong to Him, even when we rebel and don't choose to pursue Him above all else. While I was lost and before I even cried out to Him for help, He was already there. I just couldn't see Him or feel His Presence until I turned away from sin and called for Him.

We are His children, and He will never leave us nor forsake us. He will not abandon us, even when we abandon His ways. He comes and finds us when we have gone astray and lost our way. He is our Good Shepherd. It is out of His loving kindness that He comes to save us, even though we are still powerless to do good on our own, and even while we are still sinners.

It was the fear of abandonment that inspired me to abandon God's ways and to seek love from another. Ironically, it was the abandonment of others that left me deserted but inspired me to return to God. Out of

On My Own

His great love for me, He came and revealed Himself to me as I called on His name. Even though sin had led me astray and I lost my way, I was *still* saved. I still *belonged* to God. I was still one of His own, and He came to my rescue. Will you let Him come to yours?

> *But God demonstrates his own love for us in this: While we were still sinners, Christ died for us (Romans 5:8 NIV).*

Although I was still saved, I had veered away from the path that God had for me; therefore, I wasn't living the abundant life I had been called to live. I was still behaving like a rebellious child rather than a child of God. It was time for me to grow up spiritually. Not only did this letter lead me back home, but it helped me get back on track. I began to be obedient and look to God for my hopes and dreams, to trust Him for all of my heart's desires.

I began to look to Him for love.

That is all I ever wanted—*to love and be loved.* My entire life I had been searching for it. When I received God into my life as my Lord and Savior, a seed of love was planted. God is love, and He came into my heart that day and saved me from death. However, that seed was in desperate need of living water. I felt this lack deep in my soul. I turned to what I thought would help this seed to grow.

I had been seeking water from the wrong well. I had turned to a source that left me depleted and dry. Each taste of that bitter water only left me aching for more. The well of men could not satisfy my thirst for love. My heart longed for more.

I now started drinking from the right well.

CHAPTER SEVEN

The Wishing Well

In the story *Snow White*, she sings "One Song" into the wishing well. She wishes for her one true love to find her and make all of her dreams come true.

A prince hears her beautiful song. He responds and comes to stand beside her at the well without her knowledge.

Snow White continues to sing, suggesting that if she hears an echo, her wish has been heard. However, the voice she hears inside the well isn't a man's voice but her own.

Then the prince sings one word—"Today"—into the well.

Upon first seeing him, Snow White is startled and runs away inside the castle and closes the door behind her. The prince follows her and begins to sing her own song back to her to draw her out to him.

Glancing down at her rags, she feels ashamed, yet his pleasant and approachable tone pulls her out of hiding and onto the balcony where white doves surround her.

Snow White then kisses one of the doves and sends it to her prince. The kiss is a sign that she has received his song of love in her heart and is extending her love to him in return. He kisses the dove, sealing their love in spirit until they soon meet again.

Emergence

This lovely story is also much like the woman at the well in the Bible who returned regularly to fetch water. Yet one special day, Jesus met her there, and everything changed for her. He introduced Himself to her and revealed that He was the One she had been longing for deep within her soul, that He could offer her living water so that she would never thirst again. He was the One and only that could satisfy her greatest desires and was the source of everlasting love and life.

Now Jesus learned that the Pharisees had heard that he was gaining and baptizing more disciples than John—although in fact it was not Jesus who baptized, but his disciples. So he left Judea and went back once more to Galilee.

Now he had to go through Samaria. So he came to a town in Samaria called Sychar, near the plot of ground Jacob had given to his son Joseph. Jacob's well was there, and Jesus, tired as he was from the journey, sat down by the well. It was about noon.

When a Samaritan woman came to draw water, Jesus said to her, "Will you give me a drink?" (His disciples had gone into the town to buy food.)

The Samaritan woman said to him, "You are a Jew and I am a Samaritan woman. How can you ask me for a drink?" (For Jews do not associate with Samaritans.)

Jesus answered her, "If you knew the gift of God and who it is that asks you for a drink, you would have asked him and he would have given you living water."

"Sir," the woman said, "you have nothing to draw with and the well is deep. Where can you get this living water? Are you greater than our father Jacob, who gave us the well and drank from it himself, as did also his sons and his livestock?"

Jesus answered, "Everyone who drinks this water will be thirsty again, but whoever drinks the water I give them will never thirst. Indeed, the water I give them will become in them a spring of water welling up to eternal life."

The Wishing Well

The woman said to him, "Sir, give me this water so that I won't get thirsty and have to keep coming here to draw water."

He told her, "Go, call your husband and come back."

"I have no husband," she replied.

Jesus said to her, "You are right when you say you have no husband. The fact is, you have had five husbands, and the man you now have is not your husband. What you have just said is quite true."

"Sir," the woman said, "I can see that you are a prophet. Our ancestors worshiped on this mountain, but you Jews claim that the place where we must worship is in Jerusalem."

"Woman," Jesus replied, "believe me, a time is coming when you will worship the Father neither on this mountain nor in Jerusalem. You Samaritans worship what you do not know; we worship what we do know, for salvation is from the Jews. Yet a time is coming and has now come when the true worshipers will worship the Father in the Spirit and in truth, for they are the kind of worshipers the Father seeks. God is spirit, and his worshipers must worship in the Spirit and in truth."

The woman said, "I know that Messiah" (called Christ) *"is coming. When he comes, he will explain everything to us."*

Then Jesus declared, "I, the one speaking to you—I am he" (John 4:1–26 NIV).

One Love

I was once the woman at the well. Just like her and Snow White, I returned day after day, wishing and singing, pouring my heart out into an unfulfilling source. In my thirst for true love, I sought to draw water from a well that could not satisfy. Meanwhile, unknown to me, my Prince was listening to the song of my heart and standing next to me. He was patiently watching and waiting for the right moment to introduce Himself.

Emergence

I believe that when I looked into my empty well and cried out the song of my heart to Him, this was the moment He had been waiting for. He had heard my song echoing up to heaven and came to meet with me. He revealed Himself to me through the love letter He had delivered, and sang of the promise of all He could do for me.

This was the moment when we truly met. I knew about Him and received Him into my heart as a child, yet I had never really met Him for myself. Knowing about God isn't the same as knowing Him personally. It was time I had an encounter with truth of my own. It was time for me to get to know my One true love and begin developing an intimate relationship with my Prince who was calling and drawing me closer to Him.

> Listen! My beloved! Look! Here he comes, leaping across the mountains, bounding over the hills. My beloved is like a gazelle or a young stag.
>
> Look! There he stands behind our wall, gazing through the windows, peering through the lattice.
>
> My beloved spoke and said to me, "Arise, my darling, my beautiful one, come with me (Song of Songs 2:8–10 NIV).

Something spiritual happened on that special day. My Prince met me beside the well. He introduced Himself to me and revealed His sweet song of love. My Prince drew me away from my secret place of hiding and invited me to step into the light and expose my shame and filth in His presence, so that I might receive His song of love in my heart in return and quench the longing in my soul.

My Prince saw deep into my well, beyond my hidden desires and beyond my sinful condition. He saw that I was unclean, (recently divorced, presently unmarried, and living in disgrace and captivity) just like the Samaritan woman, yet He saw my true self, the one I had yet to become. Although I was currently clothed in dirty rags and covered in filth, He recognized that my heart was asking, seeking, and willing to be cleansed. He saw a different woman than what everyone else saw—a pure soul longing to escape the bondage she was in and to be set free to change and take on a new name and inherit glorious riches.

The Wishing Well

So, He met me in that current place and presented a future promise through His love letter, one that would change the course of my destiny so long as I would receive it, believe it, and live it (answer His call back). He met my ugly truth with His gorgeous truth (His gentle and loving conviction with guidance and promise), His beautiful gift of grace.

I received that truth in spirit, and the Prince sealed that promise with His kiss—His royal seal of approval and guarantee.

What a beautiful exchange! What a magnificent Prince He is, our Jesus! I wonder if the cry of my heart sounded something like Snow White's song to her prince?

Our Prince is watching and waiting for each and every one of us to sing our beautiful song for Him. He is waiting to meet us at our empty well, so that He can fill us to overflowing with His love and living water. He's not waiting for us to be perfect; He knows we're not and never will be. If we were, then we would have no need of a Savior.

Although we don't know the sound of the Samaritan's woman's song sung deep within her longing heart, Jesus undoubtedly heard the cry of her soul. In His compassion and great love for her, He chose to meet her there. He is also waiting to meet with you.

He's waiting for you to acknowledge your need for Him. He's waiting for you to confess that you're lost without Him. Then you'll hear His beautiful voice. Then He'll sing His song of love to you. Then He'll begin to fill you with His living water.

His water is forever refreshing and reviving. It satisfies and quenches our every thirst, washes away our sin and filth, and purifies our heart. He alone is the true source of the love and life we're all desperate for.

Will you call on Him for help? Will you allow Him to introduce Himself to you and to reveal His love in your heart? That is what our Prince is wishing for. You and I are His one love. Allow Him to be yours. He is calling for you. Sing out to Him.

Today!

Full Satisfaction

I continued to ask, seek, and knock on the door of my Savior's heart. I continued to pursue Him. I continued to write out my prayers and conversations with Him and meditate on His promises to me.

Emergence

What I found was contentment and peace. I began to feel satisfied in Him alone. The desire to find a husband and have the family I had always dreamed of was still very much present, yet I no longer obsessed over it. I talked to Him about my dreams and desires, but I was finding my One Love in Him to be enough. Although we were still in the beginning stages of our relationship, I began to feel I had what I needed, and I was no longer desperate for what I wanted.

Only God can change our heart's longing and desires to be in tune with His. He was filling me up. Once I began to sip from His cistern, I began to feel differently. I was tasting life. With every drop, I got stronger and purer.

I attended church, and although I wasn't yet tithing regularly, I had begun giving on occasion. One time, I placed ten dollars into the bucket. I had very little to get by on, and that ten dollars to me was a huge sacrifice at the time. However, I chose to trust that God would provide for all of my needs, and I gave cheerfully.

Not long afterward, my daughter and I drove up to a gas station to fill our car, but I ran out of gas just within reach of the pump. I tried to stretch the gas hose as far as it could possibly go but I was still just a few feet shy of my gas tank. A nice man noticed what had happened and asked me if he could help. I was very embarrassed and asked if he could help push my car forward so that I could fill up. After helping me, he offered to pay for my gas. I thanked him but kindly declined the offer.

You see, I might have stretched myself as far as I could possibly go on my own. I might have needed a push to the pump, and a man came along to help give me that boost. But I had always been given just enough heavenly resources to fill my tank. I might have been on empty, but I never once went without. Jesus was always there within reach.

I was no longer dependent on man's temporary resources to fill me up. Jesus was more than enough.

God is faithful to provide when we look to Him to fill all our deepest needs.

Idols in Our Hearts

I had finally truly met God for myself, and now we were dating. I know that sounds funny to date God, but a relationship with Him should be intimate and personal. The only way to get to know someone

The Wishing Well

is by spending time together and dating them. This was a time of learning about who the other person was. He was revealing who He was to me, and I was discovering more about myself through our relationship.

This time of learning and discovering is a never-ending process. We can never learn all there is to know about God. That is what makes this relationship so exciting! It will never get boring. It's impossible to get tired of God. And it's impossible for Him to get tired of us.

The Creator of the Universe is in love with us and has chosen us to be His bride.

How awesome is that!

He is the One love in that letter He gave to me. If we will learn how to love Him first, then everything else will fall into place. Nothing can compare to His love.

He is a jealous God, and no man, woman, or object can compete with Him. His love is perfect, and He invites us into partaking of it. I had just gotten a taste of His love and yet I was already feeling satisfied. I was being filled with contentment, flooded with hope, and sprinkled with His desires.

My selfish desires were fading away and I had now surrendered those desires to fit with His plan. I was learning to let go of my own dream so that I could grab hold of God's dream.

All of my life I had been like a curious cat who saw something sparkling and beautiful in a glass jar and had to have it. The mischievous kitty stuck its head into the jar to grab hold of the glittery object only to realize that it couldn't pull its head out of the jar without first spitting out the object.

Therefore, the foolish feline remained trapped inside the jar.

This is what Satan does to us. He tempts us by suggesting we rebelliously take hold of these beautiful shiny objects within our reach (symbolizing our dreams and desires that are contained within God's parameters). Yet when we reach out and grab hold of sin, we realize we're stuck in it.

With all our might, we begin to fight to pull our head out of the jar with the strength of our own two hands. Unable to free ourselves, we then walk around in bondage because we're still holding onto the very thing that lured us in. If we would only look up and realize that if we would let go of our own desire and repent of our rebellion, then we would be free to receive the dream God intended to give us in His timing and in His way. The enemy's false dream is contained within our own limitations to retrieve. God's true dream is revealed within our own freedom to receive.

His dream for us is so big that it's going to require both hands. He loves us too much to give us something that we're not yet ready to handle. God's love is so big that in order for our hearts to have room to receive it, He has to begin pushing other things out.

I had been crying out to Him, but until I was ready to let go of sinful behavior, rebellious ways, and my own desires, I wasn't free to receive all that He had for me.

I had to learn to begin letting go of my dream so that I could receive His dream. I was nowhere near being completely free yet, but with each passing day, as I walked in obedience with Him, I was getting closer.

I realize now that I had created idols in my heart (which is anything that takes the place of God in our lives).

In the cat analogy, the shiny object became an idol in my heart. My beautiful shimmering dream had been sealed and concealed by God for me, to be opened in His timing and His ways. I knew that it was off limits for now, yet its stunning beauty caught my attention and seduced me. I wanted it so badly that I didn't wait for it as God intended. Instead, I listened to the wrong voice that tempted me to grab hold of it prematurely. Until one day I finally did.

In doing so, I chose my desires over God's plan, instruction, and dream for me. I chose my ways over His ways. I chose my timing over His timing. I chose something or someone over Him. I desired to please myself more than I desired to please Him.

That someone or something had become an idol in my heart, and I didn't even realize it. I had allowed a worldly object to take the place of God.

It was idolatry and pride that got Satan banished out of heaven. He wanted to be higher than God. He sought to rob God of His throne. Therefore, he was cast out.

> *How you have fallen from heaven, morning star, son of the dawn! You have been cast down to the earth, you who once laid low the nations! You said in your heart, "I will ascend to the heavens; I will raise my throne above the stars of God; I will sit enthroned on the mount of assembly, on the utmost heights of Mount Zaphon.*

The Wishing Well

I will ascend above the tops of the clouds; I will make myself like the Most High" (Isaiah 14:12–14 NIV).

The Bible tells us that God created Lucifer perfectly. He was once beautiful, anointed, and full of wisdom. He had everything. Lucifer lived in Paradise, yet it wasn't enough. He wanted all. He wanted to be God. He wanted to sit on God's throne and be worshiped by all.

"Son of man, take up a lament concerning the king of Tyre and say to him: 'This is what the Sovereign Lord says: "'You were the seal of perfection, full of wisdom and perfect in beauty. You were in Eden, the garden of God; every precious stone adorned you: carnelian, chrysolite and emerald, topaz, onyx and jasper, lapis lazuli, turquoise and beryl.

Your settings and mountings were made of gold; on the day you were created they were prepared. You were anointed as a guardian cherub, for so I ordained you. You were on the holy mount of God; you walked among the fiery stones. You were blameless in your ways from the day you were created till wickedness was found in you (Ezekiel 28:12–15 NIV).

Through your widespread trade you were filled with violence, and you sinned. So I drove you in disgrace from the mount of God, and I expelled you, guardian cherub, from among the fiery stones.

Your heart became proud on account of your beauty, and you corrupted your wisdom because of your splendor. So I threw you to the earth; I made a spectacle of you before kings. (Ezekiel 28:16–17 NIV).

This is also the same tactic Satan used to tempt Adam and Eve. He told them that if they ate of the forbidden fruit, they would be like God. Thus, they chose to disobey God in order to gain the wisdom of God for themselves.

Curiosity killed the cat.

They chose to sit in God's place on the throne and desired wisdom, knowledge, and understanding above God Himself. They too had been given Paradise, yet it wasn't enough. They walked with God in Eden, yet God wasn't enough. They wanted all! They wanted to be like God. This desire became an idol in their hearts, and ultimately, they too reached out and took hold of it. They disobediently, rebelliously, and sinfully chose it over God.

Their sin of idolatry and pride and the knowledge of good and evil ultimately led to death rather than gain. Just as in Satan's case, they too were banished from Paradise, separated from the presence of God and sentenced to death. One day, Satan's time will end, and he will be destroyed, his sentence of death upheld.

The Bible warns us not to create idols for ourselves. God is a jealous God, and He will have no other gods before Him. Nothing or no one shall take His place. This is the very first commandment He gives in the Old Testament. Clearly, it's very important to Him, and He takes it very seriously.

God gives us a warning and command, but He also gives us a promise.

> *And God spoke all these words: "I am the Lord your God, who brought you out of Egypt, out of the land of slavery. You shall have no other gods before me. You shall not make for yourself an image in the form of anything in heaven above or on the earth beneath or in the waters below. You shall not bow down to them or worship them; for I, the Lord your God, am a jealous God, punishing the children for the sin of the parents to the third and fourth generation of those who hate me, but showing love to a thousand generations of those who love me and keep my commandments (Exodus 20:1–6 NIV).*

God desires for His children to love Him first and obey Him and He rewards His children with love.

I hadn't fashioned for myself any golden calves or bronze statues and worshipped any objects like the Israelites did at the foot of Mount Sinai. Or had I? Not with my own hands, of course, but *unknowingly* with my heart. I also didn't imagine myself sitting in God's place on the throne. That wasn't something I would intentionally ever desire. I didn't desire to be like God. My desire was to serve, worship, and please Him, even though I failed. No Christian in their right mind wakes up one morning and decides, "Hey, I think I'll worship and serve an idol today. That sounds fun." No. Often, we are oblivious to idol worship. We don't see it as such. That's what makes it so dangerous.

I was simply young and in love. I didn't see the threat in what I was doing. I didn't see that I was desiring someone or something so much that I was willing to disobey God in order to have it. I didn't see how I was hurting God and in danger of hurting myself or others. I didn't understand how much God loved me and how I was to love Him in return above all else. God should always be our greatest desire. He is more than enough.

Unfortunately, I have seen and also experienced the foolish effects of sticking our noses into places they should not have been. When I was a child, we had a tomcat. One day, I found him with his head in a glass jar just like I described earlier. He was stuck and barely breathing and suffocating to death. I ran to my daddy for help, but it was too late. By the time my dad came to the rescue and broke the glass jar, the cat had suffered too much and didn't recover. Its death was terribly sad.

As I said in the beginning of my story, I have always had a slight obsession for marshmallow-like substances and was guilty of sneaking into my parents' pantry and breaking into the marshmallow cream jar that was reserved for baking.

Selfishly, I desired it then and now. Although I knew it was off-limits, its sweet fluffiness lured me in. I chose to disobediently remove the lid, break the seal, and eat its sticky contents. Therefore, its true intention never saw the light of day. I will never know what delightful dish my mom intended to create with it, and sadly, no one else will either. This decision to prematurely taste the forbidden substance robbed the possibility of its future use and potential, affecting others in the process.

Sadly, this is exactly what happened when I began to obsess over living my sparkling dream on marshmallow clouds. I wanted that sweet reality now; consequently, temptation enticed me, and I foolishly stuck my nose where it didn't yet belong. I prematurely took a bite of that fluffy filling only to discover that I was trapped and had robbed myself of the original plan my Father had intended, affecting the lives of others.

The bitter reality was suffocating.

As a result, the white marshmallow clouds that I once lived upon and obsessed over had grown dark and gloomy. My glittering childhood wonder began to fade the moment I was tricked into tasting that sinful treat.

Emergence

Idolatry robs us of God's best for us and suffocates the life from us.

This is what an idol looks like in our lives today. It can be anything or anyone that takes the place of God. God should be first, and He alone is worthy to sit on the throne of our hearts. When we place something else in His seat, we're robbing God of His place and authority. In return, we're assuming command. He alone has earned the right to rule. It is, after all, His kingdom, not ours.

We may not see these objects in our lives as idols, but God does. Having idols in our hearts attracts the enemy and invites and tempts us to enter into sin, and sin creates separation between God and us. It's a wedge, a divider, which interferes with the flow and release of God's blessings.

Thankfully, God is a loving and merciful God. If we've received Christ as our Lord and Savior, then we've been forgiven of all of our sins, even idolatry, whether intentional or not. However, we still have to face the consequences of our actions, and we still receive His corrective discipline, both of which are not fun to experience.

Nevertheless, God is a loving Father who strives to protect His children from harming themselves, and we can cry out and run to Him for rescue anytime. He warns us in order to keep us safe, not to be mean or scare us away.

He also rewards His children for their obedience. His desire is always to bring us closer to Himself. The closer we are to sin, the further we are from His love, protection, and presence. Our God is a gracious God, and He gives generously to His children who love Him and obey.

Whenever I rebelliously grabbed hold of my sparkling dream before God's reserved timing (breaking the seal of my promise), I broke God's heart. Also the realization that I couldn't retrieve my dream, broke my own heart as well. My idol was worldly love, the desire to love and be loved by man more than I desired to love and be loved by God. I thought this was the love I had been searching for my entire life. Upon reaching hold of it I became trapped in my own sin and I lost my dream. I lost my paradise. I lost the man I loved.

However, in my brokenness, I chose to look up, cry out to God, and acknowledge my mistake. I chose to confess my sin, repent, and turn away from my ways. I asked for forgiveness for trying to be God over my own life and then surrendered control to Him.

The Wishing Well

He heard my cry and answered me. My Father God came quickly (before it was too late) and began to break off that suffocating captivity in His strength and breathe a fresh, new breath of life into me. He sang me a new song. Little by little, I was learning to let go of my dream so that I could be free to receive His best.

Are you holding onto a dream that has become an idol in your own heart? Has something or someone taken the place of God in your life? Is it causing you to sin in order to have it?

Are you trapped because of rebellion? Does the enemy have you in a snare? Is it robbing the breath of life from you? Are you suffocating?

If so, it is time to look up, let go, and break free!

Don't wait until it's too late.

Ask God for forgiveness today. Repent (change your mind and turn away) from your way and turn toward God's way. Put Him first on the throne of your heart, and receive His dream for your life.

Your Heavenly Father loves you, and He wants to deliver you from your idols so that He can deliver to you His best.

Will you be willing to let go so that you can be free to receive?

PRAYER

Lord,

Forgive me for drinking from the wrong well and for creating idols in my heart. I cry out to You and invite You to be God over all areas of my life. Introduce Yourself to me in a new and intimate way and pour into me Your living water that sustains my soul. Wash away the filth of my shame and guilt as I come out of hiding and step into the light of Your presence. I open up my hands to let go of worldly idols so I can be free to grab hold of Your promises. Thank You for Your perfect love that is refreshing and reviving my longing soul and depleted heart. You are enough. Help me to be satisfied in You alone. I want You to be my One true love. Sing to me today, sweet Jesus.

In Jesus' Name. Amen.

CHAPTER EIGHT

My Gift from God

About a year after my divorce, the company I worked for was going through a conversion. All of the employees from different branches would take turns going through training classes. The day was casual dress, and I happily waltzed in wearing a cute conservative top, a pair of capris, and sandals.

Unfortunately, I was also flaunting a pair of newly sunburned ankles from spending the entire day before at the pool and getting a little toasty. Nevertheless, I made my way to the mile-long rectangular table and took a seat. Glancing up, I couldn't help but notice that sitting directly across from me was an unfamiliar face (a very cute one, I might add). There was an undeniable and instantaneous spark and connection between us.

Throughout that entire meeting, every time I looked up from my notes, that cute little face was looking back at me. Our eyes would meet, and he would quickly shift his focus back to the trainer.

It didn't stop there. We had to get up for some participation activities. Every time I turned around, he was right behind me. It was awkward but adorable at the same time.

We never introduced ourselves at that meeting.

However, we continued to cross paths at other training sessions. So, his face was becoming more and more familiar to me.

Emergence

Then unexpectedly, I was chosen to help out full time at the branch he worked at for the next two weeks. This gave us an opportunity to begin getting to know one another.

Eventually, I went back to work at my own location. A few days later, I received a phone call at work from him.

The little cutie got up the nerve to ask me out!

For our first date, we grabbed some hot cocoa and drove around looking at Christmas lights. We spent hours talking and having a good time.

When he took me home, he unloaded on me. He had also recently been through a divorce and had been praying for God to bring him the right person to share his life with. He said, "I would have never gotten up the nerve to pursue you by myself. I truly believe you're exactly the person I've been praying for, so God gave me the boldness and courage to go for it."

He came on really strong for a first date, but he appeared confident I was the answer to his prayers. It must have been my bright red sunburned ankles that captured his attention and struck his affectionate heart with a blazing heat of passion.

It took me a little longer to come around. At this time, I had finally grown content where I was at and no longer needed a relationship. I was doing really well at work and was happy and satisfied on my own. I was striving to achieve the goals I had set for myself. Letting someone else into the picture was not exactly in the new set of plans I had recently made. Finally, I had dug my heels in and was determined to provide for myself and my daughter. This was the mindset I needed. This made me strong. This was how we survived.

However, he remained persistent. We started spending more and more time together. We shared the same beliefs, had common interests, and he was just fun and easy to be around.

Christmas was approaching, and I invited him to go with me to my mom and stepdad's house. All of my siblings would be there, and this would be a great opportunity for him to meet my family. If my big, loud, and crazy clan didn't scare him off, then nothing would. Remember, we were of Italian heritage.

He accepted my invitation, and on that special Christmas Day, I got to introduce my Christopher.

My Gift from God

Could It Be? Is It He?

Christopher (Chris) came from a small family. He was adopted at the age of four and raised by his grandparents.

Chris had a quiet, sweet, and humble personality, but he was also very adventurous. This guy was amazing on a snowboard and wakeboard. We had a blast together. Most important was how kind he was to my daughter. He absolutely adored her and was willing to take my tiny toddler in and love her as his own.

I found myself falling in love with him, and I began to wonder if he could be "the one" for me. After months of dating, I knew that a proposal wasn't far away. Wanting to be sure this time, I spent a lot of time talking to God about it. I couldn't afford another failure.

Everything was perfect, yet I was conflicted. A part of me was still holding on to my previous dream. I knew that Chris wanted to move forward and desired a future with me and my child, but I wasn't quite ready to let go of my past.

Before Chris came into the picture, my first love and I had become really close friends. I still believed and hoped that one day we would be together. Although I had let go of control, I hadn't let go of that image.

I was getting scared.

Life was flourishing all around me, and yet I was hesitating to flow with it. My original dream was holding me back.

I struggled and struggled with the decision to move forward or step backwards. I had to know for sure. Despite my love for Chris, I kept pushing him away in an attempt to seek answers for my previous tie. This broke his heart. He was so certain of the answers God had given him, and it was hard for him to understand that I needed to be certain of those answers as well. I needed more time to figure things out.

Fortunately, God gave Chris patience and endurance throughout that time and eventually those answers came to me.

About six months later, Chris and I got engaged!

Learning to Receive

Before Chris came into my life, in my brokenness and desperation I had cried out to God and had been praying for a husband. I had been praying that He would bring me the husband I needed, not the one I thought I wanted. I surrendered control to Him and was believing Him for my heart's desires and dreams. Rather than rebelliously attempting to find love on my own and in my own timing, I started attempting to behave obediently as a child of God.

In the meantime, I had grown content in my relationship with God. I was satisfied and fulfilled by the love He was giving me. Then when I had learned to be satisfied with Him alone, He surprised me with a gift. When I least expected it, that was when I received it.

Chris was the gift that God had given me, the gift that He promised me. In my love letter, God told me what He would do for me when I learned to love Him first. He promised that He would surprise me with a love that exemplified my relationship with Him.

I chose to have faith and believe that those promises were spoken to me personally, and God chose to honor them. The incredible thing about this was that Chris and I had both been praying and seeking God for a spouse, and God had been preparing us for one another at the exact same time.

Then when we were ready, He brought us together (just as the letter promised).

God had moved me from my old job where I was miserable and placed me into a new environment where I would meet my future husband. Then He prepared our hearts to be ready for one another when the time was right. He took two broken but faithful souls and healed our wounds as He wrapped us in His beauty. Then He delivered us to one another. He gave us both a second chance to find love in the flesh that we didn't deserve. He placed us together and was about to join us in marriage. He would soon tie the knot with a gorgeous red bow symbolizing His perfect love.

Miraculously, my love letter from God had become a reality in my life!

God blessed and honored my faithfulness, obedience, reliance, and trust in Him. He is a gracious God and a Giver of good gifts to those who love and obey Him. My story is a testament of that. None of this occurred by chance or coincidence; it occurred by divine appointment. It was the faithful and loving providence of God!

Just a year earlier, I had spent Christmas alone, broken and empty-handed. Exactly a year later, in His way and in His timing, He gave me a precious gift, one that was too big to fit under any Christmas tree and would require two hands to hold. It was my wonderful husband-

My Gift from God

to-be, a new man to love and be loved by, and an upcoming redeemed marriage. God had rewarded us both with love as we both learned to love God first. What a gift! What a blessing! What a promise! What a loving, gracious, and faithful Father!

God's promises are true. When we put our faith and trust in Him, there is no limit to what He will do. We just have to go to Him and ask.

God loves to give good gifts to His children.

> *If you, then, though you are evil, know how to give good gifts to your children, how much more will your Father in heaven give good gifts to those who ask him! (Matthew 7:11 NIV).*

This new forthcoming marriage was a remarkable gift; a do-over. However, I nearly rejected it.

Chris was God's dream for me. I nearly missed out on it because I was still holding on to my dream. I've often hesitated to receive the gifts that God is delivering because they may involve change, requiring me to relinquish control. Sometimes in order to be free to receive, we must first be willing to let go. I'm so thankful I said yes and received this gift.

I'm not saying that my dream was bad; however, God was never invited to rule over it (to come first). As a result, sin entered, corrupted, stole, and destroyed it.

I'm also not suggesting that Chris and I were perfect or without sin. It wasn't our works or performance that prompted blessings and gifts from God; rather, it was our change in heart. The difference is that we looked to God for our dream and discovered satisfaction and contentment through His love first. We stepped out of His seat and put Him back on the throne of our hearts. We looked to Him rather than ourselves.

It's not the absence of sin nor the presence of perfection that sets us up for a successful marriage but the presence of God who trains us up and teaches us how to appropriately respond within our imperfect marriage. We put Him first, center stage, and above all else.

In doing so, God gave us a chance for a new dream, and this time He was all around it and within it. He had placed us in a new garden that He created just for the two of us, and He was now walking in our midst.

Marriage was always intended to be a gift so long as God was a part of it.

Emergence

Eve was given to Adam as a gift. Their marriage and their union were blessed and perfect until the day they chose to set God aside.

A New Beginning

We had discovered that our ways lead to pain, destruction, devastation, and death. Now we were discovering how God's ways lead to healing, restoration, redemption, freedom, and life. This was only the beginning of our blessed journey.

Chris and I were married on a joyful day and had a beautiful storybook wedding and reception. I wore a stunning strapless corset-top gown. My long blonde hair was softly pulled partially up and my head was crowned with a gorgeous tiara. I carried a bouquet of stargazer lilies and pink and orange Gerber daisies as I walked down the aisle to my handsome husband-to-be.

My three-year old daughter was our flower girl, and she was absolutely adorable. She rehearsed and rehearsed for that role, but when it came time for her to finally walk the aisle, she decided she was too tired. Instead, she went and sat down on a bench and pouted. She had been playing hard with her cousin, the ring bearer, and she was worn out by the time the ceremony started.

Unsure of what to do, I asked my father to intervene. He walked over to her and knelt down. Very gently and lovingly, he explained that being the flower girl was her job (no one else's), and she had to do it. Upon hearing this news, my child remembered her responsibility, agreed with my father, obeyed his instruction, and cheerfully and beautifully carried out her duty as flower girl. Her cute blonde curls and bright blue eyes mesmerized my heart as she planted pink petals down the aisle before me. Even though she briefly hesitated, (much like her mother) she performed her role well after all.

Often, couples spend so much energy planning for and rehearsing their wedding but no time spent planning for their marriage. Then when the ceremony is over, the couple is exhausted and unaware of their roles to perform as husband and wife. Individually, they go off by themselves, taking a seat on the sidelines of their new marriage and pout.

Sweet child of God, invite your Heavenly Father to intervene in your union. Hear His gentle and loving voice, and remember your responsibility to your marriage. Then look to Him for His instruction, agree with His

My Gift from God

words, choose to follow through, and obey His commands. Don't hesitate. You'll find the strength and energy needed to perform your roles as a couple and be positioned for a beautiful, happy, and successful marriage.

My first marriage was not positioned properly for success because my Heavenly Father was never invited to intervene. This was not the case with this new marriage. We had both been communing with Him separately as individuals and had learned to put Him first in our lives before He even brought us together. Therefore, we were prepared for success collectively as a couple. We had invited God to be the center (the cornerstone) of our lives and marriage, enabling our union to stand strong and victoriously in this new covenant. This is how marriage was created to work since the beginning. As long as we have God, we have *all* that we need! He provides for His children who love Him because He is a good Father.

We were now young newlyweds in love. Chris's gracious parents (those who adopted and raised him) had given us a home as a wedding gift. How insane is that. We were beyond grateful. It was my husband's childhood home. It was outdated but massive.

We lived in a private community where there was a golf course and even a lake. We had an enormous deck that overlooked the creek behind it. Huge cottonwood trees stood all around. It was stunning. Neither of us had any idea that this next big gift was coming. It was another dream come true for both of us.

I had gone from living in a one-bedroom apartment with my little girl to what felt like a mansion. When I prayed, I prayed big. I remember *specifically* asking God for a big, beautiful home someday. Well, someday didn't take very long. God was pouring out His blessings on us and answering my prayers. It was incredible. My life was unrecognizable. God is a fulfiller of *big* dreams!

We got a wakeboard boat and had family and friends over all the time. I loved hosting parties. We were either on the water or playing golf nearly every weekend, and when we weren't doing that, we were doing updates on our home. I got to experiment with my decorating skills and textured and painted nearly every room in that house. We scraped off wallpaper, replaced old tubs and toilets, and switched out appliances.

It was quite the adventure. Together, we had stepped into a life-giving season, and we were soaking up the sunshine.

Emergence

We had started over. Although we still had much to learn, together, we had begun building our home on a solid foundation.

We were building our house on the Rock!

For more information on how to successfully build your home and marriage on the Rock, I recommend the book *Marriage on the Rock* by Jimmy Evans.[4]

For the last twenty years, I have had the privilege of growing in my personal relationship with Christ and marriage under the ministry of Pastor Jimmy Evans. Pastor Jimmy was the Senior Pastor at Trinity Fellowship Church in Amarillo, Texas, for the majority of that time (where I attend). He is now an apostolic elder at Trinity Fellowship and remains on the preaching team. However, his primary position is the senior pastor at Gateway Church in Dallas, Texas, and founder and CEO of the Marriage Today ministry. Pastor Evans is a compassionate man of God, a gifted minister of the Word, and a profound speaker and encourager of the faith.

What a turn around my life has had. At a time I felt so alone, I'm not sure where I would have ended up if God hadn't led me into such an extraordinary church home with such anointed leadership. I had come a long way since that sad day in McDonald's when I had no place to call my home.

I encourage you to find a church home that welcomes you into the family of God. Find your place. When you do, it will change your life.

A New Direction

I decided to quit my job and go back to school to become an elementary school teacher. I loved my banking job, but I wanted to spend more time at home with my family. I thought having the summers off with my daughter would be wonderful.

Going back to school was a little intimidating at first, but it took me no time to get back into the swing of things. The only time I hadn't maintained terrific grades was when I simply didn't care or didn't apply myself. This only occurred a few times during difficult seasons of my life. Even then, my grades were never bad.

I began my college courses full-time and was doing really well. I made the Dean's List and was also commended by one of my professors. I poured my heart into writing a paper about Martin Luther King, Jr. My professor wrote on my paper, "See me after class."

My Gift from God

A little nervous, I went up to his desk and handed him my paper. He saw his note and said, "I just wanted to tell you personally that you're an amazing writer. Whatever your major, whatever field you're going into make sure it involves writing."

A New Surprise

I continued on the path of elementary education. After a few years, I was nearing graduation and would soon begin student teaching. Then something unexpected happened.

We were pregnant!

This news came somewhat as a surprise. We weren't necessarily trying to conceive, but we weren't *not trying* either. We had decided to trust God with the outcome. Regardless, when it happened, it took me a few minutes to process.

My husband was ecstatic right off the bat. He started jumping up and down and hollering right away.

I said, "Just hold on a minute. Let's take another test to be sure." Holding onto his optimism, he continued celebrating in the meantime.

Having a child together was a dream of his. Just to be clear, having a family and children was my dream as well. I was certainly not against it. It was the idea of being pregnant and giving birth that frightened me a little bit. It had always been like that for me. Even though I had already given birth to one child, I still got anxious about going through it all. It was something I wanted, but for me, having children just had to happen. I was always too chicken to commit and say, "I'm ready to bring a new person into this world."

When I was in high school, I vowed to *never* have kids until I was thirty. This statement came from feeling like I, along with my older sister, had helped raise our younger siblings. Although I loved them very much, they could be giant brats at times. So as a result, I swore off having kids for a long time. Obviously, the opposite of waiting occurred, as I became pregnant with my first child very early.

I didn't realize I had made an inner vow. In doing so, I was declaring lordship over that area of my life rather than surrendering lordship to God. I was declaring that I knew what was best for me rather than trusting that only God knows what's best for me. Pastor Jimmy Evans describes inner vows as "a self-directed promise resulting from an unpleasant experience or hurt from a life situation by a parent or someone else."

I didn't realize that back in high school, swearing this oath was wrong and sinful. The very area that I swore to take control over was the very area that the enemy attacked and brought pain into my life with an unplanned pregnancy outside of marriage.

Inner vows are dangerous. Like all sin, all we have to do is repent. In order to repent, we must acknowledge that what we did was wrong, ask for God's forgiveness, and turn away from doing it. Jesus forbids inner vows and oaths for our own protection.

Jesus Forbids Oaths

"Again you have heard that it was said to those of old, 'You shall not swear falsely, but shall perform your oaths to the Lord.' But I say to you, do not swear at all: neither by heaven, for it is God's throne; nor by the earth, for it is His footstool; nor by Jerusalem, for it is the city of the great King. Nor shall you swear by your head, because you cannot make one hair white or black. But let your 'Yes' be 'Yes,' and your 'No,' 'No.' For whatever is more than these is from the evil one" (Matthew 5:33–37 NKJV).

I liked the idea of being in control and feared the idea of being out of control. I believe that was why pregnancy frightened me so much. Not only was something miraculous occurring within my own body that was beyond my control or understanding, but it would also bring change to my life and future. I didn't like change and I liked being in control of my body and my surroundings. When I wasn't, I felt uneasy.

Fortunately, this time around I hadn't made any inner vows. My husband and I surrendered control over this area in our lives to God. Despite the initial feelings, I was very happy and excited to bring another child into our lives. I quickly adjusted to the unexpected change in plans, set aside my fear, and welcomed this coming blessing and bundle of joy.

Although trusting Him isn't always easy, it is always the safest and best decision. The absence of inner vows allows for the presence of God to administer blessings, gifts, and opportunity as He deems worthy.

My Gift from God

A New Passion

I continued with my college classes up until the end of my final trimester. Let me tell ya, it was a lot of fun hauling a packed backpack and my huge loaded belly up four flights of stairs every other day. It was good for me, though. It helped me stay fit during pregnancy. I needed something to offset the jumbo oatmeal cream pie and glass of milk I ate every night before bed. See, marshmallow-like filling—I wasn't kidding about my obsession.

One of the courses I was required to take was an art class. This was right up my alley. I was very creative and artistic, and this class was a lot of fun for me. It began pulling out those creative passions that had been stored away since childhood. Being pregnant and having a nursery to decorate also contributed to this passion.

We discovered that we were having a little girl. Hooray! I began preparing right away.

For her nursery, we chose a woodland forest theme with baby animals. In my art class, we were required to create a papier mâché project. This was the perfect opportunity for me to create something really special for the nursery. I chose to make Flower, the shy and sweet little skunk from *Bambi*. Although this project was a huge undertaking, and I probably lost a lot of hair from it, (thank goodness for prenatal vitamins), it turned out beautifully.

Outside of school, I began painting a large tree wall mural with butterflies in the nursery as well. My husband got a kick out of watching me paint with my cute belly. I also created multiple canvas paintings of a darling baby skunk, squirrel, and raccoon. We stocked the room with precious clothing, baby supplies, every woodland creature stuffed animal imaginable, and eagerly waited for her arrival.

A New Arrival

The day finally came when we received another precious gift. Our sweet little girl entered the world with beautiful bright blue eyes and perfectly pouty lips. She was a rare and sparkling jewel.

Emergence

Moving Onward

A year later, we were celebrating our daughter's very first birthday in our new house. We loved our old home, but upon having our child, we decided that there were too many safety concerns with that house. One time we found a scorpion in the living room. On a regular basis, we heard screams from our seven-year-old because she had been cornered by a giant wolf spider. The worst of all was the time we were having a get together with friends, and we found a baby rattlesnake on the back deck where children had been crawling and playing. This was one I couldn't get over, especially because I am terrified of snakes, especially deadly, poisonous ones. Despite the home's beauty and charm, the proximity to water had its drawbacks.

It was a good move. As our youngest entered into her toddler years, we discovered that she was a little stinker. So the skunk, Flower, I created for her nursery set the tone well. We jokingly nicknamed her "The Destroyer" because she was always getting into mischief and making messes.

After my second daughter was born, I decided to stay home and raise my children. It was a good decision because the little one alone was a full-time job. She wore me out. I think God made toddlers adorable so that we wouldn't rip their little pigtails off their cute little heads. It's crazy how two children can be such opposites. My oldest was calm, collected, and quiet. She could entertain herself for hours without getting into trouble. My youngest was hyper, ornery, and silly. I had to entertain her constantly to keep her out of trouble.

We had just gotten a new luxurious comforter for our guest bedroom, and the little toot wanted to try painting just like her mommy. She exhibited her mixed media and special effects with paint, fingernail polish, and glitter explosions on multiple surfaces, including the brand-new comforter.

She also enjoyed body painting and used whatever was at her disposal for her supplies. One day her cousin, approximately the same age, came over to visit. We found them both partially naked and covered in vanilla pudding, hair and all.

I had started painting all the time. It became my new passion. People began admiring my work and requesting custom orders. I eventually opened up a shop online. Between raising kids, painting, and working on my tan, I kept myself busy. Even though we moved away from the water, we decided to keep our boat. We continued to go to the lake on the weekends, and our girls turned into little fish. Life was peaceful and all about enjoying our family.

Although I had majored in education, I didn't end up teaching and working in elementary schools like I had planned. However, I have no doubt that today, I am right where God wants me and know that I'm working toward His plan using the skills, gifts, and talents He has given me to write and teach others who He is. So, I am working in the field of education after all. With God, nothing is wasted.

Empowered

We started attending church more regularly, and my husband and I received the baptism of the Holy Spirit. Interestingly, this is when I began writing and journaling again. Upon receiving this baptism, something in me began to shift. My desires began to change, and I desired to know God even more. Obeying God's Word became easier. I found myself pursuing less of what the world had to offer and more of what God promised.

Upon receiving salvation as a child, I had been born again by the Holy Spirit. But upon receiving the baptism of the Holy Spirit, I had been *empowered* and *immersed* in the Spirit.

The Holy Spirit Promised

And being assembled together with them, He commanded them not to depart from Jerusalem, but to wait for the Promise of the Father, "which," He said, "you have heard from Me; for John truly baptized with water, but you shall be baptized with the Holy Spirit not many days from now."

Therefore, when they had come together, they asked Him, saying, "Lord, will You at this time restore the kingdom to Israel?"

And He said to them, "It is not for you to know times or seasons which the Father has put in His own authority. But you shall receive power when the Holy Spirit has come upon you; and you shall be witnesses to Me in Jerusalem, and in all Judea and Samaria, and to the end of the earth" (Acts 1:4–8 NKJV).

Emergence

Earlier in this book, I made this statement, "I was powerless as I kept battling life on my own, seeking to please God yet incapable of following through." This explained why I was incapable of following through—because I was powerless to do it on my own. I had the knowledge of right and wrong and the desire to obey and please God, yet I lacked the *power* to follow through with it on my own.

I continued to strive yet failed over and over again. The heart was willing, yet the flesh was weak. On our own, we are weak. We need the Holy Spirit to empower us in order to live victoriously. I had the will to do good, yet lacked the power to succeed in walking out God's good will and purpose for my life.

Receiving power through the baptism of the Holy Spirit doesn't ensure that we'll never fail or disobey God. Rather, it helps equip us to prevail and obey God as we become His witnesses.

> *And I will pray the Father, and He will give you another Helper, that He may abide with you forever— the Spirit of truth, whom the world cannot receive, because it neither sees Him nor knows Him; but you know Him, for He dwells with you and will be in you (John 14:16–17 NKJV).*

This is why Jesus told the disciples to wait to receive the baptism of the Holy Spirit first, and then He commissioned them to go out and spread the gospel. They lacked the power behind the good news until their encounter with the Holy Spirit. In order to successfully accomplish the will of God and to complete the tasks set before them, they needed to receive the power of the Holy Spirit. They needed the Holy Spirit with them to help them, to guide them, and to transform them. Like me, they too desired to please God yet were powerless to follow through. Despite their will to follow Jesus, they denied Him because they were weak on their own.

> *But when the Helper comes, whom I shall send to you from the Father, the Spirit of truth who proceeds from the Father, He will testify of Me (John 15:26 NKJV).*

The Holy Spirit is the Spirit of truth. When we receive Him, we begin the journey of being led into all truth. He begins to teach us who God is and helps us to understand His Word, the Bible. The Holy Spirit begins the

My Gift from God

process of changing our hearts and transforming us into Christ's image, so that through His power, we may successfully go out and change the world.

> *But the Helper, the Holy Spirit, whom the Father will send in My name, He will teach you all things, and bring to your remembrance all things that I said to you (John 14:26 NKJV).*
>
> *However, when He, the Spirit of truth, has come, He will guide you into all truth; for He will not speak on His own authority, but whatever He hears He will speak; and He will tell you things to come. He will glorify Me, for He will take of what is Mine and declare it to you (John 16:13–14 NKJV).*

Receiving the baptism of the Holy Spirit marked the beginning of this noticeable process in my life. It marked the moment I began truly living *for* God rather than just living a godly life. This power began to call me to a Higher Power and greater purpose. It marked the moment that I would truly begin to *follow* Jesus. I had made the decision to follow Jesus upon salvation and met Him as I cried out to Him, yet I had not yet begun walking after Him into the places He was calling me to go.

This baptism marked the beginning of an adventurous journey that Jesus and I were embarking upon together. He would be my Guide, my Helper, my Teacher, and I would learn to depend on Him for survival. Where we were headed, I would require both power and truth. These were essential items needed for the long road ahead.

If you want to receive the baptism of the Holy Spirit, you can cite this prayer. It was also taken from *Ten Steps Toward Christ* by Pastor Jimmy Evans:

PRAYER

"Father, thank You for the promise of the Holy Spirit and for sending Him into my life. I repent of my sins and forgive everyone who has hurt me, has sinned against me, or has hurt my loved ones. By faith, I now ask You to baptize me in Your Holy Spirit. I surrender my life to live for You. Holy Spirit, I pray, come into my life and fill me. Baptize me in Your presence and power and lead me daily. I surrender completely to You and ask You to lead me closer to Jesus and empower me to live victoriously for Him. I pray that You will impart spiritually gifts into my life and use me to glorify God and help others. I also surrender my tongue to You and pray that You will give me a personal prayer language to enable me to pray more effectively.

In Jesus' Name. Amen.

My Gift from God

Called To Build

    I had settled into my easy and comfortable life. Things were great. Then circumstances began to change around us. My husband lost both of his grandparents (the adoptive parents who raised him), and I lost both of my grandparents (the ones who lived next door and contributed to raising me) all around the same time. We both grieved these losses.

    Perhaps in spite of this, we chose to move again as a result of needing a change of scenery and a fresh new start. This time we chose a house that we planned to build onto. We saw great vision and potential in this home and decided to add on a second story. We understood this would be a rigorous process, but I had no idea what we were actually beginning.

    What started out as a three-month plan turned into a year renovation. It was awful. I practically lived with construction workers for a year. Most days were spent in my pajamas because they showed up first thing in the morning and didn't leave until that evening. In order to oversee the project and ensure everything went as planned, my supervision was often required. Therefore, I didn't leave the house much at all. It was stressful, chaotic, and very dirty.

    One windy day, I was taking a shower. Meanwhile, the construction workers outside were busy framing out the second story above our master bathroom. Suddenly, a powerful gust of wind caught one of the worker's large boards, sending it sailing through the air and crashing down directly above me. It hit so hard that it broke through the ceiling and pieces of sheet rock came falling down on top of me in the shower.

    Terrified, I looked up and saw sunlight shining through the new hole in our ceiling. Afraid that one of the workers may peer through, I quickly jumped out of the shower and grabbed a towel to cover myself. This took *Naked and Afraid* to a whole new level.

    What I didn't realize at the time of our home renovation was that God was also beginning the renovation of my heart. He was about to tear out the old and damaged and replace it with the new. He had already devised His own design and plan for my life, and it was now time to begin constructing it. Undergoing this renovation would not be easy *for* me, but it would be necessary in order to build *in* me, and one day, *through* me. He had called me for a purpose, but before He could use me, He had to undo me.

Emergence

What I didn't yet know was that a different type of wind was about to blow, and things were about to come crashing down on me. It would become paramount for me to look up to heaven and see the light shining through the chaos all around. Before the new can be put in, the old must be taken out. Everything must be stripped away. I was soon to become naked in the face of God and afraid in the face of fear.

The winds of change were coming.

It was my time for a makeover. I would learn to look through a new mirror where true beauty is revealed and no longer concealed.

CHAPTER NINE

Mirror, Mirror

The stress of the renovation had begun to take its toll. A year of being confined to my loud, dirty home without any privacy was almost too much. The stress created some minor skin issues, which I perceived as small imperfections. Still, I couldn't help but to obsess over them. After praying and asking God to help me with my skin, I finally decided to visit a dermatologist. Hopefully, that would fix my problems. Boy, was I wrong!

I began treatment and was told that my skin might get worse before it got better. This was not what I wanted to hear, but I chose to ride it out. The dermatologist was right. My skin went from having very minor blemishes, which wouldn't have concerned most people, to a full-fledged nightmare. Thinking this reaction was normal, I continued treatment, assuming that eventually improvement would come. It didn't. Instead, I had a terrible reaction and developed a horrible acne rash all over my face and also deep cystic blemishes. It was extremely painful and humiliating. I began getting very concerned and depressed.

Christmas arrived, and we went to my mom's for the holiday. My skin flared up so badly while we were there that I began crying from both the pain and embarrassment. We actually ended up leaving early because I was having such a hard time and didn't want to be around anyone.

Emergence

For the next month, I didn't leave my house at all. I was so ashamed of my appearance that I would stay home while my husband and kids went out to eat or catch a movie. I wanted to go with them so badly, but I found it too difficult to face people at the time. Most of all, having my husband see me like that every day was difficult.

I was in a bad place. Every night as I looked in the mirror to wash my face, the condition of my skin made me want to cry, and most nights I did. I would go into my closet and sit on the floor and cry out to God for healing. Eventually, I contacted my dermatologist and explained the situation. They told me to stop the treatment and gave me some recommendations that might help. Although I listened and took the advice, nothing changed.

Scrambling for answers in desperation, I researched and researched and researched, and nothing seemed to help. I had tried numerous topical solutions and finally decided to try to heal my body from within, applying what I had learned with juicing. My husband bought me a juicer for my birthday. I thought that this would be beneficial for my overall well-being as well as bring healing to my skin.

Again, I thought wrong.

I began a three-day juice fast and ate nothing solid during that time. After buying an abundance of healthy fruits and veggies, I made different flavored juice drinks for every meal and snack. By the third day, however, a strange burning sensation developed in my esophagus. I thought it would go away once I stopped my three-day fast, but it kept getting worse.

Finally, I went to see a doctor about my esophagus. They discovered that I had H. Pylori. Apparently, this is a common bacterial infection in the stomach that many people get and don't even know they have. It can cause ulcers and other issues. Most likely, the stress from the house renovations had created ulcers, and the acid from the juice fast aggravated them and caused horrible heartburn.

They prescribed the necessary double round of antibiotics, and I went on my way. This treatment cleared the infection, but it would take time to heal my stomach. As a result, the heartburn continued. It got so bad that I was unable to eat many of the foods I normally ate and loved, especially pizza. I blame my pizza and pasta addiction

Mirror, Mirror

on me being one-quarter Italian. The remaining three-quarters of my genetic heritage must be Marinarian. If tested, I have no doubt that traces of oregano, garlic, and basil would be present. Marinara sauce is in my blood, baby!

As if it wasn't bad enough having to avoid all of my favorite foods, experience horrible heartburn, and suffer from a painful and embarrassing skin condition, the antibiotics caused a urinary tract infection I couldn't get rid of over the course of several months.

My immune system was shot. I went from being perfectly healthy to having multiple health issues in no time. I had never experienced anything like this. I had always had my health, and admittedly, my beauty was something I had taken for granted. Now, I had seen how quickly things could spin out of control, and I began to worry if I would ever bounce back to the person I used to be.

Everything the doctors prescribed either made no difference at all or made them worse. They couldn't help me. I was on my own. I began researching again for natural healing remedies to the point of total confusion. With so much information on the internet, getting lost was easy. Everything I tried on my own failed. I was in an overwhelming state of desperation, and depression.

I didn't understand what was happening to me. Why couldn't I get better, and why couldn't the doctors fix me? I had prayed, fasted, and cried out to God for answers and healing, yet I was still suffering.

After a while, I gave up trying to solve this dilemma on my own. I couldn't try to fix myself anymore. I had done everything I knew to do and it had all failed. That's when I gave it all to God, asking Him to take over and heal and restore me. That decision meant that I stopped everything I was doing and surrendered complete control over to Him.

After all else failed, I decided to rely solely on God for my healing. Not myself, not the internet, not the doctors and their prescribed medications or recommendations. I began to believe Him for healing as I meditated on His promises through Scripture.

I didn't see changes right away. Regardless, I just kept praying and believing that God was working on me. I continued my morning quiet time with the Lord and tried to continue living a normal life. As a result, I learned to put into practice the discipline of training myself to ignore and bear my suffering while believing, hoping, and anticipating God's healing.

Little by little, I started seeing improvement.

Emergence

Pursuing Perfection Beyond the Surface

Meanwhile, my husband and I were planning a trip to Hawaii to celebrate our ten-year wedding anniversary. I was excited about the trip and needed to get away from everything. However, I wanted to be completely healed before our trip so that I could fully enjoy it. I wanted the conditions to be perfect!

I had bought a beautiful white dress to wear during pictures with my husband on the beach, capturing the gorgeous backdrop. They were going to be our special anniversary photos. I was supposed to look and feel beautiful and healthy while on vacation to a tropical island. At least that is what I thought must first take place in order to fully enjoy this special time together. But I didn't feel that way at the time and feared I wouldn't feel that way by then either. How can you celebrate and have a good time when you look and feel terrible?

Initially, a part of me wanted to cancel our trip, but my husband convinced me that we needed to go regardless of my circumstances. So, we agreed that regardless of how I looked or felt, we were going to be together. That was all that mattered.

Chris was amazing throughout all of this. He always did his very best to make me feel beautiful. Never once did he make me feel unattractive and treat me any differently, even when I felt I looked awful. He loved me anyway and unconditionally—for better and for worse—and looked beyond the surface and past my imperfections. Chris didn't expect me to look what I would call "perfect" in my own eyes all the time; in his eyes, I just was. He saw me differently than I saw myself. We would pray together as a couple every night, and he would pray over me for healing. It was all that he could do to help. I needed him in that moment, and he was always there. We walked through these difficult seasons and trials side by side. Also, God was in the middle, even when it didn't feel like it. He was still there.

We chose to celebrate our ten years of marriage in Hawaii and have a great time together and enjoy God's beautiful creation. His presence was invited to go with us as well. The beautiful gift of our marriage and one another was worth celebrating and enough reason to still experience *joy*, even in the midst of pain and suffering.

I'm so thankful we didn't cancel our trip or put our lives on hold due to these "setbacks." We would have missed out on something very

Mirror, Mirror

special. That week I chose to forget about all of my problems and focus on the serene environment that was around me, who was beside me, and Who lived within me. This trip was a setup that provided an incredible opportunity for me to experience a comeback. It was a time of being intimate as a couple and intimate with God in paradise. It felt like we were in the Garden of Eden, if only for a moment.

I felt His peace come over me as I let go of all the heavy burdens I had been carrying. I experienced His freedom and His joy in that place and moment of time. It reminded me of what truly matters in life and brought my focus back to where it needed to be. It brought me back to a place from which I never should have strayed, a place of recognizing my gifts from God. Although I might not have had all that I really wanted, I had everything I really needed.

I learned that *joy* is not something we experience based upon our circumstances, but it is something we embrace based on a certainty. Joy comes from the Lord. You too can find it wherever you go, whenever you need it, no matter what you're going through. Joy is always present within His presence. It wasn't an escape from reality that brought about my healing but embracing my reality that welcomed it.

I took my white dress just in case my face miraculously healed overnight, but I didn't end up wearing it. We decided we didn't want to deal with the stress of hiring a photographer, and I didn't want to put my focus on my appearance and worry about looking perfect for the camera. I wanted to be free of all of that and just focus on us and enjoying the moment and the beauty before us.

Even though, I didn't heal overnight, I do believe that God gave me a special dose of His healing while on that trip. With each passing day, I got better. There is something to be said when we let go and let God and learn to embrace joy as we put our hope, trust, and focus in and on Him. That's when the healing comes.

I had been standing in my own way, trying to heal myself. While I had prayed to God for healing, I didn't wait for Him to respond. Instead, I grew impatient and chose to take matters into my own hands by seeking outside help from a dermatologist before waiting for God to respond to my call for help. My desire for instant results brought instant problems upon myself. Then I scrambled to clean my mess. All my endless striving exhausted me and made me realize I couldn't fix me.

Emergence

Finally, I chose to trust the One who could. I chose to get out of my own way and give God a chance to be God. No topical solution or magical concoction of my own hands could heal the blemishes that tormented me deep within my soul. This time I cried out and waited for Him to respond. I waited on His healing and found joy in the meantime. God forced me to confront those flaws daily in the mirror as He began to pull them to the surface.

Finally, it came. As a result, I was healed by God alone, not of my own works. He alone and no one else would get the glory. I praised Him for His mighty works.

O Lord my God, I cried out to You, And You healed me (Psalm 30:2 NKJV).

God was teaching me many things throughout these trials, one being that despite my conditions, I couldn't just check out of life and put everything on hold. I couldn't stop celebrating life because I didn't feel good or look good in the moment. I discovered that life goes on, and so must I.

The enemy saw my weakness as an opportunity to come in and torment me in that area until I acted on it. However, I believe that God allowed that to happen because He saw it as an opportunity to take what the devil meant for harm and use it for good. He used it to teach me lessons I needed to learn. I was on a journey of transformation to become more like Christ, and my heart had many issues (blemishes) that needed to be treated before I would fully be able to embrace my calling. Where God was taking me there was no room for unhealthy obsession, jealousy, envy, vanity, insecurity, and uncertainty.

It was time to get rid of some nasty bugs so that they wouldn't destroy the entire crop. We are constantly sowing, reaping, and preparing for a harvest. There is a time and a season for all things. God doesn't waste any season. Some seasons are brutal and others fruitful. All seasons are important and necessary for growth and a successful reaping.

I was in a brutal winter season, a time of facing harsh conditions yet necessary in order to kill off the pests that threatened the harvest. Although I had been sowing many good seeds and working toward God's plans, there were nasty little things that were eating away at the beauty of what God was trying to build through me. These pests had to be removed, and the only way to kill them was by sending a long, cold, and brutal frost.

Mirror, Mirror

The good news, however, is that God replaces whatever He removes. After the bugs are removed, fruit abounds. The bad news is — the fruit doesn't appear until the next season. There is a waiting period. There is a time and season where painful things are brought to the surface, but God is working beneath the surface, hidden from sight. There is a time where beauty is concealed.

> *Now we see but a poor reflection as in a mirror; then we shall see face to face. Now I know in part; then I shall know fully, even as I am fully known (1 Corinthians 13:12 NIV).*

Beauty Concealed

I had taken my health for granted and also my beauty. I had become obsessed with my imperfections. When I used to struggle with my insecurities and desiring perfection, billboards and commercials displaying beautiful models distracted me. These images of perfection were everywhere, lurking around every corner. When I looked at these images, what I actually saw was my own flaws. They screamed that I wasn't enough! They begged me to do something about it, and each time I saw my own reflection, I felt inadequate. This feeling pummeled me until I finally broke down and took matters into my own hands.

There is nothing wrong with visiting a dermatologist. However, in my case, my motivation for seeking help was wrong. Although I had a minor medical condition, the underlining problem was that I had a mental condition which rooted from a heart condition — an unpleasant case of self-absorption stemming from a place of shame, pain, and fear. My diagnosis occurred because I spent too much time focusing on myself rather than on others and God. The underlining treatment that I had been seeking was worldly perfection and acceptance. (That bad seed I had ingested in my youth had grown to consume my thoughts — the lie that beauty equals acceptance and acceptance equals love)!

Rather than appreciating the beauty that God had given me and being thankful for it, I wanted more. I didn't value what I had been given because I was looking around at what others had. What I had was never enough for my own standards because deep down, I feared I wasn't enough.

Emergence

I wanted more, more, more! I wanted her skin or her legs or her hair. This was sin, and this was wrong. I failed to acknowledge self-acceptance and recognize my own self-worth. The underlying reason was listening to the degrading voices around me long enough that I started to believe them.

I always felt the need to fight to improve and prove myself so that others would love and accept me. Because I had spent so much time in the past alone and in distress, I had developed the "me, myself, and I" mentality. I thought of myself more than I thought of others.

My insecurities caused me not to feel pretty enough, special enough, that I was enough to be loved and feel secure for better or for worse. I didn't know who I was if I didn't look and feel beautiful in the moment. My worth and value in the eyes of others were based on my beauty; therefore, I was becoming caught up in promoting and preserving it. I was becoming so wrapped up in myself that I was becoming like a mummy burying itself in a tomb.

This is exactly what our enemy wants, to distract us with petty matters on the surface so that we forget and ignore deeper matters of the soul. Instead, we wrap up these crucial issues, such as shame, pain, and fear and then we conceal, hide, and bury them. We get caught up in pointless priorities that prevent us from promoting our planned purpose until the promise putridly perishes. Our enemy loves this. He wants to keep us so beaten down with lies so that we won't ever stand and rise up in truth.

My husband would tell me numerous times every single day how beautiful, perfect, and loved I was; however, unless I believed it for myself, his encouragement wasn't getting through. People can speak the truth over you all day long, but unless you choose to believe it, you can't receive it.

Not only had I failed to listen to and believe my husband's voice, but I had failed to listen to and believe my Father in heaven's voice. Simply put, I failed to receive the truth about who I really am. On the other hand, if lies are spoken over you, and you choose to receive them as truth, they can become your reality. We must choose carefully and wisely which voices are worth listening to and whose words we will *agree* with.

I had struggled with these feelings of inadequacies my entire life, feeling the need to try to be perfect according to the world's standards.

Mirror, Mirror

If I didn't feel beautiful, I felt discouraged or depressed. So much time, effort, and energy would be spent getting myself ready every single day, trying to get my hair and makeup just right. It was exhausting.

My husband always told me that if I knew how beautiful I was, then I never would have married him. He also said, "Despite how beautiful you are to me, your heart's your best feature. That's why I married you."

He measured my beauty by the standard of godliness and righteousness (measured by the inner beauty of the heart), not by worldly perfection (measured by the outer beauty of the flesh). My husband could see clearly through me, but my vision of myself was tarnished and blurred.

This standard for weighing beauty is also true of God. If we only knew how precious we were to God, we would never question our self-worth. The reason I struggled with my image so much was because I had been looking to man, not my Creator, to discover my identity, self-worth, and unique beauty. I was looking into the wrong mirror.

Not only was this a season of teaching, but also it was a season of training. God was teaching and training me to look differently (not from the outside, but from the inside.) He was correcting my vision in many ways. The Bible says that we are fearfully and wonderfully made. God meticulously crafted every unique feature and characteristic of each of us. Out of the billions of people on this planet, no two are alike. God is perfect; He does not make mistakes. He created us with precise thought and intention.

My pastor, Jimmy Witcher (Senior Pastor of Trinity Fellowship Church in Amarillo, Texas) says in his book *Kingdom Come*, "The Kingdom of God is where we discover who we are and who we were created to be. Our identity was handcrafted by God. There are no accidents or errors with God. Finding our identity in Him—seeing ourselves as he sees us—sets us on the path He destined for each of us to take."[5]

This is where God was taking me—on a journey toward real kingdom living and a place of seeing myself clearly through the Father's eyes.

Rather than believing what God's Word said about me, I believed what the enemy's lies said about me. Rather than believing I was uniquely designed by God, I believed I was defective and that others (including myself) couldn't love me this way.

One of the lies the enemy told me after my painful divorce was that I was ruined for men. Sadly, I believed it for a very long time and even spoke it out loud and confessed it to be true.

Emergence

First, the enemy gets us to take a bite of the apple by promising us love and acceptance. Then as we do and all falls apart, he changes his tone, and promises the very opposite, insisting we will never find love, we are not worthy, and we are unlovable. If only I knew the way God loved me.

> *You are altogether beautiful, my darling; there is no flaw in you (Song of Solomon 4:7 NIV).*

If we all only knew the perfect way God loved us, we would stop punishing ourselves for being ourselves. Then we could learn to fully embrace who we are, and then we could learn to fully embrace others. When our arms are wrapped up so tightly around our own bodies out of desperation to feel loved, they aren't free to wrap around someone else. Don't get so wrapped up that you become bound up.

We were wonderfully created and delivered from our mother's womb, not to be shamefully covered and buried in a mummy's tomb. Don't become so caught up in striving to preserve the flesh of your body from seeing decay that you allow your heart and soul to rot and fall into ruin.

You weren't created for decoration. You were created for intention.

> *For you created my inmost being; you knit me together in my mother's womb. I praise you because I am fearfully and wonderfully made; your works are wonderful, I know that full well. My frame was not hidden from you when I was made in the secret place, when I was woven together in the depths of the earth. Your eyes saw my unformed body; all the days ordained for me were written in your book before one of them came to be (Psalm 139:13–16 NIV).*

I had bitten another apple. I had believed another lie, a lie that suggested I was unworthy (not enough) to receive unconditional, everlasting love. Not only had I looked to others to find my value, but I had looked at others and wanted what they had, all the while ignoring what I had been given. I had failed to see and appreciate the beauty and wonder of God's most treasured creation and possession—me.

Mirror, Mirror

Of course, I didn't recognize the sin in this mindset at the time because I was too focused on feeling sorry for myself. I didn't realize that in being envious of others' beauty, I was coveting my neighbors' gifts. I didn't realize I was offending God by doubting His goodness and questioning if He had possibly held out when making me. I wasn't seeing things from God's perspective because I was too busy looking inward. I didn't recognize the deceiver or the lies. Apples come in many different colors, shapes, and sizes. Often, it's difficult to detect the devil behind the disguise.

In the Garden of Eden, Satan tempted Eve by getting her to focus on what she did not have. He got her to put her eyes on herself and see what she lacked. She was in the middle of paradise, surrounded by perfection. She had plenty, she had enough, she had what she needed, yet even in the midst of such perfection, she wanted more. If she would have opened her eyes to the beauty that was around her and been thankful for all she had been given, she would have seen and realized just how much she was loved by God. Instead, she listened to the lies. She believed that God was holding out on her. She doubted His goodness, and she questioned His affection for her. Then she invited Adam to do the same.

This is the mirror that Satan wants us to look into. This is how Satan gets our attention. He gets us to focus on ourselves so that we don't see the beauty and the blessings that surround us, and the light of the world fades into darkness. Self-pity is dangerous, deceiving, and destructive.

When our eyes are on ourselves, they aren't on others, and they aren't fixed on God. We are most radiant when we're staring into God's eyes and looking at His glorious face as His light is reflected upon our own. He is the mirror we should be gazing into.

Those who look to him are radiant; their faces are never covered with shame (Psalm 34:5 NIV).

Once the enemy has distracted us by getting us to look at ourselves and focus inward, he whispers lies about us and convinces us that we are not loved. When we aren't looking to God, we lose our vision and the ability to see clearly. We then forget who we are—children of God. We forget that we are a reflection of Him. We lose sight of our blessings. We lose sight of our purpose—to look outward, loving God and loving others.

Emergence

When we feel unloved, it's difficult to express love. Often, we overcompensate by doing whatever is necessary to find it. We cover our nakedness. We conceal our blemishes. We mummify ourselves as we get wrapped up and entangled in insecurity, fear, obsession, and doubt. All the while, the clear truth is that God sees right through us and loves us just as we are.

Mistakenly, we look into the enemy's tainted mirror. We see what he wants us to see. Then we take a bite of the poisoned apple he feeds us. We fall into the trap of the Sleeping Death—not fully dead, yet not fully awake. Our eyes are covered and concealed to the truth of the beauty that is really before us.

The Poisoned Bite

Distraction was a successful tactic used by Satan to tempt and trap Eve. Likewise, it's a powerful tactic the enemy still uses to tempt and trap us, especially women today. Distraction prevents someone from giving full attention to something else, causing extreme agitation of the mind or emotions. Synonyms include *diversion, interruption, disturbance, interference, hindrance, frenzy, hysteria, mental distress, madness,* and *whirl.*

Satan uses any distraction necessary to poison our minds and throw us off course. He prevents us from giving our full attention to God by disrupting our normal day-to-day activities and disturbing our peace. He tries to interfere with God's work in our lives, hindering our progress in an attempt to divert and derail us from the path, purpose, and calling that God has for us, causing us extreme agitation of mind and emotions.

Satan used this tactic on Eve until she became so mentally distressed that she literally took the poisoned fruit into her own hand. She gave into temptation, diverting her, Adam, and all mankind from the path of life into the Sleeping Death. Satan also used this tactic on me.

I was following Jesus and walking on the path of life when the enemy sought to distract me by getting me to put my focus on myself. I became mentally and emotionally distressed to the point that I too took matters into my own hands. I found myself temporarily off course heading down a difficult road.

This is exactly what the enemy wants. He wants us to trip up and make a wrong turn. We make choices each and every day. We must be mindful of the choices we make. We have an enemy. He tries anything and everything to keep us from moving forward on the path of life. He not only wants to derail us, but he wants to take us out.

He knows that when we're following Jesus and walking on the path of life, we are a threat. He understands that each of us has a call on our lives and a part to play that has a tremendous impact in the kingdom of God. Therefore, he loves to play with our emotions, and women often make the easiest targets. He doesn't want to see us walking with God and blessing others, because he knows that's when people get saved. He wants to destroy us all, and he feeds on our insecurities.

Satan used to torment me every day as I put on my makeup, styled my hair, and got dressed. This was his bashing session. He used to pound on me as I looked in the mirror. I hated getting ready. I shared my insecurities with my husband, and although he couldn't understand why I felt this way, he wanted to help.

One day he offered a solution that changed my life. He made the suggestion for me to listen to sermons online while I got ready. That way I would be focusing on something other than myself and my appearance. This was genius. I took his advice, and started right away, I began spending that time either listening to different Christian speakers and pastors I enjoyed or just worshiping to Christian music. My time was no longer wasted. I turned something that I dreaded doing each day into something I actually looked forward to. Not only was I now putting the truth of God into my mind and thoughts, but I was also drowning out the enemy's voice. I replaced the enemy's poisonous lies with God's encouraging Word. It was a win-win situation. Rather than getting beat down on a regular basis, I was being lifted up.

Thanks to the painful but valuable lessons that God was teaching me about myself and Him implementing truth into my routine, I was on a path of discovering who I truly was.

Beauty is Pain

When my husband and I decided to build onto our house, we added a spectacular theater room I put a lot of time into designing. Despite how torturous the process of remodeling and planning was, the result turned out to be a thing of beauty and was totally worth it in the end. We now enjoy countless hours together as a family watching movies, playing games, entertaining guests, and having bumper pool tournaments in that room.

Emergence

One of Chris and my all-time favorite movies to watch is *Kingdom of Heaven*.[6] It's a remarkable movie about the Christian crusades and the attempts to regain the Holy Land of Jerusalem. There is an incredible and powerful scene where Orlando Bloom transforms an ordinary servant boy into a knight. He has everyone kneel as he gives the boy his oath, "Be without fear in the face of your enemies. Be brave and upright that God may love thee. Speak the truth, even if it leads to your death. Safeguard the helpless. *That* is your oath."

Then he strikes the boy across the face and tells him, "And *that* is so you'll remember it. Rise a knight. Rise a knight!"

As the boy is caught off guard, he astonishingly wipes the blood from his nose and then stands to his feet in front of all—a changed man prepared for battle.

The boy's old master is astonished. He questions, "Who do you think you are? Will you alter the World? Does making a man a knight make him a better fighter?"

The new master slowly turns his face toward the old master who is offended by what right he has in changing this man's identify from a servant to a knight.

The answer undoubtedly is, "Yes."

Yes! You gotta love that. I just want to scream, "Booyah! In your face old master!"

Sometimes in order for us to learn a valuable lesson, change for the better, or to accomplish God's will and bring change to this world, it's necessary for us to go through a painful experience that we will never forget. That way, we are sure to remember it. At the time of suffering, we don't yet know what it is God is trying to produce in us, but God knows, and in the end, so will we.

> *Not only so, but we also glory in our sufferings, because we know that suffering produces perseverance; perseverance, character; and character, hope (Romans 5:3–4 NIV).*

My lovely grandma used to say, "The rose is beautiful, but it still has its thorns." I believe that God created the rose with thorns; otherwise, it would just be too perfect, too beautiful for our eyes to handle. Our thorns remind us of our humanity. They remind us that we're not perfect in our own eyes and were not created to be. Our thorns remind us that we need Him. Our thorns keep us dependent upon Him. Our thorns keep us humble, and make us more empathetic and compassionate toward others who also have thorns. Our thorns keep us from growing arrogant, conceited, and too full of ourselves. Our pointy thorns point us to our Creator.

Our thorns, however, don't distract from our beauty. In fact, they enhance our true beauty within and build character. When we look at the rose, we see its charm, and we smell its sweet aroma. We pay little or no attention to its thorns.

God looks at us the same way. He knows they're present because He created us to have them for a purpose. Yet He overlooks them because He sees much more in us.

We are more than our thorns. Paul knew this agonizing truth, and learned to accept it in order for the kingdom and himself to benefit from them.

> *Therefore, in order to keep me from becoming conceited, I was given a thorn in my flesh, a messenger of Satan, to torment me. Three times I pleaded with the Lord to take it away from me. But he said to me, "My grace is sufficient for you, for my power is made perfect in weakness."*
>
> *Therefore I will boast all the more gladly about my weaknesses, so that Christ's power may rest on me. That is why, for Christ's sake, I delight in weaknesses, in insults, in hardships, in persecutions, in difficulties. For when I am weak, then I am strong (2 Corinthians 12:7–10 NIV).*

When we spend too much time focusing on our thorns, we fail to see the beauty in the way He created us, and we fail to release the sweet aroma that's inside us to give. When we accept who God made us to be and learn to love ourselves and give to others, to not strive to extract our thorns from our flesh, we bloom, and are at our most beautiful.

My wise grandma had discovered this truth, and she exuded it with such heavenliness. Women shouldn't seek after worldly perfection but after godly wisdom. Proverbs 31 describes the wife of noble character as a woman who fears the Lord. This chapter goes on to explain that such a wife is almost a personification of wisdom, which is of greater value than rubies.

Emergence

Gaining wisdom leads to rewards, such as honor and praise earned through humility and the fear of the Lord. I now earnestly seek wisdom over perfection and desire to honor and please my King by exuding a pleasant perfume within me that entices and engages others to draw nearer to Him rather than myself.

> *"Many women do noble things, but you surpass them all." Charm is deceptive, and beauty is fleeting; but a woman who fears the Lord is to be praised. Honor her for all that her hands have done, and let her works bring her praise at the city gate (Proverbs 31:29–31 NIV).*

Our thorns can be painful and uncomfortable, but it's our thorns that make us blossom into God's unique design and beautiful creation. Sometimes suffering is the only way to get us to give off a delightful fragrance that is pleasing to Him. Sometimes God will allow us to suffer through hardships because He knows what it will produce in the end.

Just as God allowed Jesus to suffer death on the cross in order to save us all, God knew it was necessary for our salvation. It was the only way. Even Christ begged God to remove His thorn when asking God to take this cup from Him. But in the end, Christ accepted His thorn and surrendered to do God's will rather than His own. This was the ultimate act of true beauty and perfection brought only through His suffering.

In the end, I am so thankful that God didn't remove the thorn from His flesh! That thorn produced salvation for us all. Jesus rose and His thorn altered the world.

> *"Father, if you are willing, take this cup from me; yet not my will, but yours be done" (Luke 22:42 NIV).*

God is training us to *rise* as knights in order to do the same. He is training us to step out from under the rule of our old master, who seeks to tear us down and hold us back, and step under the reign and rule of our new Master, who aims to build us up and send us out. He is developing our character, making us stronger, and equipping us for battle so that we will take the truth and love that has been produced in us and use it to alter the world. We are fighting for His kingdom to come and His will to be done here on Earth as it is in heaven.

Our thorns make us better fighters.

> *I consider that our present sufferings are not worth comparing with the glory that will be revealed in us (Romans 8:18 NIV).*
>
> *But we see him who for a little while was made lower than the angels, namely Jesus, crowned with glory and honor because of the suffering of death, so that by the grace of God he might taste death for everyone (Hebrews 2:9 ESV).*

In the end, God replaced His Son's crown of thorns with a crown of glory. Will He not do the same for you and me, His sons and daughters? Yes, if we will embrace our suffering and allow God's perfect will to train us up so that we can be like Jesus—and lift others up.

The Fairest of Us All

God is training us to become better fighters by training us to shift our focus. He is also healing our brokenness. A wounded soldier makes for a poor and weak fighter. Today, women are obsessed with their appearance. The pressure on women to always look their best is relentless, and comparison is a concerning epidemic and a disheartening truth of our society. I was one of these women, tormented daily to measure up and cover up.

Like the Evil Queen from *Snow White*, I too used to look in the mirror at my own reflection and measure my own beauty in comparison to others. Unrecognizably, in my own way, I would also say unto my mirror, "Who is the fairest of us all?" If I didn't like what I saw staring back at me, I got discouraged or depressed.

I used to compare myself to others on a regular basis. If there appeared one that competed with or surpassed my beauty, I would enter into a jealous rage. Okay, I didn't actually rage, but I did become jealous and envious. Being around others who were blessed with beauty was difficult. It brought out my insecurity and other unattractive features. Beauty was something I wanted only for myself. I wanted to be the fairest in all the land.

That is an ugly characteristic, and I'm ashamed to admit it. However, it's the honest truth. This is how I used to often think, and if being honest, it's how many women think. They fall victim to what I call the "Evil Queen disorder," a sickness that hardens and darkens the heart. Why else would women try so hard?

Emergence

The underlying reason I tried so hard and wanted to be the fairest was because I didn't want my prince to notice anyone else. I wanted his eyes, attention, and affection all for myself. I wanted to be loved so badly, and I feared that if I wasn't beautiful enough, I would lose the one I loved.

Fear was the root cause of my obsession. I feared that if I failed to uphold what I perceived to be the image of perfection in my own eyes, then I would be unlovable in the eyes of others.

Also, pain caused from experiencing rejection, and shame caused from experiencing disgrace were to blame. That was why I always tried so hard to be perfect. I thought I had to maintain being the loveliest in the land, or my prince would grow tired of me and run away with someone else. Maybe some of you can relate.

For the longest time, I fought this grueling inner battle every day. In high school, I got so upset when the Internet became widely available. At the time, I would hear and see things that the boys were talking about. Unfortunately, as distasteful images (pornography printouts) were passed around school, it disgusted me and threatened me at the same time. I felt I had to compete not only with the beautiful women around me, but now with beautiful women all over the world. How do you do that? This reality in my mind tormented me. My heart was deeply scarred by seeing images that twisted the beauty of God's gifts (sex and the human body) in such an evil way.

Later on in some of my relationships, these images replaced me. This was the world, or shall I say prison in which I lived. My greatest fear had come true. I just wanted to be enough for one person to love me, and I never felt that I was.

I struggled with my image in my first marriage, not feeling desired. I wanted to change my appearance. One day my husband said to me, "It will never be enough." I don't believe he meant that in a hurtful way. He was speaking the truth.

He also told me that my looks were never the problem in our relationship. He was right. Nothing I could do on the outside would ever be enough to change me on the inside. I needed help, but not to change my appearance; I needed my heart and mind to change. I needed inner healing from these scars and to discover my true identity.

That was exactly what God was bringing forth. How can we discover who we are when we're constantly looking at and comparing ourselves to who others are?

Mirror, Mirror

Help finally came to me. One day I learned the truth—I was enough for God, and fear is a liar! Jesus loved me just the way I was. I didn't have to be perfect for Him. He promised to love me unconditionally for all eternity. It didn't matter to Him how I looked on the outside because He was in love with who He created me to be on the inside. That was enough for me, knowing that I was enough for God. I could finally rest from the tiresome labor of working toward perfection. This revelation didn't mean I no longer sought to look *my* best with each changing season of life or that I could let myself go; however, it meant that I no longer sought to look *the* best. Now, I could be enough just being me.

When I discovered this, I found that God had blessed me with a prince on Earth who exemplified this same understanding and promise. My new husband Chris regularly overlooked my thorns and loved me in spite of them. Our relationship beautifully mirrored that of my relationship with God, just as His love letter to me promised.

Jesus was teaching and training me to do the same. I'll admit that this is still an area in my life where the devil continues to try and torment me. God hasn't removed my thorns (painful difficulties in life, imperfections, etc.), although I have begged. Instead, He's training me to overlook them daily. He's shifting my focus to remember what He says and thinks about me, to make the choice to love the person He has created me to be (flaws and all), to concentrate on the blessings and beauty before me. It's a battle I continue to face but one I'm seeing great victory in as I continue to look to God for my value and identity.

I'm being set free! Now the only person I'm seeking to look like is Jesus, truly the fairest of us all. The person I am now choosing to see when I look into the mirror is a reflection of His lovely creation smiling back at me. When the enemy tempts to distract me in this area, I quickly divert my focus back onto Christ, the true standard of perfection.

God loves me, I love God, and I love others. God loves you. He desires for you to love Him and to love others. We were created in God's image. God is love. Therefore, we were created in love's image. Without first discovering the person who is love, Jesus, we're incapable of true and perfect love. When we discover who love truly is and we discover who we truly are, then we can love the person God truly created us to be. We were created by love, for love, and to love.

Emergence

So God created man in His own image; in the image of God He created him; male and female He created them (Genesis 1:27 NKJV).

Whoever does not love does not know God, because God is love (1 John 4:8 NIV).

There is a beauty that is everlasting, One that will never fade. It lies deep beneath the surface and longs to live within us. This beauty has the power to transform even the ugliest soul into the most divine creation. His name is Jesus.

Earlier, I shared how I had been suffering through my skin condition. God used that tormenting season of my life to teach me where true beauty lies.

Here is something I wrote about it. I call it "Wrapping Paper."

Wrapping Paper
Mistie House

I'm sure most of us have received a gift at some point in our lives because someone wanted to bless us by selflessly giving something of value. One of the first things we do when receiving a gift is to admire the beautiful packaging or wrapping paper.

Usually, we do this for a moment, and then we move on. We typically rip off the pretty bow or pull out the colorful tissue paper and discard them with the wrapping. Although we admire and appreciate the beauty of the perfectly wrapped gift, we are eagerly focused on retrieving what is on the inside.

However, some might be so infatuated with the stunning appearance of the packaging that they hold onto the wrapping paper and store it for later use. In fact, their admiration may have even led them to completely lose sight of the gift in hand.

I'm here to share that each of us has an *amazing* gift to offer. Outside of that gift we are beautifully and individually wrapped. However, we can't hold onto our wrapping paper

Mirror, Mirror

forever. Over time, the outer beauty and perfection will fade, and the packaging will be discarded. So why put so much time and energy into preserving it? Admire it, and appreciate it for what it is, and then move on, and let it go in order to reveal what is inside and what *truly* matters.

I want to encourage all of us to not get so caught up in perfecting our wrapping on the outside, that we rob people of the true gift we have to offer on the inside.

We live in a world today that makes getting caught up so insanely easy. I can tell you from personal experience that getting caught up in seeking perfection and allowing the idea to consume your thoughts only leads to brokenness.

I have wasted so much time being infatuated with trying to perfect my own wrapping paper that I lost sight of the treasure inside.

Each of us is a gift from God. If we'll take our eyes off ourselves, stop obsessing over our presentation, and spend more time focusing on what we have to offer others, then we won't lose sight of our purpose.

We are a gift, and the purpose of a gift is to selflessly give something of value to bless another.

Maybe you're reading this book, and you feel you have nothing to give because you haven't yet received the precious gift of Jesus inside you. You can receive that gift today!

You are a beautiful gift, and there are people who desperately need what you have to offer. You are much more than just a pretty face. You're God's gorgeous creation, and He wants to make your heart radiant.

God also used that season of my life to heal deep wounds and scars that had been covered up and buried away. He began to unwrap me as I learned to look into His mirror and see what He sees.

That exposure was painful in the beginning. But in order to heal the wounds, first they had to be exposed. They had to be brought to the surface and uncovered so that they could breathe and receive fresh air and Son light. I told you earlier that God doesn't waste any season, and that what He removes, He also replaces.

After God removed the wrapping I had hidden myself under, He replaced that covering as He wrapped me in His love and embraced me in His arms. That is beauty beyond compare.

PRAYER

Lord,

I confess I struggle with "Evil Queen disorder." Please forgive me, deliver, heal, redeem, renew, and rebuild me. Set me free from envy, jealousy, insecurity, self-pity, and comparison. Tend to the root cause of my struggles. I want to be a confident and honorable woman who fears the Lord. Make me a knight for the battles ahead. Help take my eyes off of me and instead look into Your face, reflecting Your heart, mirroring Your character, and radiating Your beauty. Help me to look more like You and love and accept myself the way You made me. Thank you for loving me and forming me wonderfully and beautifully.

In Jesus' Name. Amen.

CHAPTER TEN

War With The Wind

When I was going through the difficult season with my skin and my health, I also wrote something else. At the time, I thought this represented what I had been going through with God and discovering about myself.

I called it "I Am Yours."

I Am Yours
Mistie House

I am Beautiful . . .
When I feel ugly,
I am Perfect . . .
When I feel I am not.
I am Strong . . .
When I feel I will break.

So Break me, O God,
So that I may Hear you.
Tear me down,

Emergence

So that I may Feel you.

When I have fallen . . .
When I am broken . . .
When I see no light . . .
No Hope . . .

Let me know I am not alone.
Lift me Up.
Plant my feet,
To bear more weight.

Build me Again . . .
So that I may be Strong . . .
To live for You.

I Am Yours.

This writing expressed my brokenness at the time and also the hope I was experiencing. I was expressing where I was currently at in my struggles and my walk with God. What I didn't realize was that this wasn't just a heartfelt writing about my feelings and encounters; it was a prayer to God. Not only was I expressing my deepest pains and yearning to Him, but I was actually granting Him permission to go deeper. What I thought was describing where I had been was actually describing where I was going.

God wasn't finished with me yet.

Just Getting Started

It was the beginning of 2015. I was glad to say goodbye to the previous year. It had been such a difficult one for me, and I was ready to start fresh and new, and hopeful for a year of peace and quiet.

Every year we had a gifted guest speaker visit our church and bring a prophetic word for the New Year, transcribed and recorded. It was always an accurate account of what God was doing in the world, the Church, and in the lives of individual believers. According to Chuck Pierce, president of Global Spheres, Inc. and president of Glory of Zion Ministries, the year 2015 was to be one of pouring out God's grace as the number five is linked with grace.[7] Some of the highlights given were:

> *"This will be a year that God is moving us, a year to let our faith be seen, a year our identity is going to shift, a year old cycles will break, a year a testimony will arise, a year linked with breaking captivity, a year of the wind blowing loudly, storms and whirlwinds, a year of discovering rest and stability, and a year of the eye of God watching and the advancement of God's people. It was also said that the enemy will take his stand in August and try to stop the manifestation and power of our grand testimony, but we will triumph."*

This prophetic word caused me to feel very hopeful but also a little cautious. I loved hearing how God's people would triumph, but I didn't like hearing the enemy would take a stand against us in August. Couldn't we just be triumphant without any resistance? That sounded like a much-better idea to me, especially after the year I had experienced. We would just have to wait and see.

One January morning, my husband and I were sitting around the kitchen table after breakfast. We were discussing the hardship and trials I had gone through in 2014. I began to cry as we discussed the difficulty these lessons had brought, yet also the beauty in what they had produced. I was just glad that it was over and praying that the worst was behind me. My husband teared up alongside me, and he started speaking an analogy of a sword.

He spoke of how the sword is first shaped and refined through fire to mold into form. Then it's polished to shine, reaching its final state. Then he prophetically said to me, "God is polishing you to shine once again."

These words were very encouraging to me. I believed he had just given a beautiful word of what God was going to do for me that year, and I was excited at the thought of being beautifully polished so that I could shine again. The cold weather and harsh conditions from the previous spiritual winter season had caused me to lose my luster.

I was ready to *shine!*

Emergence

There's a Storm Coming

Little did I know, the winter season wasn't yet over.

We began the year hopeful, optimistic, and encouraged, believing smooth sailing was ahead. Finally, I was healthy, our construction was finished, and we were actually enjoying life again. I began painting more and was working toward expanding my business, whipping out and shipping off paintings right and left. I was in the zone!

Then something began to shift. Although it seemed as if the dust had settled for me, things began to stir and rise up in my oldest daughter. She was now in her teenage years and was experiencing a lot of change mentally, physically, emotionally, and spiritually. It is completely normal to experience change on certain levels and to a certain extent; however, she was experiencing changes in behavior and personality to an entirely different degree. It wasn't normal.

My daughter and I had always been close. She had always treated me with respect, love, and admiration, rarely misbehaving and quickly responding to correction. Bright, creative, beautiful, she was a sweet girl, kind and considerate to others. My daughter was dedicated to hard work, committed to learning, working diligently to maintain perfect grades, and she excelled in extracurricular activities. For instance, she had earned a black belt in Taekwondo, eventually becoming a first-degree black belt and instructor and was extremely talented in the field of art. We were very proud of how well-rounded she was, marveled at her level of maturity, and commended her achievements. She was a huge blessing in our lives!

My husband and I had always done our best to support and encourage her in everything she did. We loved her very much. She had many fans, and we were among her biggest. We wanted to see her succeed and have fun while doing it. Nevertheless, we always tried our best to move her forward without pushing her too hard.

We are a Christian family and uphold Christian beliefs based on God's Word. That doesn't mean we don't like to have fun as a family. We love spending time with our kids and have a blast engaging in activities with them. They are nowhere near-deprived.

We do, however, believe in censorship. As I mentioned earlier, I'm a firm believer in, what goes in is what comes out. Accordingly, we monitor what we and our children put into our minds, and what and who we bring into our home. The enemy is always looking for an open door or window. I prefer not to give him easy access.

We raised our children upon the foundational upbringing of God first, marriage second, children and family third, and everything else falls underneath. This includes friends. I know that's something a teenager doesn't always understand. They would probably argue that they should come first, their friends second, and their education and activities third. It is probably safe to say that family time and church was way down there on the list. I get that. I thought the same way as a young teenager.

However, raising your children based upon their opinions isn't parenting. Our job is not to become our children's best friends; our job is to teach, train up, and prepare our children in the way that they should go. Our job is to protect our children, build a healthy and loving relationship with them, and encourage them to develop an intimate relationship with God. Despite how unpopular we may become or how invalid our opinions may appear to them at the time, that's the proper role of a parent in my opinion. One day, God willing, they'll understand and hopefully will appreciate and thank us for looking out for what we believe to be in their best interest.

I had amazing parents, but if there's one thing I wished they could have done, it would have been to have paid closer attention. They did their job to train me up in the way I should go, but I wish they would have noticed every time I began to slip off course. I wish they would have intervened and helped me find my way back home before devastating, life-altering decisions were made.

Of course, I realize now that this is an unrealistic expectation to put on any parent. Our parents can't be God in our lives. They can't always be our saving grace no matter how badly they wish they could. They trusted me and didn't see the harm coming my way; otherwise, they would have done everything in their power to stop it.

Like my daughter, I was a smart kid with a good head on my shoulders. I worked hard, and for the most part, avoided trouble. I loved God and desired to obey Him as well as my parents. I knew better. I had been taught right, and yet I still slipped.

When circumstances in children's lives get tough or begin to change, they tend to lash out and rebel against authority. They test their limits and seek answers for themselves. Despite my intentions to do the right thing and my parents' guidance and trust in me, I had let them down as well as myself. Children may appear to have it all together, but they still need their parents' wisdom, protection, involvement, and intervention.

My parents weren't perfect. However, they did their best, and they did very well. I'm extremely grateful for all they have done and still do for me. I never expected them to be perfect, and I have forgiven them for all of their shortcomings. Please understand that I also am in no way claiming to be a perfect parent. There is no such thing. A perfect parent on this earth is an oxymoron. The only perfect parent is God, and we are not Him.

However, the Bible teaches us that we are to model His example and teachings in everything we do, including parenting. I'm only claiming to have attempted to model His teachings and example the best—nevertheless imperfect—way I knew how. I hope that my children will also forgive me for my shortcomings.

God loves His children unconditionally, and yet He still disciplines them and says no at times in order to protect, guide, and teach them. I also love my children unconditionally. They are precious to me, my flowers and my jewels, and I continue to do everything in my power to keep them safe, shining, and blooming.

> *As you endure this divine discipline, remember that God is treating you as his own children. Who ever heard of a child who is never disciplined by its father? If God doesn't discipline you as he does all of his children, it means that you are illegitimate and are not really his children at all. Since we respected our earthly fathers who disciplined us, shouldn't we submit even more to the discipline of the Father of our spirits, and live forever?*
>
> *For our earthly fathers disciplined us for a few years, doing the best they knew how. But God's discipline is always good for us, so that we might share in his holiness. No discipline is enjoyable while it is happening—it's painful! But afterward there will be a peaceful harvest of right living for those who are trained in this way (Hebrews 12:7–11 NLT).*

I don't expect my children to be perfect. Again, there's also no such thing as perfect children while on this earth. They'll make mistakes as we all have. They'll fail, stumble, and cry. I wish as a parent I could protect them from all of this, but I'm aware I can't. However, I do expect my children to listen and obey our instruction and respect our authority. Then when they begin to fall, stumble, or lose their way, I can do my best to intervene. I can lovingly reach out and help pick them up and get them back on track by correcting them and showing them the way back to safety, freedom, and abundant life.

Fathers, do not provoke your children to anger, but bring them up in the discipline and instruction of the Lord (Ephesians 6:4 ESV).

Those who spare the rod of discipline hate their children. Those who love their children care enough to discipline them (Proverbs 13:24 NLT).

This is what my husband and I attempted to do for my daughter once we discovered she too was slipping. Like my parents, we trained up my daughter in the way she should go, but like me, she too began to slip. Although, we eventually discovered this, I wish I could have seen it sooner or prevented it altogether much like I wish my parents had done for me.

That's not always possible though. There are times when our supervision is limited, especially when your child resides in two separate households and is not always in your care. We are human, and we can't see all. We can only do our best to see most. Still, I'm grateful that we intervened before devastating life-altering decisions and consequences were made in her life.

Somewhere, the enemy found an open window despite the boundaries and protection we provided in our own home. I believe he snuck his way into my daughter's thoughts through other means and had been torturing and tormenting her by whispering poisonous lies and deception into her ears, heart, and mind. As a result, she became very conflicted and confused. Much like me when life wasn't going in the direction I had hoped for, she too began lashing out in ungodly rebellion. She began to withdraw from us more and more, questioning who she was, what she believed, and who she believed. She began to question the way. At the discovery of this news, my heart was broken, not only for my daughter who was lost and in pain, but also because trust between us had now been broken.

Emergence

I'm purposely not going into detail in regards to this behavior because it's not my story to tell. I hope to do my best to protect and respect that. Perhaps my daughter will one day write her own beautiful story, telling how God showed up and intervened in her precious life. But for now, this is my story and is being told from my perspective. I love my daughter with all my heart and am sharing our story so that others may be blessed and helped through it and that God may be glorified by it.

My daughter has grown exponentially since that time. She's no longer a child but has blossomed and matured into a beautiful, godly adult woman. Throughout the making of this book, she has stood at my side and has approved the telling of this story. Collaborating together, we determined its title, and us joining forces for this book's development is something I hold so dear to my heart. I'm so proud of the woman she is, and I know her relationship with Christ will only continue to bloom. Undoubtedly, He has extraordinary plans for her future. As her mommy, I am thrilled to watch as these glorious plans unfold in the life of my little buttercup.

Although my husband and I were hurt, disappointed, and shocked to learn of her behavior at the time, we didn't judge or condemn her for it. There were, however, consequences for her behavior, and we chose a form of discipline to help correct it. Our goal was to simply help turn her around and get her safely back on course.

> *Young people are prone to foolishness and fads; the cure comes through tough-minded discipline (Proverbs 22:15 MSG).*

Once we discovered that my daughter had been slipping away and heading down a dark and dangerous road, we intervened. Before we opened up a conversation with her, we went to God and opened one up with Him. We surrendered the situation to Him and asked Him to also intervene. We knew we could not lead her back to safety on our own. We prayed for His guidance, wisdom, knowledge, understanding, and peace over this situation. Then we lovingly and supportively engaged in a conversation with our daughter and tried to help her find her way back home.

We sat down and listened to her, and all of the darkness was brought into the light. We cried with her and prayed over her. We comforted her and spoke life, forgiveness, and grace over her, not judgment, condemnation, or shame. Together, we were committed to helping guide her into freedom and truth.

This is a picture of what Christ does for us all in our times of rebellion.

Sin, deception, and confusion come from the devil. Now that he was exposed, we were focused on getting him out of the picture and replacing him with God so that through building a relationship with Him, her true identity could be revealed, and her pain could be healed. Jesus alone is the Healer.

It was a difficult and painful moment but also a beautiful one. I felt the presence of God with us, directing us through the conversation, giving us wisdom, and guiding us into a place of peace and safety. I felt confident about where God was leading our family.

Our daughter left our home that weekend admittedly feeling optimistic, hopeful, and lighter after having the weight and burden of sin and secrecy lifted off her shoulders and brought into the light. However, after coming back home from spending the weekend at her father's house, something had drastically shifted. She was a different kid than when she left. It was as if she had dismissed or forgotten our entire conversation. Our loving and encouraging words of life over her seemed to have been snatched away, and the weight of the heavy load had been put back on.

I feel my daughter believed that because we were enforcing discipline to correct her behavior, my husband and I were against her and holding her back. This could not have been further from the truth. We had always been there for her and were especially there for her in this. Our intentions were to correct the behavior, to redirect our child toward the path of life, safety, freedom, peace, joy, and hope, and to help guide her into a relationship with God in order to reveal her true identity in Him. We were deeply concerned for her and compassionate toward her. All of our decisions were rooted in Love.

But, upon listening to the influence of other opposing voices, I concluded that she grew confused and misguided regarding our motivation and intentions. She mistook our discipline for mere punishment. She believed our restrictions and concerns were unjustifiably limiting her freedom and the ability to do as she pleased. She mistook loving conviction and our means to correct, protect, and impart wisdom within her as judgment and condemnation.

Despite our recent attempt to rid the enemy's voice, replace it with God's truth, and express how much we loved our daughter despite her actions, it appeared to make no difference in her.

Emergence

My daughter grew increasingly restless, rebellious, and disrespectful. The more we tried to intervene, the further she pushed us away. Instead, she chose to ignore our attempts and turned to her equally troubled friends and other set of parents for guidance and direction, shutting us out completely. She was becoming unrecognizable to us. I was losing her.

It's About to Blow

Our home, once a place of peace, had turned into utter chaos. My daughters were constantly bickering, and my oldest daughter seemed to be becoming more and more impossible for us to please. No matter how hard my husband and I tried to make her happy, it appeared to never be good enough. I constantly felt like I was competing for her approval but was always on the losing end.

She would excitedly tell me about her weekend with her other parents and how much fun she had over there; meanwhile, I would mostly just listen in silence. She would rave about the food at their house or this or that, and I always felt inadequate and hurt by her remarks. It wasn't that I didn't care. I wanted her to be happy over there; I just wanted to hear her say she was happy here as well. She rarely did at that time. So much had changed which hurt me, and it made it hard for me to share her enthusiasm.

I once again wanted her to be as proud of me and as loving toward me as she now appeared to be for her dad. I wanted her to remember and recognize how much I had done for her and sacrificed for her over the course of her entire life. I wanted to be her hero as well. I didn't know what else I could have possibly done to demonstrate to her how much I loved her. She didn't appear to have noticed any of it. Her eyes seemed to have become so focused on all that she believed she was missing over there, that she failed to notice or appreciate all that she had and was being given right here in front of her.

I can't help but to think that this must be similar to how God must feel when we treat Him, our loving Father, in this same way.

Although we had done everything in our power to make her happy, it was no longer enough. No matter how good she had it, how good we were to her, or how much additional time (outside of standard visitation requirements) I gave her with her dad (which was very generous I might add, and well-above standard), it wasn't enough. I think she still felt as if she was missing out on her freedom and time with her other family and friends. She was beginning to resent me for it, and she was determined to be unhappy and miserable while with us. The only thing we could have done to make her happy in that situation was to give her what she wanted.

The problem was, we believed what she wanted was not what she needed or was in her best interest. Therefore, I said no. I refused to give in any further. I had already bent the court-ordered papers in their direction as far as I could. If bent any further, I feared her life would have been thrown out of proper balance and stability. I was doing my best to do what I felt was best for her. I was trying to protect her.

This refusal to give in completely to her request angered and upset my daughter. Again, my job was to be her parent, not her best friend. She didn't have to understand my reasoning, but she should have respected my authority. Instead, I gathered she remained convinced that everything was greener on the other side, and she was determined to find out for herself.

One day, my daughter and I were arguing, and it was going nowhere. We just kept going round and round. I couldn't get through to her. I was about to break down, so I left the house for a little while and drove to the nearest park. After pulling up alongside the curb, I sat in my car in complete silence for a few minutes just to quiet the noise. Then I started confiding in God as tears streamed down my face. I told Him I didn't know what to do; I was trying so hard to get through to my daughter, but nothing was working. I couldn't force her to believe the truth or to see my heart for who I truly was and not for who the enemy was portraying me to be.

I felt worthless in her eyes, and it was killing me. I loved her so much and wanted her to see that. I wanted to feel her acceptance and love for me as well.

Our family was in so much pain, and I couldn't fix it. Crying out to God, I pleaded, "God, I don't know what to do. I am so broken and lost. I feel like I'm nobody to her. I feel like I'm nothing. It hurts so much. Help me. Comfort me, Holy Spirit, and speak to me!"

Immediately, my eyes caught focus of a tree right in front of me. The Lord said, "You are like this tree. The wind is going to come, and the tree is going to sway. Stay rooted in Me, in My foundation. The wind may cause the tree to sway, but if it stays rooted, it will not fall. It will not be swept away. It may lose its leaves, but new fruit will come."

His words gave me a feeling of peace, comfort, and a sense of direction came over me. I wasn't in this alone.

A Moment of Peace

Strangely enough, things had quieted down. For a few months, my daughter had been noticeably nicer, more respectful, and I thought things were improving between us. We had a wonderful Fourth of July weekend at the lake as a family. We watched our girls laugh and play together on our boat as we pulled them around on the tube. The younger sibling giggled as the older one struggled to hold on to her at every turn. They were working together as a team, and both looked so happy. We hadn't seen them have fun like that together in a long time.

We played all day and into the night and had a great conversation that evening while looking over the lake and up at the stars. It felt just like old times. It was a wonderful weekend!

My husband and I felt refreshed and hopeful that things were finally settling down and our daughter was coming around. We felt like a family again.

A False Sense of Peace

Unfortunately, our feelings were wrong.

We would soon learn that this had only been the calm before the storm. Just a week later, I had a strange visitor come to my door.

I had been served papers. I was being sued for custody of my daughter.

She had finally made the decision to go her own way.

This was the wind God had warned me about. It was here; it was now.

It came suddenly and powerfully. It was a force like nothing I had ever known. Its harshness cut through to the very bone. Its brutality was numbing to the core. It took my breath away.

In a single instant, I had been hit by a mighty storm.

My first reaction was confusion and disbelief. Shocked and stunned, I couldn't believe what was happening. Nothing made sense to me in that moment.

War With The Wind

Then heartache and despair set in. I felt betrayed, deceived, and rejected, like a failure and lifeless. I couldn't understand what I had done to deserve this and how God could allow this.

My husband and I had been seeking God and living for Him. Throughout every decision, we had sought His wisdom, counsel, and guidance. We loved our children and had been doing our best to raise them according to His Word. In my heart, I knew the safest place for her to be was with me.

So why was this happening? What did I do wrong? Then anger and frustration set in. I was angry with her dad and frustrated with my daughter. I wasn't going down without a fight. I was not going to stand by and let my daughter be taken from me. It was going to get even uglier.

Then lastly, surrender came.

I had been being prepared for the wind and the rain to hit. God had warned me through the prophetic word given from Chuck Pierce earlier that year about the coming whirlwind and again when He spoke to me at the park. God had also informed me what to do in the midst of it. He told me to stay in the eye of God, aligned with Him, and rooted in Him. It was simple. I was to look up and put my trust and faith in Him. All of the teaching and training I had recently gone through was to help equip and strengthen me for this very battle. He had made me a knight for this fight. God knew what I would soon be up against; He helped get me ready and prepared me for the storm that was to come.

Throughout every argument and battle with our daughter, I had been going to God and praying life and victory over her. I had been fighting for her before the battle even began. The enemy had gone after my daughter and now was attempting to wipe out my family. When I discovered this was happening, I sought the help of the Lord's army. I went to Him and declared victory over my daughter and over our family. I had been praying that we would all be triumphant regardless of the enemy's attacks. We would win the battle because God was fighting on our behalf. We would rebuke the wind; we would resist the devil and he would flee. We would have a grand testimony.

We were a family committed to serving God and loving others. That made us a target. The enemy had set his sights on us and was making his move. We were now at war.

Emergence

The Battle

Despite God giving me a strategic battle plan to ensure victory through the prophetic word earlier that year, winning the war, unfortunately, is easier said than done. War is brutal and not without sacrifice, loss, and pain. It takes everything out of you and threatens to take everything from you. It is dark, dreadful, and it is dangerous.

There is no such thing as an easy victory; it is a fight to the finish. In order to survive, you must endure, outlast, and overcome your enemy. In order to win, you must believe, hope, trust in God, stand your ground, and never submit to fear. Your response to attack determines your outcome for victory.

My husband and I had been summoned to a fight and custody battle that we didn't want. We were forced into something over which we had no control, yet we made a decision in the midst of this mighty whirlwind to trust God and believe that He is good, even when it didn't look good or feel good. As His children, we didn't need to understand His reasoning; we simply needed to respect His authority.

We chose to surrender our child to Him and trust that He would take care of her and provide for her, despite where she lived. We also believed that He was taking care of us. We acknowledged that she was God's child before she was ours, and He alone knew what was truly best for her. That was a hard pill to swallow.

Upon realizing our daughter was of age to choose which parent she wanted to live with and that the child's choice took precedence over most other issues, we chose not to contest the court battle. We didn't want to put her through a difficult trial; therefore, we let her go and agreed to their terms. Even though, I was given joint custody, the roles were now reversed. I was granted less-than standard visitation rights. Despite the fact that I had always generously given more than required to the other parents, I was now receiving less-than standard visitation rights from them. This was a slap in the face to say the least. It was absolutely degrading as a mother.

However, I chose not to wage war against her parents because they were not my enemies. The real enemy was Satan. He was the one seeking to destroy my family and steal my child. He comes to steal, kill, and destroy, and he wants people to battle amongst themselves and destroy one another. This makes his job much easier.

War With The Wind

Well, I was finished being a part of his plan. The enemy wanted me to look at them as enemies, hate them, and retaliate against them. Instead, I chose to see them as God's creation and to forgive, love, and extend grace to them, praying that God would bless them, even if they didn't love me, forgive me, or bless me in return. I didn't seek revenge but sought to humble myself before God. This is how we waged war against the enemy. I chose to be in right standing with God by laying down anger, pride, bitterness, and past offenses. I also asked God and the other parents to forgive me of my part played in all of this mess. None of us involved were without fault or blame. I can't control their actions, but I could certainly take responsibility for my own.

We fought to bring her back to her spiritual home, not our physical home. It no longer mattered where she lived; this battle would take place in the spiritual realm. Our place was to war alongside God, fighting the enemy in an unseen battle. Satan's plan was to create division by isolating and pulling our daughter away, separating her from truth, from us, and from the Lord.

I had been trying everything to bring her back and win this battle in my own way. Now was the time to let God battle in His way. This battle was to be fought with complete surrender, love, forgiveness, mercy, and grace, and love never fails.

> *"You have heard that it was said, 'Love your neighbor and hate your enemy.' But I tell you, love your enemies and pray for those who persecute you, that you may be children of your Father in heaven. He causes his sun to rise on the evil and the good, and sends rain on the righteous and the unrighteous. If you love those who love you, what reward will you get? Are not even the tax collectors doing that? And if you greet only your own people, what are you doing more than others? Do not even pagans do that? Be perfect, therefore, as your heavenly Father is perfect (Matthew 5:43–48 NIV).*

This was one of the hardest decisions I had ever made. In previous situations, I had chosen to let go and let God, but never like this. As a mother, you always want to be able to hide your baby under your wing in order to hold them close and keep them safe. Yet there is a time that you must let them go, to leave your nest, so that they can learn to fly on their own.

Emergence

I had done what I was supposed to do—train her up in the way she should go. Now it was time to let God do what only He could do and pray and believe that one day, upon finding her wings, she would be led into all truth, return to her roots, and soar back home. I may have been forced to let go of her hand as she was pulled away from me, but I never let go of her heart. I held on in love, trusting and believing that love would reunite us again.

Love is the strongest bond of all.

The comfort I had in this was knowing that God was love. He loved my child more than I could ever know, and He was a better parent than I could ever hope to become. She was safer in His hands and under His wing than my own.

In letting her go, God would go after her and bring her heart safely back to me. Even though I didn't understand His ways, I could trust in His faithfulness.

Although the loss I experienced throughout this battle was extremely painful at the time, I stood on God's promises that in the end we would triumph and be victorious. Everything the enemy tried to take from us would be returned, redeemed, and restored.

> *No weapon formed against you shall prosper, And every tongue which rises against you in judgment You shall condemn. This is the heritage of the servants of the Lord, And their righteousness is from Me," Says the Lord (Isaiah 54:17 NKJV).*

> *Now David was greatly distressed, for the people spoke of stoning him, because the soul of all the people was grieved, every man for his sons and his daughters. But David strengthened himself in the Lord his God (1 Samuel 30:6 NKJV).*

> *So David recovered all that the Amalekites had carried away, and David rescued his two wives. And nothing of theirs was lacking, either small or great, sons or daughters, spoil or anything which they had taken from them; David recovered all (1 Samuel 30:18–19 NKJV).*

Throughout this section of the writing, I have specifically left out details of the situation as to not distract from its theme and purpose. My intention was not to discuss who said this or who did what through it all; it was to discuss what God said and what God did through it all. That was the purpose behind my testimony. The finger was meant to point at none other than God.

This is my story, but it's not about me; it's about God and what He has done for me and what I know He can do for you.

He is the subject of this writing, and *you* are its purpose.

While experiencing my storm, I wrote a poem called "The Storm."

The Storm
Mistie House

**In the distance it approaches . . .
The racing Clouds
swirl above as darkness looms.
The vocal Wind
charges in announcing her presence with her
beastly performance.
The pounding Rain
takes her stand with her rhythmical beat,
Yet is no match for
the obtrusive Thunder.
She arrogantly parades her flashy bolts
in clamorous fright.
It is here . . .
The Storm.**

A Wild Ride Through the Storm

It was now August. Our daughter would be visiting us for the first time since everything blew up in mid-July. Chris and I took our daughters out of town for the weekend and visited my dad, thinking this might help break the ice. We had a nice time while we were there, going to an amusement park and trying to relax and have fun as a family despite all of the cold tension in the air. It helped; however, I was still a wreck inside. My heart was so wounded, and no amount of distraction could take that away.

Emergence

As the weekend came to a close, we dropped my daughter off at her dad's and said our goodbyes. I was used to having her at home with us throughout the week. Now I would only see her every other weekend. This transition was going to be very difficult.

I especially worried about my youngest daughter. I didn't yet have the strength to explain the situation to her, knowing this news would devastate her. Her older sister was the only sibling she had. Now to her, it would feel as if she was an only child most of the time. She adored her big sister, and this was going to be difficult for her to understand or accept. She was going to require special attention and affection from her mommy and daddy. This affected all of us a great deal.

A few days later after our eventful weekend, I started experiencing vertigo. According to Web MD, vertigo is described as a sensation of feeling off-balance. These dizzy spells, might make you feel as if you're spinning or that the world around you is spinning. I had ridden a roller coaster while we were all at the amusement park and noticed a trace of it after getting off the ride. However, it progressively worsened over the next few days. I began to research how to get rid of it because I didn't want to go to the doctor; I didn't want to be put on any antibiotics. Therefore, I chose once again to self-medicate.

There are specific maneuvers that treat vertigo. So, after my husband got home from work, I got him to help me by reading off the maneuver steps. It was a specific process of lying down and changing positions in a particular sequence in order to move tiny, unwanted particles out of your inner ear canal. These particles bounced around in the ear canal, sending signals to the brain and causing dizziness and head spinning. It was a horrible sensation.

My husband read off the instructions, and I began transitioning into each position required. We did this a few times because we kept missing steps; therefore, it wasn't working properly. Each attempt was nauseating, and I started to feel strange. This process caused severe head spinning at the time of transition. We decided to try it one more time to see if we could get it right.

We should have taken a break or stopped altogether.

Immediately after I completed the maneuvers, my body began to go into shock. I knew right away that something was terribly wrong. My arms became numb; my hands began to curl up and then my feet.

War With The Wind

My body locked up on me. I had no control over what was happening. I panicked and told my husband to call 911, believing I was experiencing a stroke. I was having difficulty breathing. My chest felt like it was closing up, and then my mouth puckered up.

It was terrifying!

The ambulance and the fire truck finally arrived. The entire time they worked on me, I prayed silently to God. I was experiencing terrible discomfort and was extremely frightened, not understanding what was happening. Was I dying?

Thoughts raced through my mind. I wasn't ready to die. I didn't feel like I had accomplished my purpose here yet. I didn't want to leave my husband and my children. I wondered that if I got through this, would I still be able to use my hands? Would I ever be able to paint again? Would I be able to speak or walk? What legacy would I leave behind?

I wanted the paramedics to explain what was going on and to alleviate my discomfort, but none of that happened. They just asked me questions about how I was feeling and what I was experiencing and tried to make me as comfortable as possible. They encouraged me to relax, stay calm, and breathe slowly. Miraculously, I was able to listen and respond. I kept my eyes closed throughout it all because I didn't want this horrific image and memory stuck in my head.

Eventually, my muscles began to let up slightly, and they were able to put me on the stretcher and load me into the ambulance. They began hooking me up to machines, closed the doors, and headed to the hospital emergency room. My husband followed behind us. Fortunately, my youngest daughter was at a birthday party that evening and didn't have to witness any of this. God completely took care of that for us.

Once I arrived in the emergency room, I was immediately taken into a room and given some medication to help me stay calm and relax my muscles. Finally, a doctor came into the room and explained that I had experienced a severe panic attack. Although extremely uncomfortable, it was not life-threatening, and I would recover.

I was relieved to hear that I was going to be all right and that there should be no permanent damage as a result. My body had been under an incredible amount of stress; it had finally had enough. We were able to go home, but I was extremely weak. It was similar to how you feel after having a baby or undergoing surgery, and they make you get up and walk for the first time afterwards. I could hardly do it. My body had suffered a traumatic experience. It was going to take some time to recover and rebuild from the aftermath of the effects of this storm.

The ferocious wind had knocked the breath out of me. I was paralyzed in fright as the torrential rain poured, and the thunder roared. The crashing lightning sent a jolt of terror through my veins with every flash. My sense of safety and control had been completely wiped out. This horrific storm had obliterated what used to be "my norm."

The medical staff encouraged me to take it easy and to rest and relax as much as possible. The weekend came around, and my oldest daughter returned home for our weekend visitation. I was a little nervous of how things would go because I couldn't afford any further stress. She knew nothing of what had happened, and I wanted to keep it that way and not add more stress upon her as well.

Everything was good until a little drama occurred that Saturday afternoon with an outside family member. Unfortunately, all it took was a little tension and pressure, and again my body wasn't happy. I experienced a minor anxiety attack. Although not near as severe as the other, it made me realize something—I was now vulnerable.

I had become weak, fragile, and unstable. These were the perfect conditions the enemy had been waiting for. Remember, the enemy attacks when we are at our weakest, lowest, and most vulnerable state. That's what creates his window of opportunity for making his move. Now he was attacking my sense of security and peace of mind.

Over the course of the next several months, I encountered daily attacks mentally, emotionally, physically, and spiritually. The enemy had introduced me to the spirit of fear. It would torment me relentlessly day and night.

CHAPTER ELEVEN

Deep in the Dark Forest

After realizing how weak and vulnerable I had become, I grew increasingly fearful of experiencing another attack like the first one. It had become a nightmare from which I couldn't wake up. I thought about that attack all the time. Although I had closed my eyes during the original panic attack in an attempt to shield myself from the memory, it didn't work. It was clear and present in my thoughts and mind as I was engulfed in this whirlwind of darkness.

My physical weakness scared me. I no longer trusted my own body and was constantly afraid I would lose control of it again. I began battling with worry and anxiety on a daily basis, having attacks every single night and occasionally throughout the day. This carried on for months and months.

I barely slept. I would have to wake my husband up in the middle of the night to pray over me and help me calm down. Although he did his best to comfort me and stand by my side, I felt this was a battle I was forced to fight on my own. I felt so alone. Many nights, I wanted him to take me to the emergency room, but instead, I fought through the darkness. I had become so weak that I struggled to even walk around our cul-de-sac.

Emergence

Just a few months earlier, I had been jogging around our neighborhood and was strong and active. Now I was afraid to even be left alone. I could no longer do the things I loved or enjoyed. Often, I couldn't even finish watching a movie upstairs in our brand-new media room because it would trigger an attack. I didn't have the physical strength to even paint. I had never, ever, experienced torment or weakness like this in my life. This was not me. I was not a worrier. I was a joyful, hopeful person.

This was something else, something that had grabbed hold of me. This wasn't just a feeling I could shake off. We all have a healthy sense of fear that we are born with that protects us. This was not a healthy sense of fear. It was a spirit of fear that had come upon me and wouldn't get off, like a blanket that was smothering me. It's much like people who battle depression (a spirit of depression or a chemical imbalance) as opposed to others who feel depressed (a temporary feeling that passes) in the moment. A hovering spirit of fear doesn't just go away; it lingers and torments.

I was afraid for my life. I was afraid of dying, yet I didn't know if I wanted to continue living because of the mental torment I experienced. It was the darkest and scariest time of my life and the absolute worst feeling I ever had. Every day was a fight to see any trace of light and color. Every day and every night were filled with agony, pain, and torture.

Fear had crippled me.

No matter how hard I tried to fight back on my own, I couldn't win. Believe me, I tried. However, fear sought to destroy me mentally, physically, emotionally, and spiritually. Every front was under attack.

Once again, my husband and I turned to God for answers and help. We remembered the prophetic word and my personal word from God. We were told the enemy would take his stand in August, yet we would triumph. I also remembered that God told me to stay rooted in Him, and I would not be swept away. He was establishing a grand testimony, and the enemy would do whatever it took to prevent it from manifesting.

This was exactly what was happening in my life. The enemy was attempting to take me out through fear in order to stop the testimony from manifesting the mighty works God had done for me and my family. He was attempting to shut me up for good.

My husband and I knew that we had to stand firm under the eye of God and remain rooted in Him in order to triumph over the enemy in

Deep in the Dark Forest

victory. We would have to be still and know that God was in control. We would have to submit to God, resist the devil, and he would flee. We would overcome by the word of our testimony. God promised that as we did this, we would triumph.

He says, "Be still, and know that I am God; I will be exalted among the nations, I will be exalted in the earth" (Psalm 46:10 NIV).

Submit yourselves, then, to God. Resist the devil, and he will flee from you (James 4:7 NIV).

They triumphed over him by the blood of the Lamb and by the word of their testimony; they did not love their lives so much as to shrink from death (Revelation 12:11 NIV).

So that was what we did. However, this was no easy task for me. It sounded so easy. Even though I knew what I was supposed to do, it felt impossible for me to do it. It's easy to stand firm when nothing is opposing you; however, when the raging winds are coming at you, and the storms are all around you, it's a different story. You are in a wilderness where you feel all alone while tests, temptations, and trials are pressing you from all sides.

The condemning noise of the enemy is so excruciating that you struggle to hear God's voice. Visibility is so limited that you struggle to see God's direction. The feeling is so overwhelming that you struggle to grasp God's faithfulness. The stench of life is so potent that you struggle to smell God's goodness. The taste is so bitter that you struggle to indulge in God's sweetness. It's easy to panic in this type of environment no matter who you are or how strong you think you are. These conditions will test, unsettle, and unravel you.

Even the beautiful, sweet, and graceful Snow White experiences fear and panic when her life is threatened. She fearfully runs away into the dark, haunted forest in sheer terror. There she is tormented by her own thoughts. Fear has settled into her mind, and she can no longer see the beauty or peace around her. Here is where her imagination got the best of her. The wind chases after her, the branches reach for her, eyes watch her, and creatures attack her. The world around her is spinning out of control. Eventually she becomes so dizzy and overwhelmed that she falls to the ground in agony, anguish, and tears.

I too experienced an initial feeling of being overwhelmed by fear when faced with what seemed like a near-death experience. This event later became a near-death experience due to my own response to it. For a time, I panicked in the midst of my storm. In the midst of chaos, I struggled to grab hold of truth and find my way back home to safety, stability, and peace. The only way to seek shelter from this type of storm was to go to the Word of God and prayer. It is the sword of the Spirit that has the power to cut through fear, silence the wind, and calm the storm inside of you.

One day while feeling lost, confused, and defeated, I reached out to my oldest sister—the Guardian. While confiding in her over the phone, she said, "Get into the Word, Mistie. Read it out loud and over you."

When I struggled to see that day, she became my eyes. She helped direct me back to the path of life. She was a strong Christian voice that gave me direction toward the light and encouragement in the dark. When facing spiritual attack, it is vital to surround yourself with trustworthy Christian influence, people who speak life, not death, and truth over you and into you.

My husband was my greatest encourager throughout this time. He walked with me through every test, trial, battle, and storm. He saw it all. He saw me in my weakest and darkest moments. When I wanted to give up or give in, he would tell me what I needed to hear to help me hold on and not give in to temptation. There were times I was so desperate for help and was tempted to get on anxiety medication. Instead, he encouraged me to press through my suffering and look to God for true healing and deliverance, not for temporary ways to mask the pain and manipulate the situation. He reminded me that I wanted God to receive the credit for my healing and the glory of my testimony.

I always made a joke and told him that "God is my Rock, but you are my little pebble." He was more than a little pebble; he was wonderful. This experience was terrible, but it did bring us closer together as a couple and increased my love for him. He manned up and put on the armor of God during this battle and fought for me when I didn't have the strength to fight for myself as a watchman on the wall. He carried me in prayer and protected me in spirit. Our marriage, which had always been wonderful and strong, had grown even stronger. We were being united in a way like never before. We were a cord of three strands. We were an unstoppable and unbreakable team, and God was coaching us to victory. We would remain undefeated. That's a powerful testimony in itself.

> *A person standing alone can be attacked and defeated, but two can stand back-to-back and conquer. Three are even better, for a triple-braided cord is not easily broken (Ecclesiastes 4:12 NLT).*

Throughout this time, I sought encouragement from many Christian sources with the ultimate one being the Bible. I dug into God's Word and searched for Scripture that encouraged, empowered, and protected me. In order to silence the enemy's noise, I had to replace it with God's Word. I meditated on it day and night.

I also leaned on my church for prayer and encouraging sermons to help me remain hopeful and focused on truth rather than my problems. Series like Pastor Jimmy Evans's How to Think When Life Stinks was a life-saver for me.[8] Also helpful was, *A Woman Who Trusts God: Finding the Peace You Long For* by Debbie Alsdorf.[9] *Hinds' Feet on High Places* by Hannah Hurnard was another treasure for me.[10]

However, Jesus was my ultimate encourager. As I looked to Scripture for comfort and direction, I found Jesus as the prime example. He had faced every trial, every temptation, every storm, every hardship, every battle, and every fear; yet Jesus overcame it all. He alone was the ultimate victor. If anyone could give advice or direction, it was Him. He could understand everything I was going through. While here on Earth, He had seen it all, done it all, been through it all, and died for *all*. He had been beaten, broken, rejected, betrayed, mocked, scorned, tempted, tormented, and murdered. There was nothing I was going through that He couldn't relate to.

Jesus the Great High Priest

> *Therefore, since we have a great high priest who has ascended into heaven, Jesus the Son of God, let us hold firmly to the faith we profess. For we do not have a high priest who is unable to empathize with our weaknesses, but we have one who has been tempted in every way, just as we are—yet he did*

not sin. Let us then approach God's throne of grace with confidence, so that we may receive mercy and find grace to help us in our time of need (Hebrews 4:14–16 NIV).

I cried out for Him: "Jesus, come to my rescue!"

It was Jesus who the disciples cried out to in the midst of their storm. It was Jesus who walked on water to them. It was Jesus who silenced their every fear. It was Jesus who spoke, "Peace, be still," and quieted the storm. It was Jesus!

Jesus Calms the Storm

Then he got into the boat and his disciples followed him. Suddenly a furious storm came up on the lake, so that the waves swept over the boat. But Jesus was sleeping. The disciples went and woke him, saying, "Lord, save us! We're going to drown!"

He replied, "You of little faith, why are you so afraid?" Then he got up and rebuked the winds and the waves, and it was completely calm.

The men were amazed and asked, "What kind of man is this? Even the winds and the waves obey him!" (Matthew 8:23–27 NIV).

When Snow White comes to her senses after her battle in the dark forest, she is ashamed of the fuss she has made because of her response to fear. She has a heart of gold, yet even she temporarily freaks out under pressure.

The disciples had hearts that were willing to follow Jesus anywhere. Still, even though He was with them in the boat, they grew hysterical when the waves came crashing into it.

Everyone in each of these examples experienced the same fear, the ultimate fear, the fear of facing death.

The fear of death, discomfort, and pain is also what inevitably threw me into a frenzy as well. I too was ashamed for how I initially reacted to fear when the huntsman came chasing after me in "the woods," and the battle of war was waged.

Deep in the Dark Forest

Jesus went further and said, "You of little faith, why are you so afraid?" In other words, "I'm right here with you. Do you not trust Me to take care of you? Where is your faith?"

Those are good questions and ones I would spend the next year of my life discovering the answers to. I would face fear and discover true faith and trust in the midst of it. Before tragedy hit, I could easily say that I trusted Jesus and demonstrated great faith. Yet faith untested is not really faith at all. Knowing about faith and trust in God is not the same as having it. It is something you have to encounter on your own through intimacy with Jesus. It is not something you can read about or borrow from others' experiences. It's personal and unique.

Sometimes it's the storms of life that force us to go deeper beneath the surface in order to discover and reveal who we truly are underneath. It's at the very bottom where we'll find hidden treasures of our identity and that of God's tucked away for us to explore, retrieve, and to share.

The storm is a place where our faith and trust are tested in the midst of fear and panic. It's a place where we learn to rebuke the wind as we dive deeper into His Word and into His arms in order to calm the storm inside of us. It's a place of moving us out of the stagnant water where we have comfortably sat for too long and moving us into the flowing waters where we belong. The stagnant water is murky and still, full of moss and no life. The flowing river moves and is alive. It twists and turns along its path to new destinations, bringing life with it to all it touches. It flows into the vast ocean, a place full of endless discovery, creation, and beauty. This is where Jesus was leading me. He was calling me deeper into the unknown, deeper into relationship and intimacy with Him.

Deeper Still

When I was in Hawaii, my husband and I spent one special evening at the beach. We packed some lawn chairs, a bottle of wine, and headed out to watch the sunset. After finding a secluded cove, we unpacked and got comfortable in our cozy spot, enjoying the final warmth of the sun. With our toes stuck in the sand, we gazed out upon the ocean, stopping now and then to take cute photos of one another. I sported an attractive white bikini, cool shades, and a trendy floppy hat. I was all set up.

Emergence

Then suddenly, I realized something. I hadn't come all this way just to sit and stare at the ocean from a distance. I hadn't come to just witness a glorious and miraculous event. I came to encounter and experience one.

I took off my shades, then my hat, and I stood up. My husband, who was taken by surprise, turned to me and said, "What are you doing?"

I said, "I'm going in."

He raised an eyebrow and questioned astonishingly, "Now?"

With boldness and assurance, I answered, "Now."

"Mistie, he said, looking around at others on the beach, "Have you noticed how everyone else is coming out of the water now that it's getting dark, and you're the only one going into shark-infested waters? There's probably a good reason for that."

"I don't care," I proclaimed with my chin jutted upward. "I'm going in, and I'm going to trust God."

He sat back and watched and took pictures of me as I eased my way into the unknown waters as the bright and beautiful sun was going down behind the horizon. I first went in just a little ways. I was surprised at the strength of the waves and the pull of the water as it returned to the ocean. It pulled from the sand underneath my feet and made it hard not to fall. I decided to sit down in it, thinking I would be able to sit comfortably as the waves rushed back and forth around me. That's not what happened.

Instead, waves mixed with sand began to crash into me, pushing me backwards and nearly head under. Startled and a little out of control, I awkwardly washed ashore. My hot momma moment had instantly faded. Feeling humbled, and a little embarrassed, I turned to face my husband who was now laughing at me as I wiped the mucky sand and water from my face and body.

He yelled to me, "You can't sit down. You have to get up and go out further past the waves."

I thought, *Really, genius, I hadn't noticed.* That is husband and wife talk for "I hate it when you're right."

I firmly stood back up to my feet and went deeper, past the opposing waves. At that point, I was able to hold my ground, stand steady, and explore without wavering and being washed backwards to shore.

With God, nothing is wasted.

Deep in the Dark Forest

Later as I looked back at that experience in Hawaii, God used that imagery and encounter to reveal something to me. He showed me that in that moment, spiritually, I was cute and comfortable sitting on the beach, watching and waiting for the miraculous to take place in my life. However, God was calling me to go deeper, deeper in intimacy and relationship with Him. It was what my heart was longing for as well. I was tired of sitting on the outside. I was ready for an encounter of my own like nothing I had ever known.

I answered His call and entered into the dark and dangerous unknown where evil was lurking beneath the surface seeking to devour me yet where the presence of God was hovering over the deep seeking to protect and promote me. If I thought I could encounter Him by still sitting cute and comfortable, then I had another thing coming. The pounding reality check made me realize that in order to encounter Him beyond my wildest dreams, I would have to stand firmly to my feet and move beyond the opposing forces and my weakness. There I would find a stability, strength, identity, and purpose unknown to me.

Who knew *Moana* was actually written about me? Kidding, it was written for all of us Disney lovers.

God is always present in our midst, waiting for us to answer the call, to go deeper and further into the unknown in order to discover the unimaginable. Our encounter with Jesus doesn't always happen the way we expect or want. It's not up to us. Sometimes, the experience leading to the encounter catches us off guard and sweeps us off our feet, but we have the choice to humbly get back up. That is a choice that's up to us.

It's okay to get knocked down. It happens to the best of us, even Snow White. In fact, it's good for us. Getting knocked down humbles us and sends us to our knees in prayer.

However, it's not okay to stay sitting, cowering in fear. We have to stand up and move to where He is calling us. We must also surround ourselves with loving and godly voices that encourage us to keep going forward. We may be the only one experiencing the encounter in the water, but that doesn't mean others aren't witnessing, assisting, and interceding from afar.

I came out of the water looking nothing like I did when I went in. My white swimsuit was now full of tiny particles of black sand that had woven its way into the layers of my fabric. I tried and tried to remove all traces of the dark sand, but it wouldn't completely come out. My swimsuit would never be the same. It had an encounter with that ocean in Hawaii that was forever embedded into the very fabric of its being. It would forever carry a part of that journey with it and serve as a reminder of what it had been through.

Likewise, after having gone through the storm, I tried and tried to erase the dark particles from my memory, but I couldn't completely eliminate them. That experience had woven itself into the deepest layers of my being and was now a part of me. I nor "my norm" would never be the same. I would forever carry a part of that journey with me, and it would serve as a reminder of what I experienced and who I encountered along the way. It was an experience I wasn't meant to forget but to share.

If you want to experience an encounter with God and go deeper with Him in relationship, then you have to be willing to move. You have to be willing to go outside of your comfort zone and into the deep and mysterious places He is calling you. God is on the move. If we want more of Him, it's up to us to move with Him.

If we're brave enough and willing to answer the call, then we must be brave enough and willing to stand to our feet, move beyond opposition, and hold our ground in the unknown in order to unlock the mystery of our calling. The encounter will not leave you traumatized; it will leave you mesmerized. I promise you, He is worth it in the end.

Here is a powerful prayer for overcoming fear, anxiety, and panic. Rest assured, dear one, for God's power is greater than our enemy and mighty in our weakness. Declare His strength at work in your life with confidence. Declare your freedom in Christ in Jesus' Name. Praise Him!

PRAYER

Jehovah Shalom (the Lord is peace),

I know You are not the source of fear and anxiety. It is Satan who desires to cause Your children pain. You are a God of peace and do not torment us with worrisome thoughts or burden our hearts with fretfulness. You give power over our worries and victory over our enemy as we rely on Your love and trust in Your sovereignty. I lay my panic and anxiety at Your feet. When I'm tormented by fear and worry in the midst of storms and whirlwinds, remind me of Your power and Your grace. Help me to walk on water by filling me with faith, confidence, and peace that surpasses all understanding as I believe in You to keep me safe and secure.

Help me remember, when fear and anxiety attack, to respond with powerful Scripture—to hold on to Your goodness, faithfulness, and truth. Replace my worries and destructive thoughts with Your promises. Jesus, calm the storms inside of me. Help me to be still and know You're in control. May the peace of God guard my heart and mind in Christ Jesus. I need You and I thank You for carrying my burdens. I command the spirit of fear to leave now in the name of Jesus. Holy Spirit, come and help me to rest in Your perfect love that casts out all fear. I declare, You are my strength and shield. I will trust in You. Thank You, Lord, for rescuing me from drowning in a sea of fear and taking me deeper into the mysteries of who You are.

In Jesus' Name. Amen.

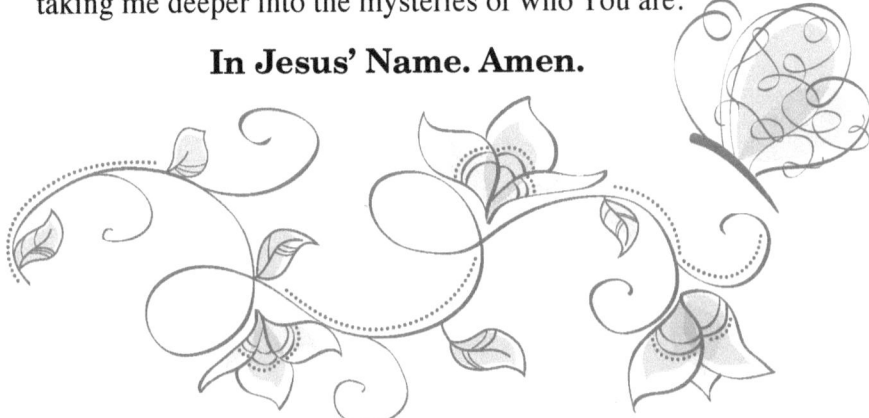

CHAPTER TWELVE

Polished For Purpose

The year 2015 was said to be a year that God's people would demonstrate their faith and receive grace. The storm brought out a demonstration of faith that I wasn't always proud of. However, it created an opportunity for me to receive God's grace like never before. It exposed my areas of weakness, revealing where I required extra doses of grace in order to build strength.

The 2015 prophetic word said that God would send a fire down from heaven that would activate our faith and unlock our identity.

The enemy uses storms and seasons of hardship as opportunity to ravage and ruin us, but God uses storms and hardship as opportunity to rebuild and refine us.

> *But now, this is what the Lord says—he who created you, Jacob, he who formed you, Israel: "Do not fear, for I have redeemed you; I have summoned you by name; you are mine. When you pass through the waters, I will be with you; and when you pass through the rivers, they will not sweep over you. When you walk through the fire, you will not be burned; the flames will not set you ablaze (Isaiah 43:1–2 NIV).*

> *See, I have refined you, though not as silver; I have tested you in the furnace of affliction (Isaiah 48:10 NIV).*

Emergence

Looking back to when I was suffering with vertigo, Web MD states vertigo is the result of an inner ear problem; a problem of unwanted particles entering the ear and sending disruptive signals to the brain. In the same way, Satan had been sending tiny lies, or "particles," into my ear, which traveled to my brain and entered into my mind and thoughts, resulting in an unpleasant sensation of instability, anxiety, worry, fear, and panic. Satan thrives on throwing us off balance in such a way through life's trials and tribulations.

The treatment of vertigo is similar to the process of refinement. Both involve removing impurities or unwanted elements from a substance. Synonyms for refinement include purify, treat, polish, improve, fine-tune, hone, perfect, cleanse, filter.

One might say that the unpleasant spinning sensation I experienced with vertigo in the physical world was connected to the refinement process I was experiencing in the spiritual world. Necessary for achieving a state of purification, or refinement, is the process of a filtering treatment which can be unpleasant. Both created an intense sensation of feeling off-balance and unstable, of instability and discomfort as impurities are removed. The two were directly linked. In both the physical and spiritual realms, particles "lies" were being strained from my ears. This treatment was taking place so that I would experience stability and purity in my thought life and mental state.

Throughout this refinement process, I was forced to discover my faith and trust in God. The world around me felt as if it was spinning out of control, and I had to look to God for grounding. It was a transition period as I maneuvered into multiple positions with Him. Each stage of transition was uncomfortable but necessary in order to flush out the impurities, lies of the enemy, and unwanted elements in my life.

> *So that the tested genuineness of your faith—more precious than gold that perishes though it is tested by fire—may be found to result in praise and glory and honor at the revelation of Jesus Christ (1 Peter 1:7 ESV).*

As I moved with God, things that threatened to hold me back from my freedom, identity, and purpose were eliminated. Much like the process of forging a sword, the constant heat, pressure, hammering, and grinding from the refinement process brings hidden things out into the open, transforms us into who we were created to be, and reveals what we were created for.

Heat is first applied in order to make us pliable, flexible, and movable. Intense pressure is applied immediately afterward. Then God molds and shapes us into our proper form by hammering His Word into us. Lastly, we're polished and refined, revealing our true nature and purpose to be used as a strong, sharp, powerful, and shining weapon of God.

But he knows where I am going. And when he tests me, I will come out as pure as gold (Job 23:10 NLT).

And after you have suffered a little while, the God of all grace, who has called you to his eternal glory in Christ, will himself restore, confirm, strengthen, and establish you (1 Peter 5:10 ESV).

God allows us to suffer temporarily in order to establish us as His righteous children. He uses this time to transform our hearts, purify us, set us free from bondage, and prepare us for our purpose. It is for our good.

And we know that in all things God works for the good of those who love him, who have been called according to his purpose (Romans 8:28 NIV).

So knowing that God is good and working on our behalf even in the middle of storms, trials, and fire, how do we believe this when we can't see it or feel it in the time of our suffering? The answer is simple—we must *choose* to believe and trust in our faith.

As I began to meditate on God's Word and pray and speak it over me and my circumstances, I still couldn't find peace right away.

Do not be anxious about anything, but in every situation, by prayer and petition, with thanksgiving, present your requests to God. And the peace of God, which transcends all understanding, will guard your hearts and your minds in Christ Jesus.

Finally, brothers and sisters, whatever is true, whatever is noble, whatever is right, whatever is pure, whatever is lovely, whatever is admirable—if anything is excellent or praiseworthy—think about such things (Philippians 4:6–8 NIV).

Anxiety, fear, worry, and doubt still flooded my mind and thoughts. I struggled to replace them with God's Word. I knew what I was supposed to do, and I was doing it, but I wasn't *receiving* the relief God promised. God eventually revealed to me the reason why—I wasn't choosing to believe.

Although I was saying all of the right words and doing all of the right things, something was missing. The knowledge was present, yet the belief was absent. The Bible works on faith and trust. My trust and my faith were weak in my moment of suffering because they had been overpowered by the spirit of fear. In order to begin receiving, I had to tip the scale and begin believing the Word in order to activate the Word. Once I began to put faith, trust, and belief at the forefront of my thoughts and focus, the truth caused the fear, anxiety, worry, and doubt to be flushed and filtered out of the other side of my mind. It took time and persistence, but eventually my faith was activated and strengthened by the fire that God sent down.

The two types of fire are a controlled, refining fire, and a wild, consuming fire. The controlled fire is sent from heaven. It seeks to refine and promote new life and growth. The consuming fire is sent from hell. It seeks to destroy and kill all in its path.

The two fires raged war at the same time as a spiritual battle took place in my mind. The consuming fire had to be extinguished in order for the renewal of my mind to take place.

The Spiritual War

Now I, Paul, myself am pleading with you by the meekness and gentleness of Christ—who in presence am lowly among you, but being absent am bold toward you. But I beg you that when I am present I may not be bold with that confidence by which I intend to be bold against some, who think of us as if we walked according to the flesh. For though we walk in the flesh, we do not war according to the flesh. For the weapons of our warfare are not carnal but mighty in God for pulling down strongholds, casting down arguments and every high thing that exalts itself against the knowledge of God, bringing every thought into captivity to the obedience of Christ, and be-

ing ready to punish all disobedience when your obedience is fulfilled (2 Corinthians 10:1–6 NKJV).

Do not conform to the pattern of this world, but be transformed by the renewing of your mind. Then you will be able to test and approve what God's will is—his good, pleasing and perfect will (Romans 12:2 NIV).

It only takes one coal (one thought) and one spark (one unfortunate event) to ignite a roaring fire (consume your mind). That is why taking your thoughts captive is so important. It can prevent a raging wildfire. Once a consuming fire is ignited, it can be difficult or a challenge to put out. It must be extinguished with truth.

The fire in my mind represented the fear, worry, doubt, and anxiety that I allowed to take residence through one coal and one spark. It began with the storms of life (rejection and difficult, painful circumstances) that led me to question who I was and who God was in my life. Maybe I never really had a strong enough foundation to begin with, and it was time to establish one. It was time to fight fire with fire—God's refining fire against the enemy's consuming fire.

When the conditions were just right for the enemy, that coal and spark finally ignited a flame that quickly spread into a roaring fire.

The problem was in knowing how to put the enemy's fire out. I was in need of living water (God's Word). I knew where to get it and what you should do with it, but I didn't personally know how to receive and apply it to my own circumstances.

There was a roaring fire in my mind, but there was a barrier over it that was preventing the water from coming through. It was like a giant umbrella that I was holding over the flames that prevented the water from touching it; therefore, it kept on blazing.

I had gone to the Source, and yet as the living water began pouring out like rain, it wasn't able to get through.

The barrier (umbrella) was symbolic of not knowing enough of who God was to me intimately, not knowing who I was in Him, and not trusting and believing what He could and would do for me. This is what was preventing me from believing and trusting His promises in His Word. I was uncertain of my identity and of His.

In order to put out the flames that threatened to consume me, I had to remove the umbrella so that I could receive the water.

Emergence

The problem was that I didn't know how. I had to learn, and Jesus had to teach and instruct me one on one. I had to learn it was a choice to remove the umbrella that I didn't even realize I was holding. I didn't know I wasn't allowing God in by being unwilling to truly trust and believe in the midst of pain and fear.

The overwhelming heat of the fire was so intense that it nearly consumed me. Confusion set in. I was unable to think properly or process accurately. The smoke was too thick to see clearly.

I had to learn to receive Him and know Him intimately and to learn who I was to Him in order to trust and believe. Again, knowing about Him is not the same as knowing Him personally.

In order to remove the umbrella, I had to choose to let Him in and allow His living water to penetrate my mind, soul, and heart. As I began to discover more of who God was and more of who I was in Him, the umbrella finally began to come down.

Then the rain began to fall on the flames and put the fire out. The living water began to rise and flow in me and eventually washed away all traces of ash that was left behind.

Then the calm came after the storm (peace) and the rainbow after the flood (promise). The smell after the rain was refreshing, invigorating, reviving, and uplifting. Then new life began to spring forth, blossom, and grow. The beauty and fragrance were alluring, captivating, and astonishing.

I can now say,

I am Grateful for that one *Coal*, and that one *Spark*
That Ignited a *Fire*
That Required *Living Water*
That Exposed an *Umbrella*
That Prevented *Saturation*
That Promoted an *Opportunity*
That Changed an *Identity*
That Established a *Relationship*
That Propelled a *Promise*
That Produced an *Abundance*
That Prompted *Praise*!

Without the hand of my enemy, I would never have been *delivered* into the hands of my Father.

Once the barrier of unbelief that stood between God's truth was removed, I was able to receive the living water. The renewal of my mind began to take place. My identity began to be established, and I began to encounter God in a new way. I was being transformed! The old was being washed away, and the new was beginning!

God is so good. He is so faithful when we are willing to put our trust and faith in Him. He will show up in a mighty way on our behalf. When we encounter God's Word, we encounter Jesus, we encounter love, and it is His perfect love that casts out fear.

> *There is no fear in love; but perfect love casts out fear, because fear involves torment. But he who fears has not been made perfect in love (1 John 4:18 NKJV).*

To Love, to Be Loved

> *God is love. When we take up permanent residence in a life of love, we live in God and God lives in us. This way, love has the run of the house, becomes at home and mature in us, so that we're free of worry on Judgment Day—our standing in the world is identical with Christ's. There is no room in love for fear. Well-formed love banishes fear. Since fear is crippling, a fearful life—fear of death, fear of judgment—is one not yet fully formed in love (1 John 4:17–18 MSG).*

The Fire

In the Bible, Shadrach's, Meshack's, and Abed-Nego's faiths were tested when they were thrown into the fiery furnace for not bowing down and worshiping other gods. No doubt, I'm sure they were afraid; regardless, they chose to trust God in the midst of fear despite their circumstances. They refused to submit to the enemy. They chose to stand their ground and believe that God was with them in this trial. Nevertheless, they were bound as prisoners and thrown into the fire, but they weren't harmed. God showed up on their behalf and protected them from the flames. They were not incinerated; they were liberated! Jesus did the same for me.

When tested by fire, it is easy to feel as if you're being consumed by the heat and flames. However, if you *put* your trust in God, the temperature and the pressure of the furnace will drop. If you choose to stand your ground, despite your feelings and circumstances, you will be protected and come out unharmed and unbound. This is God's promise to us. Trust in Him, and He will deliver you from all of your fears. He will perfect His love in you.

Sometimes our faith and trust muscles grow weak due to non-use. Sometimes it's necessary to work them out in order to build them up. This is the process of how strength and power is developed. It isn't fun; it isn't easy, and you may feel as if you might die, but it won't kill you; it will build you. Therefore, again, I urge you to submit to God during the process. Trust Him in the midst of pain and fear. Believe that God is with you and for you, and know that God loves you no matter what. You'll come out unharmed, unbound, unincinerated, liberated, and covered with the presence of God.

Saved in Fiery Trial

If that is the case, our God whom we serve is able to deliver us from the burning fiery furnace, and He will deliver us from your hand, O king. But if not, let it be known to you, O king, that we do not serve your gods, nor will we worship the gold image which you have set up."

Then Nebuchadnezzar was full of fury, and the expression on his face changed toward Shadrach, Meshach, and Abed-Nego. He spoke and commanded that they heat the furnace seven times more than it was usually heated. And he commanded certain mighty men of valor who were in his army to bind Shadrach, Meshach, and Abed-Nego, and cast them into the burning fiery furnace. Then these men were bound in their coats, their trousers, their turbans, and their other garments, and were cast into the midst of the burning fiery furnace. Therefore, because the king's command was urgent, and the furnace exceedingly hot, the flame of the fire killed those men who took up Shadrach, Meshach, and Abed-Nego. And these three men, Shadrach, Meshach, and Abed-Nego, fell down bound into the midst of the burning fiery furnace.

Then King Nebuchadnezzar was astonished; and he rose in haste and spoke, saying to his counselors, "Did we not cast three men bound into the midst of the fire?"

They answered and said to the king, "True, O king."

"Look!" he answered, "I see four men loose, walking in the midst of the fire; and they are not hurt, and the form of the fourth is like the Son of God."

Then Nebuchadnezzar went near the mouth of the burning fiery furnace and spoke, saying, "Shadrach, Meshach, and Abed-Nego, servants of the Most High God, come out, and come here." Then Shadrach, Meshach, and Abed-Nego came from the midst of the fire. And the satraps, administrators, governors, and the king's counselors gathered together, and they saw these men on whose bodies the fire had no power; the hair of their head was not singed nor were their garments affected, and the smell of fire was not on them.

Nebuchadnezzar spoke, saying, "Blessed be the God of Shadrach, Meshach, and Abed-Nego, who sent His Angel and delivered His servants who trusted in Him, and they have frustrated the king's word, and yielded their bodies, that they should not serve nor worship any god except their own God! (Daniel 3:17–28 NKJV).

The fire was a place where God burned away my barrier that prevented me from believing Him to be who He says He is, knowing who He truly is to me, and trusting who I am to Him. It was a place where my faith and belief were tested and proven genuine, and my identity purified and refined.

The Wind taught me to *Hold On***,**
The Battle taught me to *Let Go***,**
The Storm taught me to *Go Deeper,* **and**
The Fire taught me to *Stand Firm***.**

Emergence

The opposing wind of the enemy may have come up against me to knock me over, strip my leaves, and sweep me away, but the allied wind of God came up behind me to straighten me back upright, give me new fruit, and root and establish me in perfect love.

God is my Rock, my Fortress, my Refuge, my Strength, my Shield, my Redeemer, my Deliverer, my Protector, my Everything! His prophetic promise to me held true. I am like a tree now rooted by His stream of living water. His unfailing love enabled me to withstand the buffeting winds, to not wither, but to flourish and mature, producing righteous fruit and shade to offer and bless others.

> *Blessed is the one who does not walk in step with the wicked or stand in the way that sinners take or sit in the company of mockers, but whose delight is in the law of the Lord, and who meditates on his law day and night. That person is like a tree planted by streams of water, which yields its fruit in season and whose leaf does not wither—whatever they do prospers. Not so the wicked! They are like chaff that the wind blows away. Therefore the wicked will not stand in the judgment, nor sinners in the assembly of the righteous. For the Lord watches over the way of the righteous, but the way of the wicked leads to destruction (Psalm 1:1–6 NIV).*

When I hear the song "Jesus" by Chris Tomlin, I weep because it isn't just a song to me; it's a personal reflection of my relationship with Jesus. My encounter with Him was personal and real, and I will forever praise Him for what He has done for me!

> *The Lord is my rock, my fortress and my deliverer; my God is my rock, in whom I take refuge, my shield and the horn of my salvation, my stronghold (Psalm 18:2 NIV).*

> *God is our refuge and strength, an ever-present help in trouble (Psalm 46:1 NIV).*

> *He will cover you with his feathers, and under his wings you will find refuge; his faithfulness will be your shield and rampart (Psalm 91:4 NIV).*

Polished For Purpose

    Although the rain fell hard, the floods rushed in, and the wind blew and beat against our house, it did not fall. We had built our house on a solid foundation rooted deeply in God's Word. It may have taken on a colossal amount of damage and was in serious need of repair; however, it stood and held its ground in the face of opposition.

    Likewise, I faced fear in a grueling battle, yet I refused to bow down and submit to it. I held on to my faith in God. The Lord watched over me, protected me, and nourished me as I revered Him alone, resisted the devil's temptation, and sought to do His will. Eventually, fear fled as promised.

    God promises to watch over you too.

    Thank you, Jesus, for Your promise to watch over the righteous as we delight and meditate upon Your living Word.

    Truly, there is no one like You, Jesus!

PRAYER

Lord,

Polish me for purpose. The winter seasons of life have dulled me. Make me shine anew. Forge me as a strong weapon and refine me in the furnace of Your love. When I face tests, trials, or tribulations, stand beside me in the fire and keep me safe from harm. Help me to stand firm and never bow down or worship other gods when feeling the heat and pressure of this world. I submit to You and You alone. Remove the barrier of unbelief that prevents me from trusting You when afflicted. Thank You for liberating me and establishing me as Your righteous child. You are my refuge and my strength, my ever present help in times of trouble. I declare I believe in who You are and I trust in You.

In Jesus' Name. Amen.

CHAPTER THIRTEEN

Every Sheep Needs A Shepherd

I cried out to Jesus in the midst of my storm, the battle, and the fire. He came into my boat, taught me to walk on water, extinguished the consuming fire in my mind, and rescued me from drowning in a sea of fear.

> *I sought the Lord, and he answered me; he delivered me from all my fears (Psalm 34:4 NIV).*

Perfect love isn't something. It is someone. It is Jesus! One encounter with Him and you are never the same. His perfect love rushes in and flushes out all that has come against you and sought to destroy you. Take just a minute to really *absorb* some of these truths and acknowledge all that Jesus's perfect love has done for you and me. The list goes on and on.

Perfect love forgives you, calls you, cleanses you, saves you, heals you, delivers you, renews you, restores you, rebuilds you, redeems you, transforms you, identifies you, establishes you, prepares you, anoints you, blesses you, favors you, protects you, leads you, purposes you, commissions you, and above all loves you.

Emergence

**The enemy seeks to *take* all; God seeks to *replace* all.
He exchanges:**

**Darkness for Light
The Old for New
Sin for Forgiveness
Shame for Redemption
Guilt for Grace
Condemnation for Compassion
Who I Was for Who I Am: A Sinner for a Saint
Pain for Healing
Weakness for Strength
Rejection for Acceptance
Insecurity for Security
Unloved for Loved
Unwanted for Chosen
Orphaned for Adopted
Bondage for Freedom
Mourning for Joy
Ashes for Beauty
Death for Life!**

Therefore, if anyone is in Christ, the new creation has come: The old has gone, the new is here! (2 Corinthians 5:17 NIV).

My encounter with Jesus was a process of me learning to trust in Him, rely on Him, and depend on Him for all of my needs and desires. It was an experience of me learning to receive all that He promised me, and took place by spending time alone with Him daily. This is how we developed an intimate and personal relationship and how I learned to hear God's voice and sense Him leading me.

The Bible is filled with Scripture and examples of God's promises to us if we will choose to follow and obey Him. As we make Him the Lord of our lives, He circumcises our hearts. He cuts away the old and reveals the new. Abraham answered God's call, and God made a covenant blessing with him. As descendants of Abraham, we're inheritors to receive those same spiritual and physical blessings and promises.

The Call of Abram

The Lord had said to Abram, "Go from your country, your people and your father's household to the land I will show you.

"I will make you into a great nation, and I will bless you; I will make your name great, and you will be a blessing. I will bless those who bless you, and whoever curses you I will curse; and all peoples on earth will be blessed through you" (Genesis 12:1–3 NIV).

As I continued to follow Jesus, He continued to lead me to green pastures as promised. I came to know Him as my good, good, shepherd.

A Psalm of David

The Lord is my shepherd, I lack nothing. He makes me lie down in green pastures, he leads me beside quiet waters, he refreshes my soul. He guides me along the right paths for his name's sake.

Even though I walk through the darkest valley, I will fear no evil, for you are with me; your rod and your staff, they comfort me. You prepare a table before me in the presence of my enemies. You anoint my head with oil; my cup overflows.

Surely your goodness and love will follow me all the days of my life, and I will dwell in the house of the Lord forever (Psalm 23: 1–6 NIV).

When I was a kid, we raised sheep. The thing I remember most about having sheep was feeding them. All of the sheep needed to be fed, but not all were fed the same. When they were first born, we would bring the helpless lambs into the house out of the cold and put them in our bath tub. We would make a soft palette, add a heat lamp, and then feed them individually with a bottle. This was my absolute favorite part! These precious little lambs were so cute and cuddly. They were born black and would later turn white. They were adorable.

When feeding the older sheep, we had to be careful. One day when my dad was feeding them, he wasn't paying attention to the large male sheep we named "Big John." He came up behind my dad and butted him in the back. My dad was sore from the experience. Then there was the time when another sheep chased him up the fence. Dad would often warn us to keep our eyes open and remain watchful while feeding them because they might turn on you.

Sometimes, the very sheep you have raised, nurtured, and fed will come when you aren't looking and ram you from behind. Sometimes, your own sheep you have loved, protected, and cared for begin to grow and think they're big enough to take care of themselves and that they don't need you anymore. They become arrogant, resentful, and unappreciative. They want to be their own master, their own shepherd, so they butt you out of their way, out of their business, and out of their lives. These are the sheep that turn and go astray.

However, every sheep needs a shepherd!

We as believers are all His sheep. We all have One Shepherd—Jesus. Even though we sometimes leave Him, He will never leave us. We all must first be taught how to be a good sheep—one who obeys, trusts, and listens to the Shepherd. We must learn to hear His voice and do what He says. Then we'll be able to shepherd our own flocks, in the same way He shepherds us. We can be a sheep and a shepherd at the same time, just as we can be a daughter and a mother, a child and a parent, and a student and a teacher at the same time.

In addition, these little lambs were born black and later turned white. We as believers, are all His lambs born into sin, but we can be washed clean by the blood of the Lamb—Jesus. We have all gone astray at some point, but thankfully, we have a loving and forgiving Shepherd who welcomes us back home.

Even Jesus became a sheep so that He could become a Shepherd and lead His people. The very people He loved, birthed, and fed since the beginning of creation in the Garden of Eden went astray. Later, Judas came up from behind and brought forth the ultimate betrayal, even though Jesus knew ahead of time. Over and over again, His own brothers and creation hated Him, rejected Him, mocked Him, belittled Him, chose life without Him, and crucified Him.

However:

Every sheep needs a shepherd!
Every soul needs a Savior.
Thank heaven everyone has one.
But not all will choose Him.

Every Sheep Needs A Shepherd

For those who do, our Good Shepherd commands us to take care of His sheep and feed them. Jesus asks us to feed His lambs, those who are newly "born again," those who are young, helpless, and need tender care, those who aren't yet able to feed themselves, those who have been out in the cold and the dark. Take special care and bring them into the warm and inviting light. Feed them individually and tenderly until they grow and mature and are able to feed themselves. Look for the lost sheep, those who have gone astray, and lovingly and warmly welcome them back home as He has welcomed us back home. He says to take care of His sheep and feed His sheep, His people.

Jesus asks us to serve others as He served us. If we truly love Jesus, then we will love and take care of what He loves—His people (His flock).

When they had finished eating, Jesus said to Simon Peter, "Simon son of John, do you love me more than these?"

"Yes, Lord," he said, "you know that I love you."

Jesus said, "Feed my lambs." Again Jesus said, "Simon son of John, do you love me?"

He answered, "Yes, Lord, you know that I love you."

Jesus said, "Take care of my sheep."

The third time he said to him, "Simon son of John, do you love me?"

Peter was hurt because Jesus asked him the third time, "Do you love me?" He said, "Lord, you know all things; you know that I love you."

Jesus said, "Feed my sheep (John 21:15–17 NIV).

My parents shepherded me, yet I still lost my way. But Jesus, my Good Shepherd, found me and led me back home, but not before being led astray and having made a life-changing decision.

When I told both of my parents that I was pregnant outside of marriage, I was so ashamed. I didn't want to disappoint them, and I was afraid of how they might react. My parents were both still and quiet as I broke the news. They sat there with disbelief, shock, and sadness on their faces. Thankfully, they didn't yell at me, and they weren't ashamed of me.

Their hearts grew sad. They knew the hardship that was ahead of me because they had gone through a very similar experience. They didn't want their daughter to face the same consequences. They were hurt because I was hurting. They knew and understood my heart, and they didn't judge me for my error. Instead, my loving parents embraced me, and they helped me through this difficult time. They stood by my side and continued to guide me. They wiped away my tears and helped pick me back up.

This is also how our loving Father in heaven embraces us all as His children, His sons and daughters, when we come to Him and repent for our wrongdoing. When we return home to Him, He warmly welcomes us with compassion and understanding. He loves us, and His heart breaks every time our heart breaks from the decisions we make when we choose to leave home and rebelliously do life on our own. He knows the price we will pay when we disobey and go astray. Nevertheless, He affectionately reaches down, picks us up, wipes away our tears, and celebrates our homecoming treating us as if we never left or went our own way against His will.

> *So he got up and went to his father. "But while he was still a long way off, his father saw him and was filled with compassion for him; he ran to his son, threw his arms around him and kissed him.*
>
> *The son said to him, "Father, I have sinned against heaven and against you. I am no longer worthy to be called your son."*
>
> *But the father said to his servants, "Quick! Bring the best robe and put it on him. Put a ring on his finger and sandals on his feet. Bring the fattened calf and kill it. Let's have a feast and celebrate. For this son of mine was dead and is alive again; he was lost and is found." So they began to celebrate (Luke 15:20–24 NIV).*

I shepherded my own little lamb, but she too wondered away. I prayed to my Shepherd to go out and find my lost sheep and bring her back home. She had gone beyond my reach and out of my care. Yet, not

Every Sheep Needs A Shepherd

only did she wander off; she wondered off. She began to wonder about God's truth. I prayed that Jesus would bring her back home safely.

God heard my prayer. He heard my cry for my little lost lamb. Although our living arrangements remained the same, that was of no matter. I had prayed that my little lost lamb would come back to me in spirit and love and back home to Him in spirit and truth. I prayed that my little lamb would find the way, to the truth, and to the life.

Jesus heard and answered my prayer.

In 2 Kings, there is a story about a Shunammite woman who cleared out space in her home for a prophet named Elisha to stay with her. In return for her hospitality, the man of God asked what he might do for her. She had no son, and her husband was old. He prophesied that she would give birth to a son. However, she hesitantly resisted and tried to refuse the promise as to not get her hopes up and dream again. She had grown content in her life circumstances and feared further disappointment. But God was calling her to stand in a doorway. He was asking her to open up her boxed-up dreams, awaken her hidden desires, and retrieve His new dream for her future in exchange for her buried dream.

God graciously intervened on behalf of the woman, and she did indeed birth a son and behold the promise spoken through the prophet's word. However, in time, as the boy grew older, he tragically died one day while working in the field.

Nevertheless, upon the death of her child, the woman quickly, quietly, and gracefully sought out the man of God. Although she was confused as to why her son was taken from her, she was determined to present the problem to the one who decreed the promise. Her faith was tested in that moment. But she didn't stop until she found him and got the answers she was seeking.

She explained to the man of God her situation, and he followed her back home to where her son lay. There the prophet prayed and stretched himself over the boy. He woke up by the power of God, was restored to life, and returned to the woman (2 Kings 4:8–37, paraphrased).

Seven years later, after a famine had struck the land and the woman was forced to leave her home, she returned and came before the king to beg for her house and her land to be restored. At that exact moment, the servant to the man of God told the king about the miracle stories performed by the prophet. He told him the story of the woman's son and how he was restored to life.

Emergence

The woman and her son appeared before the king, and he asked to hear the testimony from her. Upon hearing her story, the king assigned an official to her case. Everything that was lost was ordered to be returned to her. The Lord's hand of provision and favor was upon her because of her obedience to the word of the Lord spoken through his prophets (2 Kings 8:1-6, paraphrased).

This was the exact story I meditated on while hoping for a miracle, waiting for my child to be returned, and believing that everything that was taken from me would be restored and brought back to life. I felt a strong connection to this story and my situation. It gave me solid hope in the midst of confusion, fear, and disappointment. I too had opened up my heart to the promises of God and His new dream for my life—the dream to have a husband, a blessed marriage, and a *complete* family. Then suddenly, my daughter was taken from me. My dreams and heart were broken, and my faith was tested.

However, I too quietly and quickly sought out the man of God for answers and solutions. Because of the promise spoken through the Word of God and His prophets, I was able to faithfully and obediently pick up the lost thing, the dead thing, the stolen thing and lay it down before Jesus. I believed He would come into our circumstances, lay Himself down over it all, and breathe fresh life into it again. I believed that not only would we rise from this situation, but also that a grand testimony would emerge and be heard from it.

For a period of time, I was silent with nearly everyone but God and my husband and shared our circumstances only with those closest to us. I needed to hear directly from the voice of God and that came by spending time alone with Him in the room I had made for Him in my heart and in my home. This was where I gained wisdom, knowledge, understanding, and discernment that helped us battle and defeat chaos, confusion, and disappointment.

But that period of silence is now over. It's time to speak out and share about the miracles the man of God (Jesus) did, how He intervened on my behalf, and how the King assigned His own royal Official to my personal case.

Exactly one year later after my lamb left, the Lord brought her back home safely and brought us back together. My daughter, who had lost all interest in church and seeking after God, turned around and received the baptism of the Holy Spirit at a women's conference that she *chose* to attend *with* me. Satan had tried his best to destroy our house, separate us, and separate her from the love of God, but he failed. My daughter came back to God and back to me, just like I believed in faith she would. I prayed endlessly and declared and claimed victory over her and our circumstances for over a year. Finally, I was reaping the harvest of the faithful seeds I had sown.

Our words matter. We make the choice to speak life or death over our situations. Choose to speak life by speaking the Word of God over your circumstances. Then get ready to witness His wonder in your life.

In the same manner that we receive salvation in Christ through faith and declaration, we receive victory over the enemy through faith, declaration, and proclaiming truth. Jesus defeated Satan's temptation in the wilderness by specifically proclaiming and speaking the written Word of God in faith.

We've been given the same power and must use it. The Bible says that life and death are in the power of the tongue. I specifically prayed that my daughter would receive the baptism of the Holy Spirit, and exactly one year later, she did just that!

His promises to us are true. God is faithful.

> *From the fruit of their mouth a person's stomach is filled; with the harvest of their lips they are satisfied. The tongue has the power of life and death, and those who love it will eat its fruit (Proverbs 18:20–21 NIV).*

> *Jesus answered, "It is written: 'Man shall not live on bread alone, but on every word that comes from the mouth of God' (Matthew 4:4 NIV).*

I believed and declared that upon receiving this baptism, my daughter's heart and desires would begin to change, and she would develop a hunger for God in a new way. That was exactly what occurred. I understood she desired to go and be with her earthly father to establish a more intimate relationship with him. That's an important and fundamental need we all have and one she left home for. However, I am beyond thankful that she also found what she was truly searching for and Who she truly needed her—Heavenly Father.

My daughter had father issues in more than one way; I have dealt with these same issues. However, above all, she was missing a relationship with her Heavenly Father; it was holding her back from experiencing freedom, joy, and abundant life. I have since watched her transform from a lost, confused child, into a confident, hopeful, and joyful daughter of the King.

We did triumph just as I declared in faith we would, just as the prophet said, and just as God promised.

My child was lost and now is found! I will celebrate, rejoice, and praise God for what He has done. Thank you, Lord, for directing my little lamb safely back to You.

Now that she has returned to her true home in Your kingdom, I'm certain she is forever safe and forever loved. You are truly — wonderful.

Sustenance For The Meantime Journey

Before we could engage in this wonderful reunion celebration, there was a waiting period just as there was a waiting period in the story of the prodigal son. My prayers were not answered right away.

There was a time where the son was away doing what he desired and felt was best for him. Meanwhile, the father was at home waiting for his son's return.

Finally, the day came when the son returned home. The father was filled with compassion for him. He ran to embrace him and kiss him as if he had never left or broken the father's heart.

But what happens in the meantime, in the waiting?

In my meantime, in my waiting, I went through several stages. I grieved; I wept; I longed for my daughter. I prayed; I cried out; I surrendered. I hoped; I trusted; I believed. I praised; I worshiped; I sang; and I smiled.

I waited while God worked. I waited for many things at the same time — for my daughter and me to be reconciled and reunited, for her heart to heal and desires to change, and for her to be led into all truth. I also waited for my health and wellness to be restored physically, mentally, emotionally, and spiritually. While in a broken place for a while, a place of suffering, a place of transition, and a place of transformation, I found grace to move forward in hope and belief, knowing that beauty and life were on the other side of the mountain. Grace allowed me to press on and climb higher, even when I couldn't see or feel what was waiting for me on the other side. I believed because God's Word promised. Therefore, I was given the joy, strength, and hope to keep going in the midst of my pain and suffering.

Every Sheep Needs A Shepherd

Some days looked and felt impossible, many to the point of wanting to give up and quit. There were also days I could do nothing but rest in Him, so that I could gather the strength to climb and fight the next day.

Daily, I opened the Word and meditated on Scriptures that spoke to whatever my need was in that moment. I learned to resist the devil and receive from God by following its instruction. I received prayer from the elders of the church in all of my areas of deficiency.

> *Is anyone among you sick? Let them call the elders of the church to pray over them and anoint them with oil in the name of the Lord (James 5:14 NIV).*

My journey was exhausting. In order to make it through each day, I had to get filled up first with spiritual food in order to survive, with the Bread of Life and Living Water. I was completely dependent on God for my daily needs. Nothing else could sustain me or provide me with the proper nourishment but true, wholesome nutrients and substance.

Therefore, every morning, God's presence was invited into my day and I would feed on the Word, pray, meditate, and worship. This filled me and gave me the fuel needed to press on. At the end of each day I was completely depleted, but God always gave me just enough to get to my destination.

He faithfully provides our daily bread, our manna from heaven, just as He did for the Israelites (the chosen people of God) throughout their wilderness journey.

> *Then the Lord said to Moses, "Behold, I will cause bread to rain from heaven for you; the people shall go out and gather a day's portion every day, so that I may test them [to determine] whether or not they will walk [obediently] in My instruction (law)" (Exodus 16:4 AMP).*

> *Do you not know? Have you not heard? The Lord is the everlasting God, the Creator of the ends of the earth. He will not grow tired or weary, and his understanding no one can fathom. He gives strength to the weary and increases the power of the weak. Even youths grow tired and weary, and young men stumble and fall; but those who hope in the Lord will renew their strength.*

Every Sheep Needs A Shepherd

They will soar on wings like eagles; they will run and not grow weary, they will walk and not be faint (Isaiah 40:28–31 NIV).

My family loves breakfast, and my husband has to have eggs every morning, or he gets *hangry* (a combination of hungry and angry). You've probably seen the Snickers commercials where the main actor behaves badly, suggesting that they aren't themselves until they've had their Snickers fix.

We tease my husband that this is how he is until he gets his eggs. Otherwise, he is the nicest, gentlest, and most loving man I know, that is unless he goes without eating. Then it's like he's a completely different person. Then it's, "Get that boy some eggs so we can *recognize* him again!" You can't just give him a donut or a pastry to tie him over either. No, he needs whole food, something of sustenance, protein, and nutritional value. He doesn't want to fill up on junk, only to crash later.

That's the same for all of us. We all need to be fed spiritually first thing in the morning in order to gain the proper nutrients and fuel that's needed throughout the day. Otherwise, we don't have what it takes to adequately and successfully get through this life. We eventually crash and burn out because we are hungry for His Word and angry because of the lack of fullness and sustenance in our lives.

So, what's in an egg?

One morning during my quiet time with the Lord, He began to speak to my heart about an egg. I love sharing with others the conversations Jesus shares with me. I never know what He's going to talk to me about. That's what makes it so exciting and fun. He is by far the coolest person I know.

The following was what He shared with me.

I called it "What's in an Egg?"

What's in an Egg?
Mistie House

When the world looks at us, it sees our shell; it sees what is evident on the outside similar to how we see an egg.

But when God looks at us, He sees our inner being.

Every Sheep Needs A Shepherd

He looks past the shell, for He knows that it will be broken, peeled away, and discarded, revealing what is on the inside.

Therefore, when God looks at us, He is searching our hearts and looking to find Himself deep within it.

It is not our shells that impress Him nor our work that satisfies Him, but it is our Hearts that belong to Him.

This is what He is after.

Let's look at the anatomy of an egg and compare it to the anatomy of a Christian.

The egg is basically made of three parts: the shell, the white of an egg, and the yolk.

The shell's outer covering conceals its inner being.

The white is the protein substance.

The yolk is full of life-giving nutrients, wholesome.

Similarly, Christians are also made of three parts.

Our shell represents our flesh and body.

Our white represents our soul.

Our yolk represents the Spirit inside of us (Jesus).

The shell is the outer covering which conceals what is underneath, much like our flesh and body, and is the framework, protecting and supporting the structure inside.

The white of an egg, or the protein and substance, is symbolic of our mind, will, and emotions that make up our soul, the true essence of who we are.

If we are Christians, then our inner core, the yolk, is filled with Jesus Christ, and He is alive in us. We are nourished with His vital, life-giving nutrients, and our lives are full of flavor and blessing. Just as the yolk of an egg is the center of its source of

Emergence

life, nourishment, and flavor, Jesus is at the center of our lives. His spirit is at work within us, transforming us into His image.

We continue to grow in spiritual maturity through this work until we reach our final stage of perfection. That day of perfection will come upon His return.

Just as a new chick is created, molded, and formed within its core, eventually, it grows and matures until it reaches perfection, and then it hatches. It breaks free from the captivity and bondage of its shell and is revealed! It is a new creation.

We are also created by God, being formed, matured, and perfected into Christ's image. One day soon, we will break free from our shells and be revealed. We will be lifted up, transformed, and alive. We will see our Creator face to face, and we will reign with Him for all eternity!

We will be His new creation!

When our shells fade away and are no more, all truth will be revealed, and what was hidden on the inside will be exposed. The Christ in us will be revealed, and we will be transformed into His image. We will become a new creation, and we will receive a new shell, one that will never break or see decay, but one that will be worthy of His glory!

A life without Jesus is like an egg without a yolk.

It is no egg at all.

It is but an empty vessel, robbed of its life-bearing capability, void of vital nourishment, rid of its flavor, and absent from its very sustenance.

In the meantime, Jesus is also doing this same work in us now. Day by day, He is transforming our hearts to be more like His. This work in our hearts is done as we spend time in His Word, prayer, worship, and alone with Him in intimacy and relationship. Without dedicating time to Him to allow our hearts to be transformed, we won't fully recognize who we are and what we are called to do.

Every Sheep Needs A Shepherd

While this work is taking place, our hearts begin to sing a new song. Even in the midst of suffering, our hearts can still smile and rejoice because of the hope and truth in us that's being revealed. We feed on this truth, and our hearts are filled and satisfied. We're supernaturally given power to overcome any obstacle.

Through the power of God's living Word, we're equipped for battle, transformed under pressure, and promised victory. In order to fully *recognize* who we are, we must feed on the living Word.

Jehovah Raah (the Lord my Shepherd), You are the Good Shepherd who goes after the lost, the wandering, and the wayward and brings them home. Faithful one, here is a prayer taken from crosswalk.com for guiding you how to pray when your child or loved one goes astray.[11]

Insert their name into the following verses. While God works, make room in your day to feed on the Word and pray for their return to God's loving arms and transformation through His Spirit:

PRAYER

"Create in _____ a pure heart, O God, and renew a steadfast spirit within him/her (Psalm 51:10). Though you have made _____ see troubles, many and bitter, you will restore _____'s life again; from the depths of the earth you will again bring _____ up. You will increase _____'s honor and comfort _____ once again (Psalm 71:20-21). Thank You that Your word says I am convinced that neither death nor life, neither angels nor demons, neither the present nor the future, nor any powers, neither height, nor depth, nor anything else in all creation, will be able to separate _____ from the love of God that is in Christ Jesus our Lord."

CHAPTER FOURTEEN

Bring Me Her Heart

One morning when life was feeling gray, I was having my quiet time with the Lord. I tried to sit quietly with my eyes closed and listen for His voice. All I could hear in that moment was the sound of birds singing. It was like they were having a party or a celebration right outside my window.

I opened my eyes and said to the Lord, "All I can hear is the birds. It sounds like they're singing to you."

Then God said to me, "Go and watch."

I got up and went to my window to look outside. A male and female cardinal bounced around in a tree joyfully, dancing from tree to tree.

The Lord spoke to my heart. "This is their Garden of Eden. They're so small, yet like Adam and Eve, they have all of this beautiful creation around them to explore and enjoy with one another. They're provided for. Yet unlike Adam and Eve, they aren't focused on what they don't have. They wake up singing and rejoicing to the Father for all of the gifts they have around them. They wake up like this every morning, singing, praising, and rejoicing."

This is how Adam and Eve should have been in the Garden—content, satisfied, and enjoying their time with one another and their intimacy with God. Instead, Satan distracted them by changing their focus. They became ungrateful and unfruitful. They stopped singing. Then their beautiful garden was no more.

Emergence

With a Smile and a Song

Snow White spends a lot of time speaking and singing to the birds. When things go wrong, she sings a pretty song "With a Smile and a Song." At the end of her joyful melody, she feels quite happy.

My grandma was the same way. Singing made her happy. One of her favorite hymns was "In the Garden." I can see why. The lyrics remind us where we are to reside. Adam and Eve were created in the Garden, and we are to find our way back into the Garden. There we find intimacy, identity, and joy as we walk with Him, and we talk with Him.

Seeing the birds and hearing God speak to me made me look at my surroundings in a new way. It opened my eyes and made me think that Earth is our temporary garden. Although it isn't perfect like Eden was, it is still beautiful, colorful, and full of gifts. If we'll wake up every morning singing and rejoicing for all that He has given us and appreciate all that's in front of us rather than focusing on what we need or lack, then we won't be tempted as Eve was. We won't become robbed of our joy, fellowship, and communion with God.

We'll remain fruitful, full of God's love, joy, peace, patience, kindness, goodness, faithfulness, gentleness, and self-control. Thanks to Jesus, we have the freedom to still walk with God and enjoy the beauty and blessings that surround us, even when life isn't a perfect paradise.

God is still good. He's still with us, and there's still plenty to sing and dance about. God gives us hope, even in our suffering. Therefore, we can choose to rejoice and praise God as we wait patiently in faith and trust for His promises to be revealed. We can choose to focus on the promises rather than our circumstances. We can sing and dance before the production of His work even begins because we know and believe in our hearts that it is coming. He is *at work* all around us and deep within us.

In the meantime, while we wait, He works, and while He works, we worship in song.

I have always loved theatre. In high school, I played Miss Brooks in our three-act play *Our Miss Brooks*. So much work went into preparing for this production. There were auditions, castings, memorizing lines, rehearsals, and finally, production. A lot goes on behind the scenes before the curtain reveal.

Bring Me Her Heart

One of my daughter's and my favorite things to do together is to go see the holiday production of *The Nutcracker*. We can't wait to buy our tickets and witness the grand event. It has become a special mother-daughter date that we look forward to every year. We get all dressed up, enjoy a nice dinner before the show, and always try to arrive early. After settling into our seats, we wait patiently and enthusiastically for the show to begin.

Seeing the beauty in what other guests are wearing is always fun. You'll see shimmering gowns of every color, elegant updos, and sparkling tiaras and jewelry. Then the lights grow dim, and the auditorium gets dark and silent as the orchestra begins.

All eyes are directed to the front of the stage where the show is soon to start. Finally, the curtain is pulled to reveal the glorious work of art. We always leave mesmerized by the incredible performance and eager to return again.

Waiting on God is similar to waiting to see a grand show or production. However, in order to witness this spectacular event, first you must buy a ticket. Making an effort to set up an appointment with God in prayer and showing up to meet with Him daily is like buying our ticket. We're making a sacrifice to set aside our time and energy to spend on alone time with Him. Yet we don't have to get all dressed up to meet with Him; He invites us to come as we are. We also don't have to plan a specific date or time. He's always available to us. We just have to put forth the effort by investing our time.

Some people want to witness a magnificent demonstration of God's work in their lives, but they don't take the time to first meet with Him in His Word, prayer, intimacy, and relationship. They simply don't want to buy a ticket.

When we buy a ticket, though, we can expect to witness an incredible event take place in our lives. This is our time of hoping for and anticipating what lies ahead. We may not know what's behind the curtain, but we can know that our requests have been heard, and there will be a response in accordance with God's will.

Before the excitement begins, however, we must take our seat and wait patiently. Although we're eager to see what's behind the curtain, if pulled too soon, we'll be disappointed. God is at work moving, preparing, and setting everything into its proper place, but timing is a factor. We must wait patiently in hope.

Emergence

Similar to *The Nutcracker*, right before the production in our life begins, the lights grow dark and dim, cueing us that something incredible is about to take place. This could be the enemy trying to stop the manifestation of God's work and testimony or God catching our attention and focus. Nonetheless, this is when our faith is tested, and we must be still, quiet, and expectant of things to come.

We must quiet our souls but not our mouths so we can sing, praise, and worship at the sound of His symphony and not grow restless or weary. We must hold fast to the promise that lies ahead just beyond the curtain. Our eyes must be joyfully fixed on the stage and the light that's shining dimly before us, all the while appreciating the beauty that still surrounds us, instead of the darkness of our circumstances.

Although God sets the stage, we too have a role to play. We must trust, believe, and know that He is in absolute control and orchestrating every detail according to His precise plan. This is what keeps us in perfect peace and harmony as we patiently endure.

Finally, the time comes, and His glorious work is revealed and displayed before our eyes. We discover that this wondrous event was well-worth waiting and hoping for in the end.

This is what it's like to have witnessed a marvelous demonstration of God's work in our lives, to have our prayers answered, and to have received a wonderful gift from Him. We stand in awe, applauding and rejoicing in expression of our ample gratitude. We then walk away, marveled and eager to return to Him time and time again.

> *For from days of old no one has heard, nor has ear perceived, Nor has the eye seen a God besides You, Who works and acts in behalf of the one who [gladly] waits for Him (Isaiah 64:4 AMP).*

> *May the God of hope fill you with all joy and peace as you trust in him, so that you may overflow with hope by the power of the Holy Spirit (Romans 15:13 NIV).*

My grandma also used to sing the songs "You are my Sunshine" and "Jesus Wants Me for a Sunbeam" to all of her kids and grandkids. It's one of our favorite memories of her. She had the most graceful and joyful heart of anyone I have ever known. She sang all the time and praised God in everything, which was what made her so beautiful to me. The Son of man shone brightly upon her smiling face. She was truly fruitful, full of the fruits of the Spirit.

> *But the fruit of the Spirit is love, joy, peace, patience, kindness, goodness, faithfulness, gentleness, self-control; against such things there is no law (Galatians 5:22–23 ESV).*

> *"The Lord bless you and keep you; the Lord make his face shine on you and be gracious to you; the Lord turn his face toward you and give you peace" (Numbers 6: 24–26 NIV).*

> *Rejoice in the Lord always. I will say it again: Rejoice! (Philippians 4:4 NIV).*

Snow White's singing heart made her beauty surpass that of all others. Her inner joy made the Evil Queen so mad with jealousy that she wanted her heart cut out and brought back to her in a box. She knew that the source of her beauty was not on the outside but on the inside. She was jealous of more than just Snow White's appearance; she was jealous of her grace, compassion, kindness, and peaceful nature. Snow White's heart was full of love and the Evil Queen hated her for it.

Satan also hates us because of the song that's in our hearts. He too wants to rip out our hearts to extract the joy that's inside of us. He wants us to focus on how miserable we are so that we won't focus on God and all the blessings that surround us. If victorious, he can then slowly steal, kill, and destroy us.

However, if we will wake up with a smile and a song every morning singing and praising our King in gratitude and thankfulness, feeding on His Word, believing that He's working on our behalf, marveling at the beauty that surrounds us, and anticipating the goodness that's before us. Our hearts will be protected for the joy of the Lord is our strength.

> *Nehemiah said, "Go and enjoy choice food and sweet drinks, and send some to those who have nothing prepared. This day is holy to our Lord. Do not grieve, for the joy of the Lord is your strength" (Nehemiah 8:10 NIV).*

Emergence

The Lord is my strength and shield. I trust him with all my heart. He helps me, and my heart is filled with joy. I burst out in songs of thanksgiving (Psalm 28:7 NIV).

I wrote the following prayer called "Dear God, Make Me Like a Bird So I Can Fly Far" after my encounter with God and the birds.

Dear God, Make me Like a Bird So I Can Fly Far
Mistie House

Dear God, I want to be like a bird.

I want to rise every morning singing to you a song of praise. I want a thankful heart that admires Your beautiful creation each new day.

I want to joyfully dance and playfully bounce from place to place, soaring and enjoying all that You have for me.

I want to envision this earth as our temporary, imperfect Garden of Eden, and I want to walk in it alongside You.

I know there's a serpent that will attempt to separate me from you, Lord.

He will try to deceive me and trick me into focusing on what I don't have rather than focusing on the precious gifts surrounding me that You provide.

Help me, Lord, to not be tempted or deceived.

Give me strength and wisdom to discern good from evil.

Give me Your perspective daily, and lead me in truth.

Make me like a bird so I can fly far . . .

Far, far, away with You.

Amen.

Bring Me Her Heart

Whistle While You Work It

One of the most beautiful characteristics that Snow White also embodied was a servant's heart. She was led to the seven dwarfs' cottage in the woods that was in need of a warm touch (and a broom). She and the little forest creatures began tidying up the room. This princess wasn't afraid or too proper to get her hands dirty. In fact, she sang "Whistle While You Work." She was glad to offer a helping hand and had fun while doing it.

My grandma embodied this same charming characteristic. She worked very hard at keeping a tidy home and happy family. She often had bruises all over her arms from her hard work, yet I never heard her complain. The cheerful tunes she always hummed demonstrated such grace throughout her tiresome labor. Her garden was also extraordinary, filled with rows of fresh vegetables, blossoming fruit trees, and fragrant flowers.

As you walked up to the front of her house, you were welcomed by the sweet scent of purple lilac bushes and lustrous yellow, peach, and pink roses bordering her front porch. Her home was always warm and inviting. Food seemed to always be prepared in her kitchen, and her table was always a place of gathering and saying grace. Even nighttime offered beds covered with crisp line-dried linens that smelled refreshing. There really was nowhere else like Grandma and Grandpa's place. They gladly and faithfully served and welcomed others. It is a legacy that I hope to continue to fulfill.

> *"His master replied, 'Well done, good and faithful servant! You have been faithful with a few things; I will put you in charge of many things. Come and share your master's happiness!' (Matthew 25:21 NIV).*

True story: One afternoon while a mother and her daughter ate lunch together, the mother noticed a homeless man walking past the window outside of the restaurant and heading toward the door. As he came in, many people uncomfortably stopped and stared at him.

One by one, the man went from table to table and asked for money. The mother didn't have any cash to give him. Still, she didn't want to turn him away, but she didn't know how to help.

Emergence

Finally, the man approached her table and made his request. She kindly said, "I'm sorry, I would, but I don't have any cash." She was saddened as the man turned away. Then she silently prayed, "Lord, what can I do?" Suddenly, the mother realized that although she couldn't offer him cash, she could offer to buy his meal with her debit card.

Without hesitation, she quickly jumped out of her seat, grabbed her purse, and boldly walked over to the man standing in front of another table of guests. She said to him, "Sir, I can pay for your meal. Would you like for me to do that?"

The man nodded enthusiastically. "Yes."

The mother then joyfully walked with the man to the counter to order his food. As they stood at the register, she noticed the man's crippled arm and feet that were stained black from filth. Her heart ached for him. She knew that he needed much more than she was able to provide in that moment.

The man at the food counter asked the name for the order, so the mother turned to the homeless man and asked him his name.

"David," he answered.

A lady witnessing what was taking place came up to the mother at the register and offered to help. She held out her hand with cash, offering to help pay for the man's food. Since the mother had already paid for it, the lady turned and handed the money to David, who gratefully accepted it.

The lady said to the mother, "God bless you. You're doing a good thing."

The mother returned her smile. "God bless you too."

David then made his way to a table after placing his order while the mother collected her receipt.

The young man taking the order said to her, "You are so nice. You don't see things like that happen very often."

The mother smiled, thanked him for placing the order, and quickly and quietly headed to her seat.

The restaurant was full of spectators, but the mother didn't pay them any regard as she passed by them. She couldn't call to mind a single face in the restaurant other than those who were directly involved. Wishing to move about the busy restaurant unnoticed, she modestly kept her head down. It took all she had to maintain her composure and hold back her emotions throughout that entire scene.

Bring Me Her Heart

When she finally made it to her seat, she turned toward the wall, hid her face behind her long hair, and silently burst into tears praying no one would see. Her heart was overwhelmed with compassion for David, and all her attention and heart's affection were upon him and God. Although that event had just occurred in a public setting, it was a very personal experience and intimate moment with God. The daughter stared across the table at her mother and watched as she wept.

They finished eating and had some food left over. The mom boxed it up and suggested they give it to David, who was eating his meal just a few tables down from them. She watched as her daughter walked over to him and handed him their extra food.

David didn't look up at her, but he accepted her offer. Then she walked away. The mother and daughter left the restaurant, and once in the parking lot, they prayed for David. The mother called him "King David" and prophesied that although in this world he may be poor and needy, one day he will be mighty in the kingdom of God.

That day, the mother, her daughter, the man at the register, the kind lady, the spectators in the restaurant, and King David all witnessed a remarkable encounter with Jesus. It was Jesus who saw his helpless child's need and boldly approached him without hesitation and then fed His lamb. It was Jesus who prepared the way for His lamb to be fed and provided the food. It was Jesus who served him. It was Jesus's heart that was overwhelmed with compassion. It was Jesus who gave the extra food. It was Jesus who demonstrated an act of love. It was Jesus, the Good Shepherd, at work in the hearts of His people, His sheep who heard His voice.

It was all Jesus!

Lord, I pray that King David not only witnessed an encounter of Your love that day, but also that He received Your love. I pray that he has come to love the One who came to meet with him so that he may receive the promise you offer to those who love You. In Jesus' Name. Amen.

Listen, my dear brothers and sisters: Has not God chosen those who are poor in the eyes of the world to be rich in faith and to inherit the kingdom he promised those who love him? (James 2:5 NIV).

Emergence

The incredible back story is that weeks before this encounter occurred, the mother had been in a situation where she felt the nudge and call of God to approach another person who might be in need. She wrestled with God about it, which caused her to hesitate. By the time she was willing to obey and turned around to go greet that person, the opportunity had passed. The person had moved on and was no longer there.

Someone else would now be called to meet that particular need. She felt disappointed in herself and asked God to forgive her and give her another chance. He heard her prayer and later gave her another opportunity to respond with boldness. This time, she obeyed immediately and didn't grumble, cheerfully going to work. When she walked away, she didn't feel disappointed or depleted; she felt full of more love and energizing compassion after witnessing a remarkable encounter with Jesus. She felt God's heart for another, and that compassionate love overwhelmed her in such a way that it overflowed and caused her to burst into tears. It was an indescribably touching moment that she will not forget.

This mother was me. I continued to pray for King David and even asked God about him a year after our encounter. I wanted to know if he was all right. Again, God heard my prayer. Just days later, God showed him to me. While driving, I caught a glimpse of him walking down the street near my neighborhood. Never before that restaurant encounter had I seen him nor have I seen him since that day on the street. God arranged both of those meetings. My heart leaped with joy at the sight of him. God's heart is so caring.

I have also experienced such encounters with complete strangers approaching me and demonstrating this same love of God for me. One special encounter that happened to me was on September 6, 2016. It compelled me to write "A Simple Act of Love."

A Simple Act of Love
Mistie House

Yesterday, I had something unexpected happen to me.

I smiled at a little boy in the store as I walked by him to continue shopping. A little while later, the same boy approached me and asked if he could have a hug.

Bring Me Her Heart

Surprised, I asked, "You want me to give you a hug?"

He replied, "Uh huh."

I said, "I'll give you a hug."

After this child and I embraced in the middle of the store, he walked away.

I tried to process what just happened and make some sense of it. My mind refused to let me believe the simplest answer—this little boy just needed a touch of love, and he needed it from me.

This morning while reflecting on that child's need for a simple act of love, I was reminded that each day is a gift and that within that gift exists opportunities for unexpected beauty.

It also reminded me that each day, the possibility of someone in need of a simple act of love exits. This creates a fresh opportunity to give that love away, whether it be methodically planned or unexpected.

That is what makes each day so beautiful.

My second encounter happened in a grocery store. While doing my normal shopping, a lady passed by and asked, "How are you?"

I smiled. "I'm good. Thanks."

A few minutes later, that same lady walked back to me. Maybe, she too had been wrestling with God and had hesitated briefly. Nevertheless, she asked, "Is there something you need that I can pray for today?"

I was completely caught off guard by her question. Immediately, my eyes began to tear up.

An encounter with the love of Jesus typically catches you by such surprise and often overwhelms you to the point of tears. These are good tears. They fill your empty bucket and water your soul. I was in the midst of my difficult season of battling fear at that time, and I was in need of refreshment, peace, and strength. This woman was sent to help. Together, two complete strangers prayed in the middle of a grocery store on an ordinary day.

Emergence

In the movie *The Hobbit: An Unexpected Journey,* an ordinary hobbit was chosen by a wizard and a companion of dwarves to accompany them on a dangerous adventurer in an attempt to regain their home in the mountain along with their treasured possessions.[12] Dwelling in the mountain and standing guard over the treasure was a fire-breathing dragon responsible for invading their territory.

The hobbit, Bilbo Baggins, faced the difficult decision to leave the comforts of his home to go on an unexpected journey. Filled with compassion for these wandering fellows, he set aside fear and restraint and chose to venture out to help the homeless and needy.

A question arose from the Lady of Light, Galadriel in regards to bringing a hobbit (small folk) along for the quest of such a grand expedition.

She asks, "Mithrandir, why the Halfling?"

Gandalf, the great wizard, replies, "I do not know. Saruman believes that it is only great power that can hold evil in check. But that is not what I have found. I've found it is the small things, everyday deeds of ordinary folk that keeps the darkness at bay. Simple acts of kindness and love. Why Bilbo Baggins? Perhaps it is because I am afraid, and he gives me courage."

To this Galadriel responds, "Do not be afraid, Mithrandir. You are not alone. If you should ever need my help...I will come."

Sometimes we need the presence of folks such as these, around us most when we anticipate it the least.

None of my encounters happened by coincidence or chance; they happened by divine appointment. God saw a need in His children (His sheep), and He sent His people to help remind them of His loving presence and meet those needs.

When the boy in the store approached me, I left afterward asking, *Why that small child?* I realize now that God sent that little one on an unexpected journey. That bold and brave child came to accompany me because I was the one who needed a hug, needed help, and who was afraid. God chose and used him to help give me courage. That simple act of kindness and love, that small deed from an ordinary little boy, helped keep the darkness at bay that day and let me know I was not alone.

> *Don't be afraid, for I am with you. Don't be discouraged, for I am your God. I will strengthen you and help you. I will hold you up with my victorious right hand (Isaiah 41:10 NLT).*

Bring Me Her Heart

God loves people through people, and He wants to love His people through you. He can use anyone to serve out His love and compassion. The young, the old, it doesn't matter who the person is if they have a heart that's willing. He will equip us with what we need to accomplish His great deeds, even through the smallest of us so long as we are courageous enough to leave the comforts of home and bold enough to do what He calls us to.

One year, I had the honor of serving Thanksgiving dinner to underprivileged children. It was a wonderful experience. As each darling child came through the cafeteria line, I greeted them with a smile. Most would smile back, and one little girl even said to me, "You're pretty."

Along with the carefully portioned servings of turkey and mashed potatoes with gravy, I served warm smiles with generous helpings of unlimited love and kindness. Yet I found that they blessed me as much as I hoped to have blessed them.

What that little girl didn't know was that I was struggling with insecurity in that moment. That morning I tied my hair in a braid, threw on a baseball cap, a pair of jeans and sneakers, and was on my way. I would be working to serve food through a cafeteria pass-through line, so I made sure to tie back my long hair as to not serve any strands along with the meal.

Despite my own personal battles and struggles that day, I cheerfully showed up to offer a helping hand because I was there to serve and glorify God, not to be seen, recognized, or noticed by others. Yet, unexpectedly, that precious little girl had taken notice of me.

As I delivered each serving with a smile and a song, God graciously delivered what I lacked that day. Obviously, my outer attire or appearance didn't make me attractive to that little girl; it was an inner beauty exuding through the love of Jesus, expressed through my warm smile and greeting, that directly caught her affection. That small child saw a glimpse of Him through me as I cheerfully served out doses of His loving kindness to her. God's love (not me) is the most beautiful to look at. It's also infectious.

Receiving a portion of God's contagious love caused her to respond in kindness and pour back into me, giving me the confidence boost I needed through her encouraging word. Even though I left my home with the intentions to give of Him that day, I also left having received from Him. That little one warmed my own heart as did each child's sweet smile. Their excitement and enthusiasm from receiving a simple meal served by strangers lit up the room.

Emergence

It's amazing what a simple loving smile and kind word can accomplish and orchestrate in God's kingdom. The special encounters of others made me feel loved and cared for on those days, and I hope I was able to help do the same for those children that Thanksgiving.

It truly is better to give than to receive. I'm so thankful that our God is incredibly giving. He gives generously to those who so generously give.

> *In all things I have shown you that by working hard in this way we must help the weak and remember the words of the Lord Jesus, how he himself said, 'It is more blessed to give than to receive'" (Acts 20:35 ESV).*

When we're serving out love, we're serving out Him because God is love, but we can't give something we don't possess. In order to give and reflect God's exuberant love, our hearts must first experience an encounter with love. We then have the ability to take those seeds and sow them into another's garden.

There are many different types of seed—seeds of service, food, money, prayer, or even hugs, seeds of hope, joy, peace, compassion, courage, and much more. It's important to have a mixed variety, and all of these are beneficial.

Whatever seed you've received and choose to sow in love, just remember to whistle while you work. Don't draw attention to yourself. Help others see and experience God's heart smiling upon them so His righteous acts are glorified, not our own. This is the mark of a true servant's heart, one who gives cheerfully (without hesitation, willingly, and with the right motives) to please and honor God. Their selfless acts are not for show or seeking honor or to please man but to love. No matter the place, they give from a pure heart and with pure intentions, just like Snow White did. If God so happens to direct you to give to those in need while in a public setting, by all means, do so cheerfully without hesitation, but *whistle quietly* among yourself.

No one likes a show off.

The World Is Not a Stage

> *"Be especially careful when you are trying to be good so that you don't make a performance out of it. It might be good theater, but the God who made you won't be applauding.*

Bring Me Her Heart

"When you do something for someone else, don't call attention to yourself. You've seen them in action, I'm sure—'play-actors' I call them—treating prayer meeting and street corner alike as a stage, acting compassionate as long as someone is watching, playing to the crowds. They get applause, true, but that's all they get.

"When you help someone out, don't think about how it looks. Just do it—quietly and unobtrusively. That is the way your God, who conceived you in love, working behind the scenes, helps you out (Matthew 6:1–4 MSG).

The Cheerful Giver

The point is this: whoever sows sparingly will also reap sparingly, and whoever sows bountifully will also reap bountifully. Each one must give as he has decided in his heart, not reluctantly or under compulsion, for God loves a cheerful giver (2 Corinthians 9:6–7 ESV).

His Heart

The enemy wants our hearts so he can rip them out and destroy them. God wants our hearts so that He can repair, renew, purify, align, and dwell in them. God wants to give us His heart.

I had a pretty serious spiritual heart condition for a very long time; it wasn't functioning properly. God has been my physician, overseeing the condition.

Part of my heart had been deeply wounded from my past and had died due to trauma. Many daggers of rejection were still lodged in it. My Physician began working to perform spiritual open-heart surgery to remove the daggers and seal the wounds so that it would function properly as a whole. He wanted to resurrect it and bring it back to life so that I could love again wholeheartedly.

This treatment has been a lengthy process. Like any procedure, you have to follow proper protocol. In my case, I followed Him, His instruction, and His plan of action (not my own), and I obeyed His commands.

Emergence

First, I began to notice symptoms, problems, and pain. Then I set up a "consultation" with my Great Physician to explain what seemed to be the problem. (I cried out to God in prayer.) The Physician then wanted to take a deeper look, and I agreed to let Him examine me. (I answered the call.) He identified the problem and told me how He planned to fix it. I agreed to give Him permission to perform treatment. (I surrendered control to His plan and trusted Him.)

Then I underwent a rigorous surgery (through trials, tests, storms, and fire) to eliminate and fix the problem. My Physician then sealed me up and closed the wound. (Here is where I went through the process of forgiveness and redemption.) Then I was forced to bed rest (to be still and know that He is God and in control and to trust Him) throughout the healing process.

Next, He slowly introduced new habits and routines to me to help regain my strength. (I had to look to Him for relationship through quiet time and learn to depend and rely on Him for all of my needs and restoration.)

I began to feel like a new person and appreciate my wellbeing. (I experienced new life and grace.) I no longer took my health and life for granted; now I live every day to the fullest and experience abundant life. I am forever changed (transformed, redeemed, renewed) and will be forever grateful for the work of my Physician's hands. I have experienced freedom!

Finally, I'm privileged to tell others how great and wonderful our mighty Physician is. It is a privilege to bring Him praise, glory, and honor. I highly recommend Him to anyone with a spiritual heart condition.

My new heart is beautiful and is reinforced with a strong layer of His amazing grace—an impenetrable force field of His perfect love that sings His praises. Although my heart and dreams may have been temporarily shattered and broken, God picked up all the pieces, put me back together, and made me whole again. He created something new, radiant, and secure. Unlike Humpty Dumpty, my King was able to put me back together again, better than before.

For my entire life, I had looked to others to fill me; however, others can't fill you because they lack the power to heal you. My heart was deeply wounded. I was in spiritual bondage and a slave to my own sin. I had carried the weight of my sin, guilt, and shame around with me for far too long. God had forgiven me, but I had yet to forgive myself for the pain I inflicted upon myself. Although God had released me from this offense, I was still offended toward me. Therefore, I still carried around the heavy chains that connected me to my sin and brokenness.

In order to be set free from my past, I had to give God access to my heart so that He could reach in and touch every one of those wounds and break every one of those chains. I also had to learn to forgive myself. First, I had to change the way I saw myself. I needed to discover the way God sees me and who I truly am. Then I would be set free from the burden of my sin, past regret, shame, guilt, fear, and insecurity.

The enemy seeks to steal and *still* our beating hearts. When we come to God broken and willingly offer our hearts up to Him, He adjusts them to beat to the sound of His own drum and to dance joyfully to the tune of His own song. We begin to take on His gentle and humble nature as we find rest in His identity for us.

> *"Come to me, all you who are weary and burdened, and I will give you rest. Take my yoke upon you and learn from me, for I am gentle and humble in heart, and you will find rest for your souls. For my yoke is easy and my burden is light"* (Matthew 11:28–30 NIV).

Our dear Snow White found much-needed rest, relaxation, and recovery in the cottage after her traumatizing event in the dark forest. She found joyful company singing and serving in the presence of seven little dwarfs amongst a warm hearth in the woods. To the beat of "The Silly Song," Snow White and the dwarfs danced up quite a jig together in the friendly cottage.

I did the same after my own traumatizing bout with fear.

Soon after, the Lord gifted our family with our own cottage in the woods. A friend of ours sold us a plot of land in the mountains of New Mexico at an incredible price. The timing could not have been better. This quiet and quaint lodge nestled in the trees offered us a place to rest, relax, and recover after our family had experienced so much.

It was deep in the forest where our family began to sing a silly song and dance again with delight around a warm campfire beneath the stars.

The Great Physician healed us all.

Emergence

As we bring Him our hearts, we find shelter in His warm arms, company in His delightful presence, and we are able to serve out warmth and loving kindness to others. Only then will we truly find rest for our wearied souls, and will our hearts newly jive, jam, and jitter to the beat of His drum!

SECTION IV

Paradise Restored

CHAPTER FIFTEEN

The Father's Princess

Those times of battle with my health, skin, and past created heavy burdens for me to carry around. Matthew 11:28–30 has been one of my favorite verses. It always gave me such comfort knowing I could come to Jesus, and He would give me rest in exchange for my weary heart and soul.

Finally, I decided to accept His offer and give my heart to Him in exchange for healing, granting Him full permission to make it beat again in proper rhythm. So after the church service, I went forward to receive prayer.

Pastor Kim Witcher, the Executive Pastor of Ministry Care at Trinity Fellowship Church, warmly greeted me. With watery eyes, I explained to her that I wanted to receive prayer for physical and emotional healing.

At the end of her prayer, she said, "Close your eyes and ask, 'God, what do You want to tell me right now?'"

I did and He responded. "I've always been there. Even through the bad times, I was always there and never left you."

Then the joyful pastor prompted me to ask God another question.

"How do you see me?" I asked Him, a little afraid of His answer. Nevertheless, I closed my eyes and waited for a response.

I saw a little girl with long golden-blonde hair with curls on the end. She was running through a field of white flowers, smiling, laughing, and glowing as sparkling rays of sunshine shone down on her and the glittering field.

Emergence

The enchanting and uplifting picture in my mind caused my face to be drenched with tears. I told Pastor Kim what I saw.

She said, "Describe how the little girl felt."

"Light, free, and joyful!" I responded.

That incredible encounter with God in that moment changed my life and the way I saw myself. The image of that happy little girl replaced my prior reflection of how I felt in that moment—a sad and broken woman weary and burdened.

God doesn't view us the way we view ourselves. He sees His beautiful creation and those He has adopted as His precious children. He created a way for us to be free from the heavy burden of our sin, to be joyful for His cleansing love and forgiveness, and to reflect His glorious light and shine as His radiant child.

In that vision, God's peaceful, golden light shone down on me causing me to shimmer in incandescent beauty.

God saw me as pure and innocent as a flower, white as snow. Jesus's cleansing blood had washed over me, taking away my sin, my shame, my regret, my guilt, my pain, and my sorrow. He had cleansed me of who I once was (dead in sin) and revealed who I now am (alive in Christ). The Son of God washed away our stains so that we *could* become the children of God.

If we are born again, this is how God sees His children and how He wants His children to see themselves—no more sorrow, no more shame, no more guilt, no more pain. No more.

> *"Come now, let's settle this," says the Lord. "Though your sins are like scarlet, I will make them as white as snow. Though they are red like crimson, I will make them as white as wool"* (Isaiah 1:18 NLT).

I couldn't get that epiphany image out of my mind, and I never wanted to. Although I still looked the same on the outside, something had changed on the inside. My spiritual eyes had been opened (awakened with a moment of sudden revelation and insight). I now saw myself through the eyes of the One who made me.

This supernatural, divine experience helped me to see myself as a child of God, yet I had been living like a spiritual orphan. Until that vision, I hadn't yet fully recognized the Father's extravagant perfect

The Father's Princess

love for me nor my perfect position in Christ. I had been holding on to my feelings of shame over my past. Those orphan feelings of being fatherless, abandoned, unwanted, alone, and unloved had been weighing me down and holding me back from my future promises, including the promise of rest and freedom for which Jesus died.

We're only slaves to those burdens if we choose to remain bound to that yoke and carry the weight of our sin. Jesus has set us free from it. It is up to us to choose to be connected to Him so that we may walk beside Him as free, light, and joyful children of God. As we take His yoke upon ourselves and learn from Him, we find the rest He promises.

Realizing how God saw me allowed me to see myself in the same way. It allowed me to love and forgive myself because I finally understood how much I was loved and forgiven by God. Finally, I learned how to see Him as my Father (Daddy) in heaven and receive His love, forgiveness, and acceptance. This recognition helped set me free from the captivity and bondage I was under. No longer was I a spiritual orphan; I was adopted and chosen! No longer alone and afraid, I had found peace. No longer a slave to sin, death, and fear, I was a child of God. No longer a nobody, I was royalty.

I finally recognized and understood that I was a daughter of the King!

When God opens up your eyes to how He sees you and your heart and how He feels about you, it no longer matters how others see you or what others think about you. I no longer needed to be loved and accepted by *everybody* because I understood that I was forever loved by *Somebody*. You are loved by God, and that is always enough.

I remember telling my husband Chris when we first met that "I just want to be enough for one man, not all men, just one man." I finally realized that I would *always* be enough for One Man—my Father in heaven. And dear one, so are you!

I discovered who I am:

I am who God says I am! I am a child of God. I am never alone. And I am loved!

That encounter marked the beginning of my inner-healing journey. I went to God and asked for His yoke in exchange for my weary and burdened heart. I had begun my journey toward freedom, restoration, identification, and purpose.

Emergence

Beauty for Ashes

While on this remarkable journey, God gave me a remarkable mission.

It had been over a year since I saw the image of the girl in the field of white flowers. Then one day during my conversation with Him, another vision was given to me. This one involved me writing and illustrating a children's book built around the image I saw. The story would be of a lost and lonely orphan girl who was adopted by her Heavenly Father, the King. She is transformed into a beautiful princess and given three special gifts: a crown of beauty, a garment of praise, and a royal scepter filled with the oil of joy. In receiving the gifts, the forever grateful princess responds, "Father, you have given me so many good and perfect gifts, but the greatest gift of all is Your love!"

Before this new vision was given, while I was still in my season of suffering, I had been praying specifically that God would exchange my ashes for a crown of beauty, my mourning for joy, and my despair for a garment of praise for the display of His splendor. This was a specific verse I had been meditating on and would become one of the many verses my book would be centered upon.

Now that God had answered that prayer, He called me to write about my encounter with Him and share it with the world.

> *... And provide for those who grieve in Zion—to bestow on them a crown of beauty instead of ashes, the oil of joy instead of mourning, and a garment of praise instead of a spirit of despair. They will be called oaks of righteousness, a planting of the Lord for the display of his splendor (Isaiah 61:3 NIV).*

The princess tells her story of how she was adopted by the King, grafted into a new family, enthroned in royalty, given a new identity, and a new name, all thanks to the hands of her loving and gracious Father!

> *I will not leave you as orphans; I will come to you (John 14:18 NIV).*

> *God decided in advance to adopt us into his own family by bringing us to himself through Jesus Christ. This is what he wanted to do, and it gave him great pleasure (Ephesians 1:5 NLT).*

The Father's Princess

The princess has been transformed and now shines radiantly because of the light that's within her. She goes out into the land and invites others to come and meet her Father and inherit the kingdom, so that they too may encounter and receive His radiant light and love.

> *"Then the King will say to those on his right, 'Come, you who are blessed by my Father; take your inheritance, the kingdom prepared for you since the creation of the world (Matthew 25:34 NIV).*

The Story of the White Daisy

When my husband and I dated, he said I reminded him of a white daisy. So he started calling me *his* white daisy.

In my vision from God, I ran through a field of white flowers. Right away I knew that Daisy was to be the name of the princess in my story.

Once I began writing my story, I was curious as to what the flower and name "Daisy" meant. My research found that it symbolizes innocence, new beginning, purity, harmony, childhood, loyal love, beauty, patience, simplicity, the Virgin Mary, motherhood, transformation, and true love due to the combination of two flowers joined together—the yellow flower in the center and the white flower on the outside. [13]

Shakespeare was also inspired by the daisy's meaning and used a daisy chain in *Hamlet* representing Ophelia's innocence. The term "ups-a-daisy" was derived from being used to encourage children to get up when they fell. It was later transformed to "oopsie-daisy" or "whoopsie-daisy," which was used as an exclamation after a stumble or mistake. [14]

The daisy's bright yellow center represents a heart filled with joy and solar energy (or as I like to say, "Son Light"). Sounds a lot like the egg analogy. Interesting!

The white daisy is referred to as the day's eye because it really does open its petals as the sun rises and closes them at sunset to sleep and rest. It is also called the "thunder flower" because it blossoms bountifully amidst storms. It stands unharmed afterward, representing protection from the thunderstorm.

Emergence

Is all of this just coincidence? I don't think so. The meaning of the white daisy sums up the entire story of my life. I believe that my husband was prophesying over me when he began to call me his white daisy after God downloaded into my husband the way He saw me as His pure, white flower, His white daisy.

My husband began to speak that identity over me so that I would blossom and emerge into the creation I was intended to be. He spoke life over me, and he didn't even realize it at the time. But God knew all along who I was to Him.

The white daisy doesn't represent my story only. My life's simple story is so much bigger than me or you. All of creation points to the Creator, and as His creation, each of our lives are meant to tell a story. The stories (testimonies) of our lives as His children all tell of Him and His great wonder and love for us. Yet our story is not our own. We were made by God to belong to God. Therefore, our story belongs to Him.

The Story of the White Daisy that God was writing through me is meant to represent the story of all God's children (an allegory of the believer's journey to the kingdom). He picks them up when they fall from sin, transforms them when they look to Him, protects them through storms as they seek His shelter, and purifies them through His cleansing blood. Just like when God finishes His mighty works in us, we stand unharmed in the end and bloom as beautiful and innocent white flowers whose center is the golden Son, the light, the joy, and the source of life and true love.

God does everything with precise detail and intention. He is marvelous like that.

Just as the meaning of the daisy was noteworthy to my story, our names are also significant. God often changed names in the Bible. For instance, Abram was changed to Abraham, Sarai to Sarah, Simon to Peter, Jacob to Israel, and Saul to Paul. The change of names established a change in character (in heart), a new identity within them, and a new mission to fulfill. It marked them in a special way as God's servants, called, chosen among the chosen, and appointed to serve the Lord's purpose. As God begins to transform and change our hearts, our true identity and purpose is being revealed.

The name Daisy in my story was symbolic of this change, transformation, and work that God has and is doing in my life. He has transformed my heart to love Him, others, and myself and to live for Him. He has cleansed me, leaving me pure, joyful, innocent, and filled with childlike wonder and freedom.

I had received the Father's love and was being transformed into who He created me to be. Now I was commissioned to open up, share, and invite others to experience it as well as help them to see themselves as the Father's princesses. The name Sarai and Sarah in the Bible both mean princess; however, the change in name stressed that she would become the mother of nations and kings, serving the Lord's purpose.

As children of God, we are the descendants of Abraham and Sarah and thus carry on this same royal lineage. It is our royal mission to serve the King's command for the display of His splendor.

I was so excited to do this work for God. I loved the way He put His and my story into words and pictures for others to see and experience. Only God can do that. He can take something very painful and personal and turn it into something beautiful and expressive—beauty for ashes.

This book was to become an expression of my heart of what God had done in my life and about my relationship with Him. It was a visual illustration of our perfect love story. As the Father and I wrote it together and the colorful pages came to life, I felt my heart healed even more. It was a special time of intimacy between us. I was faithful to do His work, and He was faithful to keep His promise.

Exactly one year later to the day I received this assignment from God, I finished the book. I couldn't have planned that if I tried. On April 4, 2017, our story was published and released to the world.

On the cover of my first children's book is the image I saw—a little girl with long, golden-blonde hair, smiling with her arms stretched out wide in a field of white daisies. The title of my book is *The Father's Princess: The Story of the White Daisy*—A miraculous journey of a wonder-filled soul in search of everlasting love.

Crowned

While growing up, my town held an annual Santa Fe Trail Daze Celebration. This fun-packed festival hosted several events such as a historical tour, parade, dance, pageant, picnic, craft shows, contests, and more. During my senior year of high school, I entered the Santa Fe Trail Daze Beauty Pageant. For the talent portion, I dressed up as

Emergence

Olivia Newton John's character Sandy from *Grease* and sang her song "Hopelessly Devoted." These are often the embarrassing things you do to keep yourself and others entertained when you live in small towns. To make matters worse, members of the community most likely have these festive moments captured on video.

Performing on stage was something I had been doing from a young age, so I was fairly comfortable and confident in this area. Parading my formal gown in front of the audience was also a breeze for me. However, the same could not be said when it came to the interview. I was terrified before being called in.

In preparation, I tried to imagine all the possible questions that could be asked and how I was prepared to elaborate on my background and family life, but I failed to prepare for what came.

Finally, I was up. The very first question asked was, "If you could change one thing in this world, what would it be and why?"

I froze. All that ran through my head in that moment was the scene from *Miss Congeniality* where that same question was asked, and the same response was given over and over by every single naïve contestant—world peace.

Although world peace is a fantastic idea, in my pride and arrogance, I refused to follow that lead. I didn't want to present as if I had no original or creative thoughts, opinions, or beliefs of my own. So, I sat there in silence and disbelief, not believing they asked me that stereotypical pageant question.

I'm sure my lack of response made known to them my point and stance on this matter. Not! I'm quite sure I ended up demonstrating the very argument I was determined to refute—I was a brainless blonde.

I understood that I desperately needed to *say something*, but what I really wanted to address was an extremely sensitive issue—pornography. I knew this matter had devastating results, yet my shame, embarrassment, and lack of courage prevented me from exposing my feelings and speaking up about it.

It was very easy for me to act and perform on stage because I was portraying another character other than myself. However, I lacked the boldness and confidence to open up and express who I truly was to others who didn't yet know me. Although I was passionately against this concerning topic, I feared bringing up such a revolting subject. If nothing else, this interview exposed this truth about me to me—I was like a closed book unwilling to open up and share my thoughts, my story, and my experience with others.

Pornography was already becoming a widespread problem even in the small world around me, and I believed it was only going to continue to spread. This product of evil that sought to bring destruction to the lives of many men, women, and children across the globe absolutely sickened me to my core. Although unbeknown to me at the time, it would come to play an important role in the destruction of my future relationships.

During my interview, they skipped over the first question and moved on to more relaxed topics, which I answered confidently and without hesitation. They later came back to the first question and gave me an opportunity to form a response. Regretfully, again, I gave no reply. I left that interview feeling very ashamed and foolish over my performance. I failed to expose the truth in my heart because I was too cowardly and ashamed to say something.

At the final stage of the competition, fellow contestants told me that after having shared my talent and parading my beautiful evening gown on stage, I was going to win. I responded, "No, I blew my opportunity during the interview." I ended up receiving second place for the talent portion, but I didn't win the crown.

Ultimately, winning a beauty crown is of little significance; however, speaking up regarding important issues and speaking out against evil, is. I went over that interview time and time again in my mind, wishing I would have opened my mouth. Why did I remain silent when I had so much to say?

Beauty and talent will only get you so far in life. Our words and confession of the heart are what truly matter. Ultimately, it is God's words that will bring the change that's so desperately needed in this world.

Therefore, as the Church, we must not remain silent. We must open up the Word of God, take the sword of the Spirit out of its sheath, and use our mouths to cut through and push back the darkness with the light that has been given to us. If we are going to become the Father's princesses, then we must act and speak like royalty. We need to use our God-given authority to protect and uphold the sovereignty of the kingdom by sharing the truth of what God has placed in our hearts. The Church must not be silent on sensitive issues that threaten our world.

Emergence

Likewise, we as individuals must not remain silent on the most important issue we all face—our salvation. In order to receive our crowns in heaven, we must openly declare and publicly confess what we know and believe to be true in our hearts—that Jesus Christ is Lord. His beauty outshines all others, and His truth takes the crown.

If we're ashamed of Him and refuse to open up and speak the name of Jesus, He will be ashamed of us. We don't want to miss the opportunity to receive our crown in heaven because we were too ashamed to unveil our inner testimonies and speak of His truth from the Book of Life.

We can choose to be His hands and feet by taking a stand and walking toward righteousness and speaking out and sharing the good news of the gospel with others.

> *So everyone who acknowledges me before men, I also will acknowledge before my Father who is in heaven, but whoever denies me before men, I also will deny before my Father who is in heaven. "Do not think that I have come to bring peace to the earth. I have not come to bring peace, but a sword (Matthew 10:32–34 ESV).*

True Royalty—For Such a Time as This

On October 21, 2017, I hosted my first book signing event for my published children's book *The Father's Princess: The Story of the White Daisy*. The party was magical! I welcomed princesses of all ages to come celebrate the love of their Heavenly Father, the King. Little girls dressed up in shimmering princess gowns. We ate delicious cupcakes and treats, made crafts, sang and danced. I had the privilege of sharing my story and ministering God's Word to His precious children.

After reading my book aloud to everyone, I looked out among these little ones and asked, "What makes you a princess?"

Their initial response was "The dress, the crown, the royal scepter."

I answered, "No, the only thing that makes you a princess is becoming a child of God."

Anyone can "look the part," or "act the part," but only those who become a child of God will inherit the kingdom and wear the crown.

It's not enough to be imitators of the faith; we must become *believers* of the Word. God alone is the King, and if we confess with our

The Father's Princess

mouths and acknowledge who He is in our hearts, then He will welcome and acknowledge who we are, His own children.

Once we're born again by the Spirit, we're adopted into His kingdom and receive the right to be called sons and daughters of the King of kings. We become royalty—princes and princesses who will one day rule and reign at His side.

It's not about the dress, the crown, the royal scepter, or even the title. It's about God being the Sovereign King and shouting and proclaiming our allegiance to Him and His Word. It's not about parading around the gifts of beauty and talent He's given to us. It's about using those gifts to glorify God and benefit others. It's about honoring our Father, serving our King, and establishing His rule and truth in His kingdom.

> *He was in the world, and though the world was made through him, the world did not recognize him. He came to that which was his own, but his own did not receive him. Yet to all who did receive him, to those who believed in his name, he gave the right to become children of God—children born not of natural descent, nor of human decision or a husband's will, but born of God (John 1:10–13 NIV).*

As a child of God, if I have a choice for the imprint of my life and legacy to read beauty, talent, or truth, I choose truth. Beauty will fade, talent will be rediscovered, but His absolute truth will never die nor I with it. Therefore; I choose not to remain silent on these important issues.

As a child of God, it's my duty to use the gifts and talents He has given me to speak up and share His Word and my testimony with others. I pray you will do the same and declare that fear will never have the power to hold you back.

We can't be overly concerned with what the world will say or think about us. We must remember what God has to say and what He thinks about us. His opinion should matter most. Be bold, be brave, be fearless, be whoever God is calling you to be, but remain humble.

> *"For if you remain silent at this time, relief and deliverance for the Jews will arise from another place, but you and your father's family will perish. And who knows but that you have come to your royal position for such a time as this?" (Esther 4:14 NIV).*

Emergence

We (children of God) are to be the salt and the light of the world. Salt preserves the truth, and light illuminates the truth. Our primary role and concern as true royalty should not be aimed at preserving our beauty or reputation nor illuminating our talents, but aimed at preserving and illuminating His beautiful truth in this dark world. Remember, princes and princesses, it is the King who is to shine brightest, not us.

> *For it is by grace you have been saved, through faith—and this is not from yourselves, it is the gift of God—not by works, so that no one can boast (Ephesians 2:8–9 NIV).*

The Enchanted Promised Land

In the same year I was writing my book, my husband and I took an anniversary trip. We try to do this every year. It's important to set aside time to focus on one another and have fun together as a married couple.

That year, we went to Oregon and stayed in a dreamy resort right on the coast. Also within reach were many national rain forests. One day, we decided to go hiking. We discovered a trail that promised to lead to a beach. This sounded like a great adventure.

Before going on our trip, I prayed specifically for a couple of things. I asked God to show me a field of white daisies, to show me a beautiful sunset on the beach, and that my husband and I would experience a peaceful and wonderful time together with Him in our midst.

As we drove up to the place where our hiking trail began, the first thing we saw was a field of tiny white daisies. No joke. I couldn't believe it.

I excitedly hopped out of the car and ran into that field. My husband took pictures of me holding my arms out to the side, just like in my vision God showed me of myself as a little girl in a field of white flowers. That experience would be enough to satisfy me throughout the entire trip. I was thrilled that God cared enough about me to answer that prayer.

After taking pictures, we took off hiking down the trail. It was fantastic, like none I had ever been on. It was green and lush and had enormous trees with roots that stretched across the path. The trail wound up and down and all around. We could hear the ocean, but the forest was so thick we couldn't see it. The higher up the trail we went, the louder the ocean roared. It was so much fun anticipating when it would finally appear.

The Father's Princess

Just then, something marvelous caught our attention. We came upon a very unusual tree in the middle of the path. The trunk came out of the ground and then split in two, forming a circular shape. We were so fascinated by it that we had to stop and take a picture of ourselves kissing in the center of it. We named it "Lover's Tree."

Then together, we playfully walked through it as if it were a gate passing into a different realm. I know, we're dorks in that way, especially when on vacation, but I wouldn't have it any other way. We know how to have fun together.

Right as we reached the other side of Lover's Tree, the forest began to open up. Before us was the big reveal—the grand scenic overlook that we had been hoping for. The view was absolutely breathtaking!

We stood at the face of a lavish green cliff overlooking the secluded beach and gazed at the enchanting ocean behind it. Our vision stretched for miles.

The ocean view in front of us and the forest behind us were my favorite. It was a brilliant combination of two magnificent places morphed into one location. We just stood, stared, and took it in for several minutes. It was beyond peaceful.

Finally, we decided to hit the trail. "This is one of the best days of my life!" I proclaimed.

No sooner had I just spoken these words out loud to my husband when out of nowhere, a black snake slithered across the path right in front of me.

Before I go any further, let me tell you about my relationship with snakes. Everyone who knows me or has ever known me are quite aware that I am terrified of snakes. I hate them. Growing up in the country, we had to remain watchful because snakes were a big deal and a real threat. They could show up anywhere. Sometimes, we would see one in the garden, the driveway, or even on a few occasions, where one had slithered its way inside our house. Eek!

When I was a kid, one day while at church, my friends and I were outside looking for dandelions. After spotting a huge group of these flowering plants in a tall patch of grass, I made my way over to them and stood still to appreciate its beauty. Then I heard something by my feet. I looked down and saw two snake heads—the head of a rattlesnake inside the mouth of a bullsnake. I freaked out and took off running and screaming hysterically toward the church.

Emergence

All of the parents came running outside and found me in a panic. I thought that snakes were all around me. My parents tried to calm me down and reassure me that I was safe.

So, after the snake crossed my path on the hiking trail in Oregon, once again, I freaked out and screamed. I ran backwards to my husband and tried to jump on his shoulders or have him pick me up off the ground, but he wasn't getting the hint. He was too busy cracking up at me.

Concerned for our safety, we pulled out our cell phones and googled this type of snake and discovered they were common in this wilderness. We determined that although it was scary, it wasn't poisonous. This revelation enabled me to calm down, reassuring me that its bite couldn't harm me.

Therefore, I gained the courage and assurance I needed to continue on our journey. A few minutes later, another snake slithered across our path. This time I reacted differently. Although, it still startled me, I didn't freak out. I kept on walking down the trail.

By the time a third snake crossed the path in front of me, I didn't even see it. My husband told me I nearly stepped on it and crushed its head. It slithered under my foot, barely escaping. I hadn't been able to see it because my eyes were excitedly looking ahead and fixed on the beautiful beach we were approaching.

Finally, we had entered paradise. Chris and I made our way down to the secluded beach where we explored and played like little children filled with wonder. It was just the two of us and God, walking in this heavenly place.

We excitedly dug little hidden treasures out of the sand and the mossy cliffs. I twirled and danced around the shore freely, joyfully, and peacefully. As a loving couple, we intimately marveled at the beauty of God's glorious creation.

When we finished exploring paradise, it was time to make our journey back through the trail. However, this time before beginning our hike, we prayed for protection and that I would see no snakes. Chris walked in front of me so that his presence would startle them and bring them out of hiding.

My husband saw one snake on our journey home, but I didn't see a single one. I was able to walk safely and comfortably on the path before me.

The Father's Princess

About six months after taking this trip, God gave me a revelation about our hiking journey to paradise. This trip was not only symbolic of my personal spiritual journey with God; it was symbolic for all God's children.

As we begin our spiritual walk with God, we'll experience beauty and new life, but we'll also have to overcome some obstacles in the wilderness (snakes on our path). These seemingly giant obstacles attempt to stand in our way and threaten to derail us from continuing our journey and following the dreamy path God has planned for us.

We have a choice in how we will respond to these serpents. We can panic and run backwards trembling in fear or we can keep going.

God is calling us forward, toward Him and toward the prosperous territory He has provided for each of us to claim and possess as our promised inheritance!

> *Now they departed and came back to Moses and Aaron and all the congregation of the children of Israel in the Wilderness of Paran, at Kadesh; they brought back word to them and to all the congregation, and showed them the fruit of the land. Then they told him, and said: "We went to the land where you sent us. It truly flows with milk and honey, and this is its fruit. Nevertheless the people who dwell in the land are strong; the cities are fortified and very large; moreover we saw the descendants of Anak there (Numbers 13:26–28 NKJV).*

> *Then Caleb quieted the people before Moses, and said, "Let us go up at once and take possession, for we are well able to overcome it" (Numbers 13:30 NKJV).*

> *But the men who had gone up with him said, "We are not able to go up against the people, for they are stronger than we." And they gave the children of Israel a bad report of the land which they had spied out, saying, "The land through which we have gone as spies is a land that devours its inhabitants, and all the people whom we saw in it are men of great stature. There we saw the giants (the descendants of Anak came from the giants); and we were like grasshoppers in our own sight, and so we were in their sight" (Numbers 13:31–33 NKJV).*

Emergence

If we commit to move forward, we must be aware of our surroundings but not afraid of what lies hidden in them. God has given us the power and the authority to overcome any obstacle that stands in our way. No stealthy serpent or ghastly giant has the authority to take it from us.

Our promised land flowing of milk and honey lays ahead. It's a beautiful paradise (a place of rest) that God has prepared for us. It's a place of stepping into the fullness of all God has planned for us. It's the place where we enter into walking in alignment with God's will and purpose for our lives and walking in love, joy, and peace all of our days. It's an exciting place to explore and dig up hidden treasures. It's a place of enjoying intimacy with God, companionship with others, and freedom to be the person God has created us to be. It's a good land flourishing with God's fruitful blessings.

However, upon discovering this land, our sole purpose isn't just to dwell in the land. Our purpose is to go out and invite others to discover this land for themselves. That means we'll have to get back on the trail. We can pray for the Lord's presence to go before us to protect us and reveal any hidden threats. His presence enables us to go wherever we're called to go unharmed and in peace.

> *Peace I leave with you; My [perfect] peace I give to you; not as the world gives do I give to you. Do not let your heart be troubled, nor let it be afraid. [Let My perfect peace calm you in every circumstance and give you courage and strength for every challenge] (John 14:27 AMP).*

In my personal opinion, God protected me when I was a child from the poisonous rattlesnake by sending the bullsnake to swallow it up. He kept me safe by devouring the creature that threatened my life. We were miles from a nearby hospital, and I'm not sure if we would have made it in time if I had been bitten. I believe this experience was foreshadowing what I would also later experience in the spiritual realm as an adult. During my time of vulnerability, Satan came to cripple and paralyze me with fear in the hopes that I would turn away from God and away from the path that lay ahead. He sought to rob me of my inheritance and destiny, destroy my hopes and dreams, and threaten my life.

My husband and I had been seeking God together as one and as a loving couple. He gave us a beautiful vision for our marriage and ministry, a glimpse of our promised future, similar to the scenic overlook on the other side of Lover's Tree. Then Satan immediately appeared and threatened to stop us from reaching our destination. He attempted to paralyze me in fear so that I would remain motionless in the wilderness, preventing us from continuing on toward the enchanting land that God was leading us into.

Once again, the Prince of Peace showed up and empowered and equipped us to overcome those obstacles of fear, shame, rejection, insecurity, and idolatry. Although I initially panicked and ran in the opposite direction, I learned to turn around, press on, and rely on God. When He wasn't carrying me on His shoulders during my times of weakness, He was leading me along the path, making it easier and easier to overcome each obstacle. The closer I got to the promise, the more my eyes became fixed on the beauty that was waiting for me. No longer was I focused and concerned with the obstacles that were waiting to jump out at me. I was aware they existed but not overly cautious and discouraged from continuing on my journey.

My confidence, strength, and determination to reach my destination had grown because I finally recognized I was not alone. God was with me; therefore, nothing had the power to harm me. Although terrifying snakes were in my midst, when I cried out to Him, He closed their mouths (from speaking lies) and swallowed up their threats (ability to hold me back).

Upon recognizing this truth, I took up my authority and received His power to overcome. I put Him always before me. At this point, the serpents had no choice but to run and hide before they were trampled by foot, not because of anything I did but because of who my God was.

I'm a child of God called to walk faithful not fearful because He dwells in me and I in Him.

> *He replied, "I saw Satan fall like lightning from heaven. I have given you authority to trample on snakes and scorpions and to overcome all the power of the enemy; nothing will harm you. However, do not rejoice that the spirits submit to you, but rejoice that your names are written in heaven" (Luke 10:18–20 NIV).*

This adventure was the peaceful and wonder-full experience my husband and I had while on our trip. This entire vacation symbolized the closeness and the bond we had developed throughout our life together because we put God in the center of our marriage and at the forefront of our journey. As we pressed on in the midst of terror and obstacles, we overcame them together one by one. We had become like Lover's Tree, rooted in God, that had grown up out of the ground, rising above all obstacles, together as one couple united in perfect love.

When we look to God in the midst of trials, tribulations, and difficult circumstances, He promises to show up and swallow up our fears as we reach out and up toward Him in faith and trust. We then rise out of the ashes of despair and begin to grow and mature spiritually until we are firmly and securely established in love, which is God Himself.

In the story of Moses, Aaron's staff was transformed into a serpent, and it swallowed up the serpents of Pharaoh's magicians. This act symbolized freedom for the Israelites and foreshadowed the miracle that would occur at the parting of the Red Sea when the Lord swallowed up the enemy in the roaring waters that sought to kill the Israelites.

Looking back on that terrifying snake experience I had as a child, I'll never forget when someone held up the dead bullsnake after they had located and killed it in the tall grass. Although there were two heads beside my foot that day, only one snake was found and killed. To me, this story represents the story of Jesus so well.

God saw the threat upon His children's lives that occurred that day in the Garden of Eden as the serpent appeared, and He sent His Son to intervene and save us. Then Jesus appeared and swallowed up sin and death by becoming death for us all on the cross. He was killed (yet raised up) so that we may look upon Him and receive eternal freedom from the bondage of sin and death.

Our sins are washed away by His blood—His sacrifice to take our place. The punishment of death was destroyed for all who look to and believe in Him for salvation.

Throughout all of history, the serpent continues to try to steal, kill, and destroy the children of God over and over again. But his threat is turned back upon himself as Jesus comes to destroy his attempt and restore life and peace to God's children for all eternity.

Aaron's Staff Becomes a Snake

The Lord said to Moses and Aaron, "When Pharaoh says to you, 'Perform a miracle,' then say to Aaron, 'Take your staff and throw it down before Pharaoh,' and it will become a snake."

The Father's Princess

So Moses and Aaron went to Pharaoh and did just as the Lord commanded. Aaron threw his staff down in front of Pharaoh and his officials, and it became a snake. Pharaoh then summoned wise men and sorcerers, and the Egyptian magicians also did the same things by their secret arts: Each one threw down his staff and it became a snake. But Aaron's staff swallowed up their staffs (Exodus 7:8–12 NIV).

Jesus is able to swallow up (any and all) obstacles that threaten our lives, our destiny, and our freedom. No matter how big or scary our obstacles may appear, our God is always bigger and able to take them out. Not only did Jesus perform a miracle in my life when He showed up and swallowed up the rattlesnake that threatened me, but He also showed up later on and swallowed up every snake and obstacle on my path that threatened to steal, kill, and destroy the future, purpose, destiny, and promise that God had prepared for me.

Jesus has performed many miracles in my life, and He is able to do the same for you. If we'll allow Jesus to overcome and quit trying to do so within our own strength, we won't be overcome and we'll find the promised land of freedom just as the Israelites did. We don't have to wander aimlessly in the wilderness alone in search of this land. All we have to do is cry out in faith, obedience, and trust and submit to God, not our overwhelming circumstances. We can then take up our authority as Moses did. Our mighty Deliverer will show up on our behalf to part the waters for us in a powerful and miraculous way, swallow up our obstacles, and send our enemy fleeing.

So as the sun began to rise, Moses raised his hand over the sea, and the water rushed back into its usual place. The Egyptians tried to escape, but the Lord swept them into the sea. Then the waters returned and covered all the chariots and charioteers—the entire army of Pharaoh. Of all the Egyptians who had chased the Israelites into the sea, not a single one survived.

But the people of Israel had walked through the middle of the sea on dry ground, as the water stood up like a wall on both sides. That is how the Lord rescued Israel from the hand of the Egyptians that day. And the Israelites saw the bodies of the Egyptians washed up on the seashore (Exodus 14:27–30 NLT).

Emergence

I am the Lord your God, who brought you out of the land of Egypt, to be your God: I am the Lord your God" (Numbers 15:41 NKJV).

On the very last evening of our trip, we witnessed a gorgeous sunset on the beach. Every other night it had been hazy, and the sunsets were not very impressive. But on that final evening, God painted the sky with brilliant hues of gold, streaks of orange, and delightful shades of pink, purple, and blue. It was a visionary masterpiece and exactly what I had hoped for!

God had answered every one of my prayers while on our trip. He is concerned with our cares and wants to be a part of them. These were not needs I had; they were simply desires I hoped for in my heart. God still wanted to meet and exceed those simple desires.

He truly loves us, and He is a good Father. Invite Him to go before you into your journey, and trust Him to take care of you, His little princess and snow-white daisy, along the path.

Cast all your anxiety on him because he cares for you (1 Peter 5:7 NIV).

PRAYER

Abba Father,

Help me to recognize myself as the Father's princess, a daughter of the King, and to walk with great power and authority in Your kingdom. Open my eyes to see myself through Yours. Help me to discover my royal identity in You for such a time as this. Bestow on me a crown of beauty instead of ashes, the oil of joy instead of mourning, and a garment of praise instead of a spirit of despair. Help me to serve You, my King. I pray to be bold like Esther to speak truth and to shine bright in the darkness of this world. Make me salt and light. Guide me to the promised land You have for me and help me to overcome all snakes and obstacles along my path. Carry me when I'm afraid and weak. Thank You for leading me to this good land.

In Jesus' Name. Amen.

CHAPTER SIXTEEN

Heigh Ho! Let's Go!

Every day, the seven little dwarfs left home to go to work in the cold, dark mines. They dug up hidden gems, jewels, and treasures in an array of different colors, shapes, and sizes that included rubies, sapphires, and diamonds. Then they marched home from work in unity, joyfully singing and whistling the song "Heigh-Ho."

This is the same work Christians have been called to do—to leave the comfort and safety of our homes in order to joyfully go out and march united, searching and digging for lost souls in the cold, dark world in which we live. We're to help find these hidden gems so that God can polish them up to shine like the unique and rare treasures they are to Him. We're God's most treasured possession, and His people should be ours as well.

When in Oregon, my husband had been searching all week long for a whole sand dollar on the beach near our resort. All we could find were broken pieces.

Then we took our nature hike and arrived on our secluded beach, Chris had wandered off and was a pretty good distance from me. So I began taking in the scenery and capturing video on my phone when I heard a joyful shout of celebration and saw him holding something up in the air. As he made his way back to me, he revealed a perfect sand dollar.

Emergence

He said, "When we arrived on this beach, I asked God to reveal a whole sand dollar to me. Then He asked me, 'Do you believe? Do you believe in Me and that you'll find one?' I told Him yes. Then the Lord led me directly to it. Is that not incredible?"

Another hidden treasure had been found.

As we begin searching for lost souls (or hidden treasures and desires), God will reveal them to us if we ask and believe we'll find what we seek. If we're willing to go to work seeking them out, God will lead the way. He will help us to see in the dark because His light shines within us.

The search goes both ways. Sometimes we go out looking for the lost, and sometimes the lost seek us out because they catch a glimmer of our light. Either way, it's His light that leads them home. As these rare and precious gems are revealed, we should joyfully shout in celebration, for another hidden treasure has been found.

> *But you are not like that, for you are a chosen people. You are royal priests, a holy nation, God's very own possession. As a result, you can show others the goodness of God, for he called you out of the darkness into his wonderful light (1 Peter 2:9 NLT).*

> *For you are a people holy to the Lord your God. The Lord your God has chosen you out of all the peoples on the face of the earth to be his people, his treasured possession (Deuteronomy 7:6 NIV).*

Two years after our trip, I had the idea to search for any symbolic or spiritual meaning behind the sand dollar.[15] It was sacred to us because of our personal journey and experience in finding it, but was there still more to this rare treasure than meets the eye. What was so special about it that engaged our adventurous quest to find it?

I was in complete awe of my discovery.

The sand dollar is remarkably said to be a Christian symbol that represents the birth, crucifixion, burial, and resurrection of Jesus Christ. All this time, its deeper symbolic meaning had been hidden to me. It wasn't until I went searching for it that I found it. Many legends, stories, and poems are associated with this spiritual meaning. One such story or poem that I dug up was "The Legend of the Sand Dollar."[16]

According to this legend, the star on the front of the shell represents the Bethlehem star that led the wise men to the birth of Jesus. The etched

Heigh Ho! Let's Go

flower on the back represents the poinsettia, the Christmas flower. Inside every sand dollar, you'll find five doves symbolizing peace, joy, and goodwill. The four holes on each point of the star represent Christ's nail wounds on the cross. The fifth hole on the back represents the pierce to His side, symbolizing His death. The blossomed flower encircling the star represents the Easter Lily, a symbol of Jesus's resurrection.

The Legend of the Sand Dollar
Author Unknown

There's a lovely little legend

that I would like to tell,

of the birth and death of Jesus,

found in this lowly shell.

If you examine closely,

you'll see that you find here,

four nail holes and a fifth one,

made by a Roman's spear.

On one side the Easter lily,

its center is the star,

that appeared unto the shepherds

and led them from afar.

The Christmas Poinsettia

etched on the other side,

reminds us of His birthday,

our happy Christmastide.

Now break the center open,

and here you will release,

the five white doves awaiting,

to spread Good Will and Peace.

This simple little symbol,

Christ left for you and me,

to help us spread His Gospel,

through all Eternity.

Discovering this revelation was almost just as remarkable to me as actually discovering the treasure itself. The hidden mysteries we find as we seek for more of God are miraculous, and some treasures you have to seek out and dig up for yourself.

He was there on that Oregon coast. I could absolutely sense His presence through the peace and joy of that moment. To me, discovering the meaning of the sand dollar was conformation in this moment that Jesus was with us, beyond any shadow of doubt.

While walking the coastline, I thought about the poem "Footprints in the Sand." With my spiritual eyes, I believe He walked beside me. However, I wanted to see His footprint with my physical eyes. Little did I know, God answered that wish. For me, that sacred sand dollar that manifested so magically was His footprint in the sand. We were able to take it home and carry a part of that journey with us and remember that He is with us at any given moment. God is faithful to show up and deliver where He is invited. You can count on it.

There is no glamorous gem, no trifle treasure, no jubilant jewel that can compare to discovering Jesus. There is no greater peace or joy than uncovering the hidden mysteries of God in the good land He has promised us.

When we seek God earnestly, devotedly, and above all else, He leads us to this land. He meets us there and reveals and delivers on His promise.

You will seek me and find me when you seek me with all your heart (Jeremiah 29:13–14 NIV).

Heigh Ho! Let's Go

I also know that much like "The Legend of the Sand Dollar," God placed that rich treasure into the sand for my husband and me to dig up and have a story of our own to tell of the wondrous miracles of Jesus.

At the exact moment Chris searched for a sand dollar (symbolizing Jesus), I was capturing video of the enchanted land and proclaiming, declaring, rejoicing, and celebrating in faith that God was there with us because we had invited Him. In that same moment, my husband let out a shout of victory and revealed the perfect treasure from the glorious ground we stood upon.

As a couple, we had sought God earnestly in other lands, yet we had only come across bits and pieces of the treasures He had tucked away. When we finally entered into the promised land He led us to, through our unrelenting perseverance to not give up or turn back throughout our wilderness journey, only there did we discover the fullness to our lives and purpose that only Jesus could deliver.

When we examine Him closely with our whole heart, we find absolute fullness in Him. We witness the profound beauty in His nature and observe the wonder of what He created for us. As we peek inside the keyhole of His heart, we break open and release the peace and joy that can only be found inside His goodwill for our lives. This is the triumphant treasure God intends for each of us to seek out and find. Why settle for bits and pieces of the blessed life Jesus has to offer when you can step into the fullness of all that He has prepared and promised?

At the end of a day's work of searching for precious lost gems in the dark mines, I want to joyfully march home alongside my husband to our peaceful promised land, singing and whistling to the song "Heigh-Ho." I desire to know without a shadow of doubt, to *believe*, that we have found and carried with us the fullness of Jesus, the light of the world, the greatest treasure of all.

In Him, we too are made whole in His likeness. Our joy is made complete as we live, dwell, abide, rest, and remain in His love no matter where our Christian "work" calls us to go.

> *"When you come looking for me, you'll find me. "Yes, when you get serious about finding me and want it more than anything else, I'll make sure you won't be disappointed." God's Decree.*

Emergence

"I'll turn things around for you. I'll bring you back from all the countries into which I drove you" —God's Decree— *"bring you home to the place from which I sent you off into exile. You can count on it (Jeremiah 29:13–14 MSG).*

"As the Father has loved me, so have I loved you. Now remain in my love. If you keep my commands, you will remain in my love, just as I have kept my Father's commands and remain in his love. I have told you this so that my joy may be in you and that your joy may be complete. My command is this: Love each other as I have loved you (John 15:9–12 NIV).

Princess of Power

I grew up in the 80s, so I grew up playing with toys like Care Bears, My Little Pony, Rainbow Bright, Strawberry Shortcake, and She-Ra. I had the She-Ra doll, and my older sister had Catra. There was something special about my She-Ra doll that fascinated me. Maybe it was her fierceness or the combination of being a princess and a warrior at the same time.

I was recently in a women's Bible study, and we were studying Lisa Bevere's book "Girls With Swords."[17] Wonderful study, love her! During that season of study, someone posted a picture on my Facebook news feed of toys from the 80s. She-Ra was one of them. It brought me back to my childhood. I started remembering playing with my doll and how fabulous I thought she was. Then I realized something—She-Ra was a girl with a sword.

I rushed to my computer and pulled up She-Ra to learn more about her. After reading the plot and watching the 80s cartoon's opening, I was astounded.

In a nutshell, She-Ra was a princess of great power, the most powerful woman in the universe working alongside her companions to defend the Crystal Castle against evil.[18] She led a great rebellion to set captives free from oppression. Her sword was her source of power, protection, strength, empathy, and healing that enabled her to transform into a heroine. At her side was her noble steed, Spirit, who also possessed the power of transformation into a talking alicorn (a winged unicorn). She-Ra longed to settle conflict through peace rather than violence. Her long-lost twin brother was He-Man, also known as Prince Adam.

Not only did this go right along with our study, but it mirrored who we are to be as daughters of the King. For fun, I decided to write my own interpretation of the role of God's princesses in relation to Christian women warriors of faith and share it with the women in my study.

A Princess of Power
Mistie House

I Am a Princess of Power

I am a daughter of the King of kings and Lord of lords and heroine, defender of the Lord's kingdom. Holy Spirit is my beloved helper and companion. Secrets were revealed to me the day I picked up my sword, God's Word, and said, "I will serve to honor my King!" Many believers share this same secret. Together we strive to free God's people from Satan, the evil one.

The Primary Focus

The primary focus is the conflict between good and evil as God's people attempt to drive the evil one out of their world. Unlike heaven, the evil one has great power on the earth and is commonly taking over entire regions and enslaving people. There is great conflict between the evil one and God's servants. God's warriors seek to establish their relationship and identity in Christ and take up authority given from heaven above.

The Sword of Protection

The sword of the Spirit, God's Word, is the weapon wielded by God and is used to transform us into His image. The transformation is triggered by calling out to God in surrender and laying down one's life to serve for the sake of the kingdom. Our destiny requires us to tap into God's power with our sword so we can rise up and become the new creation He has called us to be as heirs to the throne.

Emergence

In addition to being a formidable weapon capable of cutting through most substances and deflecting attacks, the sword of the Spirit has the ability to change lives.

The sword is used as a variety of weapons or tools through spoken command, varying from a shield, helmet, and blade. We can use our swords to draw upon the mystical power of our Lord in heaven, increasing our strength beyond our own capabilities.

Who We Are: Our Mission Statement

We are spiritual warriors, heroines of faith, fighting battles within the unseen realms together as one in the presence of our King.

We Must Never Forget

We are powerful as long as we remain in Him and His presence.

God alone is our source of power.

Without Him, we are nobody, nameless.

We are to remain humble.

As we rise up and take our place, we should remain in our place.

We are to follow Him.

We are never to step ahead and take the lead on our own.

The higher we are lifted up, the lower we should bow down.

This is the type of princess I want to be, a princess of power. I don't want to be the type of beautiful princess who sits in her castle with servants waiting on her hand and foot. I want to be the type of princess who makes a difference in the kingdom, one who gets up, goes out, and serves others by being God's hands and feet.

Heigh Ho! Let's Go

God has given us power and authority for a purpose—to make a difference in the kingdom. We're to help set captives free from the evil oppression of Satan. We're to extend our hands with the sword of the Spirit into the dark and lonely pits where prisoners are being held captive. We're to pray and encourage them to grab hold of the sword (God's Word and truth) and help pull them out of the darkness and into the light.

> *The Spirit of the Sovereign LORD IS ON ME, BECAUSE THE LORD HAS ANOINTED ME TO PROCLAIM GOOD NEWS TO THE POOR. He has sent me to bind up the brokenhearted, to proclaim freedom for the captives and release from darkness for the prisoners, (Isaiah 61:1 NIV).*

People are hurting, and we can help them receive hope and truth. We can lead them to safety, freedom, salvation, and to a personal and intimate relationship with God. We can't be their hero, but we can put on the armor of God and go into battle on their behalf, fighting for them as warriors of Christ. We can lead them to the true hero and Savior of the world—Jesus! Together we can build the kingdom of God.

The Armor of God

Finally, be strong in the Lord and in his mighty power. Put on the full armor of God, so that you can take your stand against the devil's schemes. For our struggle is not against flesh and blood, but against the rulers, against the authorities, against the powers of this dark world and against the spiritual forces of evil in the heavenly realms. Therefore put on the full armor of God, so that when the day of evil comes, you may be able to stand your ground, and after you have done everything, to stand. Stand firm then, with the belt of truth buckled around your waist, with the breastplate of righteousness in place, and with your feet fitted with the readiness that comes from the gospel of peace. In addition to all this, take up the shield of faith, with which you can extinguish all the flaming arrows of the evil one. Take the helmet of salvation and the sword of the Spirit, which is the word of God.

Emergence

And pray in the Spirit on all occasions with all kinds of prayers and requests. With this in mind, be alert and always keep on praying for all the Lord's people (Ephesians 6:10–18 NIV).

Even more astonishing is that Sheerah, is a woman mentioned in the Bible. She was a builder of three cities and descendent of Ephraim, who received the blessing given by Jacob. This blessing rippled down to her generationally.

Then he blessed Joseph and said, "May the God before whom my fathers Abraham and Isaac walked faithfully, the God who has been my shepherd all my life to this day, the Angel who has delivered me from all harm —may he bless these boys. May they be called by my name and the names of my fathers Abraham and Isaac, and may they increase greatly on the earth" (Genesis 48:15–16 NIV).

He had a daughter named Sheerah. She built the towns of Lower and Upper Beth-horon and Uzzen-sheerah (1 Chronicles 7:24 NIV).

As a heroine of faith, Sheerah built a legacy of faith. A woman of vision, empowered by the Father, she built the kingdom in her own unique and gifted way. I too am fighting to build a legacy that will ripple down generationally. I too want to be a heroine of the faith, to know the God who has been my Shepherd all my life. I want my children and my children's children to know God as their personal Shepherd, to learn to hear His voice and obey His commands, to walk faithfully, and to be blessed and protected all of their days. I want to be a builder of the Lord's kingdom and to encourage, empower, and equip others to do the same.

They will rebuild the ancient ruins and restore the places long devastated; they will renew the ruined cities that have been devastated for generations (Isaiah 61:4 NIV).

However, I realize that in order to build, I can't do it on my own. Before Chris and I started building onto our house, we had a vision.

Heigh Ho! Let's Go

I'm very skilled in the area of creative vision and design, yet if left to my own strength and ability, my vision would never be brought to life. I have the ability to dream but not the ability to create (to build something of that stature) on my own. Thus, it was necessary for us to seek outside help for our dream to become a reality. We sought out skilled, professional contractors and worked alongside them throughout every stage of the building process until our vision was complete.

When I was a little kid, I decided to build a dog house. I found a few boards, a hammer, and some nails from my dad's supply and went to work. After struggling to even build the frame of the house, I quickly discovered that I was unskilled and unqualified in my own ability (to say the least). My vision was never going to come to pass, so I eventually gave up on the idea.

Most of us begin with a dream and vision. We strive to create it on our own, only to realize that we lack the ability to bring our vision to life. Therefore, we frustratingly give up on our dreams because we couldn't make them happen.

> *When there is no clear prophetic vision, people quickly wander astray. But when you follow the revelation of the word, heaven's bliss fills your soul (Proverbs 29:18 TPT).*

We were never created to fight or build on our own, to do life on our own. Our talents, abilities, and skills are limited. We're unqualified and we need outside help. Luckily for us, there is One who specializes and is qualified in every area of life. God is our Master Builder and Creator. He built, created, and laid the foundation of the universe and all its beauty. The Bible is our blueprint and instruction manual that He devised for us to follow and obey. The Holy Spirit is our Guide, Companion, and Helper, and Jesus is our Master Craftsman and Teacher. Together they are one.

God has *all* the resources needed to successfully create *any* project from beginning to end. Why would we ever try to build without Him? We need His help, and He is willing to give it. All we have to do is ask, seek, and knock at His door, and He will answer.

Ask, Seek, Knock

"Ask and it will be given to you; seek and you will find; knock and the door will be opened to you. For everyone who asks receives; the one who seeks finds; and to the one who knocks, the door will be opened.

"Which of you, if your son asks for bread, will give him a stone? Or if he asks for a fish, will give him a snake? If you, then, though you are evil, know how to give good gifts to your children, how much more will your Father in heaven give good gifts to those who ask him! (Matthew 7:7–11 NIV).

Like Sheerah (the builder and princess warrior), we can also work alongside God to build our homes, our marriage, our families, our dreams, our neighborhoods, our legacy, our ministry, the faith, and the kingdom of heaven. We battle safely, and we build effectively as we follow and remain in His shadow and in His vine. Apart from God, we can do nothing on our own that has real eternal value and significance.

Safety of Abiding in the Presence of God

He who dwells in the secret place of the Most High Shall abide under the shadow of the Almighty (Psalm 91:1 NKJV).

"I am the vine; you are the branches. If you remain in me and I in you, you will bear much fruit; apart from me you can do nothing (John 15:5 NIV).

PRAYER

Father,

I don't want to settle for bits and pieces. I want to step into the fullness of all You have prepared and promised me. I desire to be a heroine of faith and to be used by You in a mighty way. I want to be a princess of power. I recognize I need Your help. So I ask You to enable me to see others through Your eyes and to love them with Your heart. Empower me to fight courageously and build effectively. Equip me and use my gifts and talents to glorify Your name. Help me to remain humble and abide in You always. Train me to look for the lost and broken treasures and lead them to the light of Your presence. Bestow favor upon me so that I may help set captives free. Enlighten me to become a woman of vision, filled with true and lasting beauty and strength and one who builds a legacy of faith and fulfills my purpose. May my life's story become a testament of Your glory.

In Jesus' Name. Amen.

CHAPTER SEVENTEEN

The Sleeping Death

It's time we leave behind the shadows of the dark and come into the shadow of the Almighty. It's time we arise, awaken, and emerge from the Sleeping Death.

To me, the Sleeping Death in the spiritual world represents three things.

First, it represents our inability to be consciously awake and aware of not only Satan's schemes to steal, kill, and destroy us, but also God's plan to redeem, free, and save us from our sin. It's being asleep to the reality of truth that two invisible opposing forces are at work within our lives. One battles to tempt and lure us toward the path of death; the other battles to guide and direct us toward the path of life.

We're in the middle of this war. Conscious or not, we'll inevitably end up choosing one side or the other. Eventually our time on Earth will end as well as the opportunity to choose a side. At that point, the decision-making will be closed, and our final destination will be revealed.

Secondly, the Sleeping Death represents dying to one's self. It's the process of becoming selfless rather than selfish as we follow Jesus. It's choosing to lay down our own will, our own lives, our own desires of the flesh, and our own dreams for God's as He cuts away, or circumcises our hearts.

Emergence

We're to surrender for the sake of the kingdom so that He can raise us up and reveal a new creation for the sake of His glory. He transforms our hearts so that we die to our self-agenda. We develop a willing heart to take up and carry our cross to follow Jesus's obedient example to carry out the Father's perfect plan to the finish.

Thirdly, it represents arising to life after death or at Jesus's second coming (the rapture). For those who choose the path of life, who choose Jesus to be their Lord and Savior, they will never die. They'll simply emerge from temporary sleep into eternal life.

Death is not our permanent future address. For all believers, the instant our eyes close here on Earth, they open in heaven, our eternal address.

This emergence is what I wish to reveal. I wish for eyes to be opened to the truth as we come into the light of His presence.

> *But all things become visible when they are exposed by the light [of God's precepts], for it is light that makes everything visible. For this reason He says, "Awake, sleeper, And arise from the dead, And Christ will shine [as dawn] upon you and give you light" (Ephesians 5:13–14 AMP).*

"Emergence" by Google's dictionary definition means the process of coming into view or becoming exposed after being concealed; the escape of an insect or other invertebrate from an egg, cocoon, pupal case, etc.; the process of coming into being or of becoming important or prominent. The Latin root of the word is *emergere*, which means to bring to light. The Greek word for emergence is *emfanisi*, meaning appearance. Synonyms include exposure, appearance, arrival, springing up, cropping up, blossoming, blooming, advent, birth, rise, development, dawn, coming.

The purposes of this book are to expose the enemy's lies and tactics used to conceal truth and light. It's to reveal God's plan and purpose to help us escape death and receive everlasting life so that we may come into being an eternal, prominent child of God. Thirdly, it's to uncover what's hidden and bring it into view (out of the darkness and into the light of life).

EMERGE!

Before a butterfly is revealed, it's concealed. It's first born from a butterfly egg and hatches as an ordinary caterpillar. Then it works to eat and grow until it can grow no further. Next, the caterpillar enters into its

The Sleeping Death

chrysalis (or cocoon), beginning the transformation process. From the outside, it appears as if nothing's happening, but on the inside, miraculous change is taking place. The old body parts, tissues, and organs are remarkably transforming into the new and beautiful parts of a butterfly. This incredible stage is called "metamorphosis."

Google dictionary defines *metamorphosis* as the process of transformation from an immature form to an adult form in two or more distinct stages; a change of the form or nature of a thing or person into a completely different one by natural or supernatural means. Synonyms include transformation, mutation, transmutation, change, alteration, conversion, modification, remodeling, and reconstruction.

Once metamorphosis is complete, it enters into the final stage of its cycle, becoming an adult butterfly. It has now finished forming and changing inside, thus the butterfly emerges from its chrysalis, revealing a new creation. The butterfly rests as it pumps blood into its new parts and wings in order to get them moving. The flapping begins, and the butterfly takes flight.

As believers, we undergo this same miraculous process of transformation as we choose to follow Jesus. First, we're created and formed in our mother's womb by God, and then we're born into this world of sin. We grow on our own until one day, we can grow no further. For some of us, we make the decision to be "born again" (become children of God) through salvation. From there, we allow God to transform us through His Spirit into who we were created to be as we trust Him to lead the way. We move and enter into our hidden place with God, bound, confined, and limited of our own ability and strength as we undergo spiritual metamorphosis. From the outside, it appears that nothing's happening, but on the inside, a supernatural change is miraculously taking place.

Our old parts are being stripped away, and we're being remodeled, reconstructed, purified, and cleansed. We're being developed, formed, and mutated as our hearts, minds, bodies, and souls are being made new by the power of the Holy Spirit living within us. We're growing up spiritually and emerging into mature Christians, portraying the heart and likeness of God and His nature.

When God is finished with His miraculous work in the hidden place of metamorphosis, we finally break free from the bondage and captivity of our sin, shame, guilt, regret, pain, and past. We're revealed, entering into a state of freedom.

Emergence

As His cleansing blood continuously pumps through our new organs, we learn to spread our wings, take flight, and soar into our destiny—our promised land. Having spent intimate, personal, and private time alone in the secret place of our hearts with our Creator, we now have discovered who He is personally to us (His identity), who we are personally to Him (our identity), and what specific purpose we were created for personally (our calling, our destiny).

God has and is performing this miraculous transformational work in my own life, and He wants to do so in yours. You too can emerge and soar into a life of freedom, rest, fulfillment, and purpose. You were created for this abundant life to love and to be loved by God. As children of light, you're shedding the old way of living and putting on the new, the true, and the beautiful nature of God and taking flight.

> *If in fact you have [really] heard Him and have been taught by Him, just as truth is in Jesus [revealed in His life and personified in Him], that, regarding your previous way of life, you put off your old self [completely discard your former nature], which is being corrupted through deceitful desires, and be continually renewed in the spirit of your mind [having a fresh, untarnished mental and spiritual attitude], and put on the new self [the regenerated and renewed nature], created in God's image, [godlike] in the righteousness and holiness of the truth [living in a way that expresses to God your gratitude for your salvation] (Ephesians 4:21–24 AMP).*

We have all bitten the apple, but just like Snow White, we don't have to remain sleeping forever. Emerge! Jesus made a way for us to awaken from the evil curse of death. He is the antidote that revives us from this poisonous fate with His kiss.

We can choose to receive true love's kiss from our Prince of Peace—Jesus. He is our first true love. His kiss is the kiss of life. He alone has the power to resurrect the dead. We don't have to lie asleep in our glass coffins like Snow White, waiting for our Prince to come revive us. He has already come to set us free from death, and one day soon, He'll come back to take us home. Therefore, all we have to do is ask and receive His kiss of life, and immediately we emerge out of the Sleeping Death into everlasting life.

The Sleeping Death

I recently watched the movie *The Secret Garden* with my youngest daughter.[19] It's a story of a young troubled girl who grew up angry and bitter because she was ignored and not shown love from her parents. Her parents died so she went to live with the only family she had left. Her uncle, the master of the home, was also grieving the loss of his wife, who was the twin sister of the girl's mother. Although she had been gone for years, he fell into a state of sickness and sadness from which he struggled to recover. As a result, he stayed away from his home. Once again, the young girl was neglected.

The once-gorgeous and vivacious castle estate where they lived was now a cold, unwelcoming place of grief and sorrow. The little girl discovered a key that led to the entrance of a secret garden that had become forbidden for anyone to enter. But the little girl and her friendly companion, a boy of one of the servant's, secretly snuck in and began to restore the garden to life. They worked the ground, extracting the weeds and planting seed after seed of different flower species.

One day, the little girl heard a lonely cry and discovered another secret within the castle walls—the master's ten-year-old son. He had been hidden away, bedridden and imprisoned within his dark chambers and held captive within his own home for his entire life.

Although he was the same age as the little girl, he had never gone outside in the sunlight. His windows were boarded shut, and few were permitted to enter his room. The boy and all who knew him, except this little girl, believed he was sick and dying, having inherited the sickness of his father.

The little girl and boy became friends. Over time, she exposed the truth to the boy, that he wasn't sick and dying. He was merely weak and had been fed a lie, concealing his true nature.

The little girl helped the boy to grow strong and escape the restraint of his boarded life. She exposed him to the light and shared her secret garden with him. The boy took his first steps in that garden and grew to really live, just like the seeds that were planted.

Like the little girl, the boy had also grown up feeling unloved and unwanted by his father, who was always away. He cried out for him to come back home one day and stay.

Miraculously, the father felt the cry of his son's heart and returned home to find him walking, playing, and fully alive in the secret garden. The two were reunited in love, and the little girl was also finally accepted and loved by the master as well.

Emergence

Together as a family, they came out of the secret garden healed and emerged beautifully from hiding. All saw the father and these newly-healed children walking, playing, living, and loving again. The once-forbidden secret garden was now made available to all. The terrible grief and sadness were lifted off the castle, and peace and joy returned to the land.

This inspiring story is true for God's children as well. We all have inherited pain, sickness, and death from our fallen parents, Adam and Eve. However, much like the little girl who came to the crying boy, Jesus hears our cries of bondage and comes to find us in our dark places. He becomes our friend and promises life to us if we're willing to leave the agonizing comfort of our boarded walls and make the decision to take a stand and follow Him into the light. He takes us on a journey outside the confinement that we've known so we can discover the hidden secrets He wants to reveal. We're invited to enter this sacred garden we were once forbidden from only because Jesus made a way for us. He is the key that unlocks the gate to the entrance of this glorious paradise. Without Him, no one may enter. Behind these walls lies accessibility to abundant and everlasting life beyond our wildest imagination. The secret garden is a sacred place where magic happens and miracles grow.

Living unloved produces a cold, hard, heart of bitterness, anger, and sorrow, but discovering this truth and the love of the friend we have in Jesus brings healing to our bodies, restoration to our souls, and eternal life to our spirits. Jesus sets us free from the lies of the enemy and the curses inherited through Adam and Eve.

Upon receiving this key, we unlock the mystery of truth, escape death, and enter into a new covenant of blessings, knowing we are wanted, provided for, and loved throughout eternity by our Heavenly Father. We emerge as He transforms us into who we were created to be. We take on His beautiful nature and rejoice in singing, dancing, laughing, playing, and planting while living in peace, having received the key to the secret garden. We no longer live alone in the dark shadow of fear and death. We walk in light, new life, and freedom.

Our bodies and our hearts are healed and cleansed of sickness and lies. We become a blessed people, not cursed. This is how our loving Father wishes to find His children when our Master returns for us.

We must learn to walk as children of light!

The Sleeping Death

Walk in Light

For you were once darkness, but now you are light in the Lord. Walk as children of light (for the fruit of the Spirit is in all goodness, righteousness, and truth), finding out what is acceptable to the Lord (Ephesians 5:8–10 NKJV).

I will sing for joy in God, explode in praise from deep in my soul! He dressed me up in a suit of salvation, he outfitted me in a robe of righteousness, As a bridegroom who puts on a tuxedo and a bride a jeweled tiara.

For as the earth bursts with spring wildflowers, and as a garden cascades with blossoms, So the Master, God, brings righteousness into full bloom and puts praise on display before the nations (Isaiah 61:10-11 MSG).

Just as the dark pupils of our eyes adjust and grow smaller in the presence of light, so does the darkness within us grow dimmer as the light shines brighter. God called for Adam in the Garden of Eden and invited him to come out of hiding, reveal what he had done, and bring it into the light so that He could cover both him and Eve. Now God is calling us to step into the light so that we may emerge out of darkness. He is calling us to become who we were created to be—His resurrected beings, His bride.

As God plants His seed of love within our hearts, we begin to emerge, blooming and sharing the fragrance and beauty of our secret garden with others.

Our Secret Garden

Once we've received His kiss of life and entered into our secret garden with God, He tends to us according to our individual needs as our Gardener. While we're still here on Earth, we enter into intimacy with Jesus and are constantly growing, maturing, and evolving into new life until we reach our final destination in heaven—our eternal paradise.

His plan for us here on Earth is to produce a beautiful garden inside of us, bringing forth tasteful fruit, vegetation, and shade for others to benefit from and direct attention to His marvelous creation. Like all gardens, specific measures must take place in order to encourage further germination. This garden is a place of incredible beauty and magic, but it must be worked in order to continuously and progressively thrive and flourish.

The ground must be cultivated in order to prepare for the seed by loosening and breaking up the hard, dry soil. Fertilization must take place to enrich the soil with the nutrients it can't receive on its own. Pruning and cutting must take place to encourage further growth and development by cutting back and eliminating unwanted or spent substances. Of course, there is the cyclic seasons of sowing new seeds and reaping of harvests.

In our lives, these drastic or laborious measures don't always feel good or appear to be good for us based upon our own judgment. However, we're incapable of fully seeing or knowing God's intention, plan, or purpose behind it all. Just like the manure or fertilization process, we may encounter seasons of life that really stink, but God knows what these toxic elements will accomplish in our lives. Therefore, He allows it to run its course. He's *always* at work for our good, even when we don't perceive it to be good.

In the movie *The Shack,* Mackenzie, a man who experiences great sorrow and loss, sets a great example of how God can take a terrible situation and bring forth fruitful work.[20] Mackenzie's faith is tested as he experiences a parent's worst nightmare. He suffers incredible pain due to the tragic kidnapping and murder of his young daughter. Will he also lose sight of God in the midst of losing his child?

Don't allow yourself to lose sight of who God really is in the midst of horrific circumstances. Remember, God loves you, and He's at work on your behalf. Trust that He alone is Judge. He alone is God, and He is good. Look to Him to gain wisdom, knowledge, understanding, and discernment.

Later on in the movie, Mackenzie struggles to make sense of his world. He must choose whether or not he'll believe that God is good even in a world where bad things happen to the good and even the innocent.

In a special scene, Sarayu (a woman representing the Holy Spirit) befriends Mackenzie and takes him into a garden overflowing with gorgeous plant life and flowers. They begin digging up the ground, taking out the old in order to plant something new. As the two begin whacking, ripping, and extracting the roots from the soil, Mackenzie

The Sleeping Death

runs across a dangerous plant element. Sarayu warns him to be careful because the root is poisonous. Mackenzie is confused; he doesn't understand why it would be there if it's dangerous.

Sarayu explains in a way that suggests not all we perceive to be bad is bad, and not all we perceive to be good is good. Some poisons carry magnificent healing attributes if combined with other proper elements, for instance, the sweet nectar of a flower.

The point that I believe Holy Spirit is trying to make in this scenario, is we were not meant to discern good and evil on our own. Our opinions are not always truth. Only God is able to truly judge what is good and evil. That's why we have to look to God for wisdom rather than "play God." When we presume to have complete understanding of right and wrong, we insist on playing God in our own lives as well as in the lives of others. Often, our idea of what's good disagrees with another's idea of evil. The result is war, strife, and conflict. Arguments break loose because every man insists on being right and playing the role of God in the lives of other men.

When I was a child growing up on our farm, my older sister (the Guardian) and I had an argument one day. I'm sure we were disagreeing about who was right and who was wrong (as was the cause of most of our arguments). She became so frustrated that in her anger, she reached down and picked up a dry piece of cow manure used for fertilizing our crops and threw it at me. The dry, hard, and stinky manure hit me right in the face. Although funny now, in the moment, getting slapped in the face with that manure hurt a lot (and stunk a lot), but it hurt my heart even more. I couldn't believe she would do something like that to me. That was just wrong in my opinion! After all, we were siblings who really did love one another. We were just having a disagreement where both insisted on being right.

Anger tends to cause us to say and do stupid things that can harm ourselves and others. However, our actions and behaviors don't necessarily represent how we truly feel toward one another in our hearts. My sister had a loving, godly heart despite her temporary outburst.

God gives us the emotion of anger, but sin is an ungodly reaction to that emotion that is encouraged by evil to cause harm. Anger in itself is not a sin; it's the evil action that anger evokes that's sin. Likewise, evoking others to sin is engaging in sinful behavior ourselves. Neither my sister nor myself was considered guiltless in this scenario.

Emergence

Anger is an extremely dangerous element because it doesn't bring about the righteous life that God desires (as is explained in James 1:19–27). Therefore, be careful! Don't act on anger or tempt others to lash out because of it. Instead, get rid of that toxic behavior. Anger is like a gateway drug. It potentially can lead to worse things like retaliation, false allegations, wrongful accusations, slander, malice, manipulation, hate, judgment, unforgiveness, bitterness, sickness, and other evil behavior, including death if not handled properly.

Anger has the potential to poison you and others. Therefore, don't attempt to handle it on your own. Let God handle it. Allow Him to take your anger (or other toxic element) and combine it with the nectar of His beautiful nature. Then watch Him take that very poisonous root placed in your life to bring about the necessary healing in your heart.

Most likely, we've all been in circumstances like these where anger got the best of us, tempers flared, and we reacted in an ungodly manner because others failed to see things our way. Arguments ensued, wars broke out, and people were hurt because we all insisted on being right (or playing God).

The truth is that we as believers are all God's children. Within His family, sibling rivalry exists as long as we're on Earth. Sometimes siblings fight and argue (even God's precious little children, hard to believe, right?). Sometimes we hurt one another due to unresolved root issues in our hearts such as betrayal, rejection, jealousy, envy, pride, bitterness, misunderstandings, and differences in opinions or past or recurring offenses, etc. Sometimes we're able to work things out on our own, and sometimes we can't. When we can't, and in the same manner we ran to our parents as children, we need to run to our Heavenly Father for instruction *before* lashing out in anger. Our Father will always instruct us to love and forgive, and this we *must* do.

However, forgiving and choosing to love our brothers and sisters in Christ doesn't mean we still have to play together. Notice I didn't specify "play nicely" or "play dirty." I simply specified playing in general, meaning *associate with*. Sometimes it's necessary to separate or cut off the relationship from those we can't see eye to eye with in order for our own good and His will. If relationships cause us to *continually* sin out of anger, or anything else ungodly, then these unhealthy relationships must either be cut off or kept at a safe distance until God heals

The Sleeping Death

or changes our hearts. It doesn't mean that love and forgiveness isn't present. It just means you're taking a "time out" from the relationship in the heat of circumstances so that you can cool down.

These time-outs can be either temporary or permanent depending on the severity of the situation and the willingness of those involved to come to terms and respond in accordance with God's will. Meanwhile, God's at work in all our hearts, so we should use our tongues wisely to pray for those who offend or persecute us, and we should bless them, not curse them (Mathew 5:44).

Although we may choose to make the decision to obey our Father, our brothers and sisters may not choose to do the same (or at least at the same time we did). They may also not receive our forgiveness or even believe our sincerity. However, that's not on us. We can't control or force others' behaviors or actions. That's for our Father God to address. We must surrender these people into His hands, not attempt to force them with our own hands. We can, however, ensure that we're in right standing with God, despite what others choose to think, feel, say, or do about it.

Unhealthy ties and relationships with people with whom you don't share fundamental beliefs and morals or who lack godly wisdom hold you back from becoming the person you were created to be and walking in the way you were intended to go. They sicken the health and growth of your spiritual heart (secret garden) just like a dead or sick branch would affect a tree, preventing fruit-bearing.

Sin is a stumbling block. If relationships turn unhealthy by tempting you to trip up or fall into sin, then they must be removed from your path in order to keep you moving forward and growing upward. With my sister and me, we still shared these fundamentals and were able to work it out after just a short cool down and time-out from one another. We quickly came to terms, apologized for our foolish behavior, and recognized that we wished no real harm to the other. Both of us agreed to love and forgive. We simply had a brief misunderstanding that got out of hand, but we quickly got over it.

Trust and grace were still present in the relationship as well as humility and remorse. That short time-out allowed us time to reflect on our behaviors, remember our true feelings, respond in accordance with God's will, and remain in His vine. These are crucial components to a healthy relationship as wisdom warns us that pride comes before destruction.

Pride goes before destruction, and a haughty spirit before a fall (Proverbs 16:18 ESV).

However, when these components can't be established in the relationship, it's better for all involved to cut ties, at least until God tells you otherwise, so as not invite the temptation to sin. You've probably heard these words at some point in your life, or maybe you've even spoken them to your own children in the heat of an argument, "Okay, okay, that's enough, *break it up, cut it out,* and both of you go to your rooms (or separate corners)." God tends to His children in the same manner.

Temptations to Sin

"Whoever causes one of these little ones who believe in me to sin, it would be better for him if a great millstone were hung around his neck and he were thrown into the sea. And if your hand causes you to sin, cut it off. It is better for you to enter life crippled than with two hands to go to hell, to the unquenchable fire (Mark 9:42–43 ESV).

When I was sued for custody of my daughter, I felt much like I did as a child when that dirty piece of manure slapped me in the face. It really hurt, and my heart was deeply bruised. This time, not only was it thrown at me, but it felt like someone had dumped manure all around me. Life stunk not just in that moment, but for quite some time.

In my agony, I struggled to understand how others could do something like that and how God could allow it to happen. It felt so wrong! How could any good come from this anguish? I was losing sight of the Bible's promises that assured God was for me and working all things for my good (Romans 8:28). I was fighting to hold on to God and fighting to see beyond my pain.

My faith and trust in His goodness was tested throughout that brutal winter season (trial) as I struggled to remain in Him. The enemy fought to tempt me to separate myself from God. His lies suggested God was against me and inflicting His wrath upon me because of something I did or didn't do. He tried to get me to walk away from the life-giving vine.

However, I resisted the enemy and ran to my Daddy, my Father in heaven, who gradually helped me press through my pain. As He lovingly wiped away my tears, I began to see truth, and God began to

The Sleeping Death

enlighten me by giving me His understanding, wisdom, knowledge, and discernment in the midst of confusion and chaos.

I discovered that just because God allowed it to happen, doesn't mean that He caused it to happen. God's not responsible for man's every action, and people are not His puppets. Man is given free will and the ability to choose and make decisions for themselves. Oftentimes, man's choices hurt people. God doesn't wish to hurt us. His wrath was poured out on Jesus so that instead, we could receive His grace, forgiveness, and love.

However, God can take man's actions and turn them around for good. I came to know that God *allowed* this to occur because He knew what it would produce. Therefore, who caused it—whether God or man—really wasn't important. What mattered was the result. Either way, God saw beyond the temporary stench and into the flourishing fruit garden that would come to thrive due to the harsh conditions and elements that had been applied to it. I came to know and trust that despite how bad it stunk and how painful it felt, God produces goodness through it all because He's good and works for the good of those who love Him.

Those harsh conditions were the fertilizer I needed to encourage further spiritual growth and development in my relationship with God and with others. These toxic elements forced me to deepen my roots. They allowed God to extract and cut away the poison of unwanted or spent substances that threatened the new growth. This step of spiritual gardening, along with my communion and reliance on God, allowed for His sweet nectar to produce incredible healing properties in the soil of many hearts—mine, my daughter's, and others—who would come to hear the incredible story of what God had accomplished.

Although the circumstances were unpleasant, the end result was awe-inspiring. It made no sense to me at the time, but it made sense to God. He knew that through it all, I would further mature, the shade of my tree would increase, and I would bear tasteful fruit of love, forgiveness, humility, grace, and peace to be extended to others who would receive it (Psalm 1).

God used that season of anguish to cut out unhealthy ties to my past that needed to be omitted and replaced them with new and healthy relationships so my garden could flourish and thrive in accordance with His perfect will. He used it all to create a beautiful testimony through me.

God's prophetic promise to me remained as I remained in Him: "You are like this tree. The wind is going to come. The tree is going to sway. You may lose some leaves but stay rooted in Me, and new fruit will come. You will not be swept away."

From the Shadows to the Substance

My counsel for you is simple and straightforward: Just go ahead with what you've been given. You received Christ Jesus, the Master; now live him. You're deeply rooted in him. You're well constructed upon him. You know your way around the faith. Now do what you've been taught. School's out; quit studying the subject and start living it! And let your living spill over into thanksgiving.

Watch out for people who try to dazzle you with big words and intellectual double-talk. They want to drag you off into endless arguments that never amount to anything. They spread their ideas through the empty traditions of human beings and the empty superstitions of spirit beings. But that's not the way of Christ. Everything of God gets expressed in him, so you can see and hear him clearly. You don't need a telescope, a microscope, or a horoscope to realize the fullness of Christ, and the emptiness of the universe without him. When you come to him, that fullness comes together for you, too. His power extends over everything (Colossians 2:7–10 MSG).

Separation is never easy. But never allow the pain of this life to separate you from God who is life. Remain in Him no matter what or who comes up against you. God is good, and He is for you.

"I am the true vine, and my Father is the gardener. He cuts off every branch in me that bears no fruit, while every branch that does bear fruit he prunes so that it will be even more fruitful (John 15:1–2 NIV).

God is always *at work* in our lives to further encourage us to flourish so that others may come to see, taste, and know His sweet goodness and beauty.

The Sleeping Death

Allow Him to be your gardener and plant His seed of love in the garden of your heart so that you too may flourish and thrive beautifully as His lovely creation.

During that season of life, I wrote the following poem titled "The Seed of Love."

The Seed of Love
Mistie House

We are the relinquished fertile soil in which God uses to place HIS seed of Love.

He blesses the soil, and the seed begins to sprout and grow into a discerning bud.

He blesses the bud, and it continues to transform and bloom into a beautiful rose of velvety, soft petals and rich, vibrant hues.

He blesses the rose, and it releases a sweet, fragrant aroma that is perfectly perfumed and most pleasing to Him.

All who encounter this delectable fragrance hunger to draw nearer, for they have gotten but a taste of the exquisitely perfected aroma of God's love.

However, the soil that is reluctant and yet unfertile will reject the seed.

Until ripened, it will not see the celestial blessing of growth nor of maturity.

Thus, the fruitless soil will inevitably withhold the enticingly, sweet aroma that has yet to ensue, instead leaving only a field of weeds which scatter and take root in whichever direction the fickle wind blows.

When others hurt you, take the offense, take the accusations, take the assumptions, take the condemnation, take whatever has been thrown at you and take it to God. Ask Him how to respond; don't retaliate. We don't want to pick up the dirty pieces and start a poo-slinging contest.

Emergence

This is the response the enemy is hoping for, to create a real poop storm. God expects more from His children. According to the Google dictionary, the word "poop" has a noun form in nautical terms that refer to the highest deck or stern of ships (you've probably heard of a "poop deck"). The verb form means to be overwhelmed by a wave from behind, often with catastrophic consequences, (of a wave) to break over the stern of (a ship), to take (seas) over the stern. To "poop out" means to cease from or fail in something, as from fear or exhaustion, to break down; stop functioning.

The enemy would like nothing more than for our weakened vessels to become capsized in the midst of an unexpected poop storm due to extreme physical, mental, emotional, and spiritual fatigue and exhaustion. He wants us to pick up and take on the battle in our own hands and strength rather than surrender it to God so that we will prematurely give in, eventually give up, and ultimately give out.

Earlier in chapter ten, I made the statement, "Your response to attack determines the outcome of your victory." When we respond according to God's will rather than retaliate according to our flesh and emotions, we find healing and freedom from our pain. Don't pick up the stone or piece of poo—that's dirty business. Instead, turn the other cheek, and lay down the stone. Surrender! Forgive, pray, humble yourself, and ask forgiveness for your own doing, and turn to God for justice.

This doesn't mean you have to stand for abuse. It simply means that you take a seat to revenge. Walk in the way of love, light, and righteousness in which God would have you move. He is the Father to all His children. We are all to share a common commitment to serve and honor Jesus and the gospel. When we recognize this truth, it enables us to act in peace, not anger and strife.

Even if others don't yet recognize this truth, we can do our part to humble ourselves and obey His commands. Let God do His part in cleansing and purifying His children's hearts through His refining fire.

We're to be salt and light. Salt represents our allegiance to Jesus as His disciples and the purity and sincerity of our hearts used to preserve the gospel. Light represents Jesus living in us and is what draws others to Him through us. As salt and light, Christians are to preserve the peace and shine the light. Remember, He loves us all, and He wants

The Sleeping Death

us to love and forgive all our brothers and sisters in Christ, even when they say or do the unthinkable. Some instances might even require us to forgive God for allowing what we perceive as the unthinkable to occur.

"Everyone will be made cleaner and stronger with fire. Salt is good. But if salt loses its taste, how can it be made to taste like salt again? Have salt in yourselves and be at peace with each other" (Mark 9:49–50 NLV).

PRAYER

Father,

Awaken my spirit with true love's kiss. Arouse me to be consciously aware of the supernatural forces and spiritual war at work around me. Help me to die to self so that You may raise me up as a whole and new creation. Transform me in the hidden place so I may *emerge* into who You created me to be. Help me to soar into my destiny and walk as a child of light. I declare I am an overcomer because You overcame all on my behalf. Tend to my secret garden. Plant Your seed of love deep into the soil of my heart and make my life flourish in accordance with Your will. Forgive me when I play god in the lives of others and help me also to be quick to forgive, looking to You for justice and healing, rather than seeking revenge or retaliation. In You I am the righteousness of Christ and I am victorious as I walk in Your power, Your love, and Your light.

In Jesus' Name. Amen.

CHAPTER EIGHTEEN

The One, The Only

Oh, how our darling Snow White needed the gift of discernment when the Evil Queen came knocking on the door of her wide-open heart. Snow White's innocence and kindness made her naïve to wickedness. After her rendezvous in the forest with the huntsman, one would think she would have learned to guard her heart, which was the one thing the queen longed for most.

Snow White desperately needed the ability to see the evil behind the old hag's disguise. Failure to discern truth from lies led Snow White to take a bite of the poisoned apple and fall into the Sleeping Death. Her poor judgment of good, of evil, and of character caused her to taste death on her breath as her heart stilled and her blood congealed.

> *Above all else, watch over your heart; diligently guard it because from a sincere and pure heart come the good and noble things of life (Proverbs 4:23 VOICE).*

The most common word for "heart" in the Hebrew dictionary is the word *levav*. The heart is the center of our thoughts, our will, our affections, and our discernment.

Emergence

Satan is called "the father of lies" and the "accuser of the brethren." When we go to bed in anger against another, we give the deceiver a foothold (an open door) to step inside and begin whispering lies through his disguise and accusations toward those with whom we're angry. His poison quickly seeps into our hearts as we ingest his wormy apples. When we wake from our slumber, our mind is contaminated with rotten reason and our actions with diseased deeds because of his lies and accusations we allowed to enter.

Out of the overflow of the heart the mouth speaks forth fruit—both good and evil. It all depends on what's made its way into the heart.

> *"You don't get wormy apples off a healthy tree, nor good apples off a diseased tree. The health of the apple tells the health of the tree. You must begin with your own life-giving lives. It's who you are, not what you say and do, that counts. Your true being brims over into true words and deeds (Luke 6:45 MSG).*

This is one reason why quickly forgiving is so important. It safeguards our hearts against the enemy's poison. We must forgive others, pray blessings over them, and ask the Holy Spirit to lead us into all truth concerning them to ensure we haven't been deceived. We must also pray for those who've been deceived about us to be led into the same truth by the power of the Holy Spirit.

> *Then I heard a loud voice shouting across the heavens, "It has come at last—salvation and power and the Kingdom of our God, and the authority of his Christ. For the accuser of our brothers and sisters has been thrown down to earth—the one who accuses them before our God day and night (Revelation 12:10 NLT).*

> *Therefore each of you must put off falsehood and speak truthfully to your neighbor, for we are all members of one body. "In your anger do not sin": Do not let the sun go down while you are still angry, and do not give the devil a foothold (Ephesians 4:25–27 NIV).*

It's also unwise and foolish to make assumptions about others regarding their heart's true nature or their standing with God without

The One, The Only

having a close or personal relationship in the present. It's especially unwise when assumptions are foolishly made through the indirect opinions of others, gossip, or hearsay. God alone sees and knows all, and He can change and turn hearts at any moment.

Therefore, we should pray to ask God for discernment. In Christian context, the Google dictionary defines "discernment" as perception in the absence of judgment with a view to obtaining spiritual direction and understanding. Discernment helps us not only to see others through God's eyes but also to see through the deceiver's lies and disguise. It helps us to perceive truth instead of relying on our own limited vision.

I often pray this prayer when dealing with confrontational relationships: "Lord, give me your heart for this person. Help me to see them through your eyes, and lead me and them into all truth."

The only assumption that's safe for us to make is that we're not capable of seeing, knowing, or understanding the complete picture. Because we live in a fallen world, none of us are immune to pain, sin, or deception. We're unable to fully trace the origin of sin and brokenness in one's life or to fully discern good from evil; therefore, we're clearly unfit to justify one's motives and behaviors.

How can we judge another when we ourselves are not without sin? God is the only perfect Judge.

His judgment seat was made to sit and fit One.

> *However, when they persisted in questioning Him, He straightened up and said, "He who is without [any] sin among you, let him be the first to throw a stone at her" (John 8:7 AMP).*

When we judge others, we risk His judgment falling back on us. We should be careful not to have to face those consequences. It's likely that all of us have been found guilty of this offense, having at some point in our lives been both the accuser and the accused.

If you're feeling a slight conviction in your heart upon hearing these words, note that you're not alone. I know this feeling well as do many others, so I'm certainly not passing judgment and trying to make you feel guilty or shameful.

As you've read by now, I've made many mistakes in the past and continue to receive the gentle conviction with correction of our loving Father in the present. All His children do. But I'm no longer ashamed.

Emergence

I no longer hide in the shadows and attempt to cover them on my own through my own good deeds hoping to justify or erase my evil ones. Now I openly share how God has covered my sins and shame and has used my failures as an opportunity to take what I have learned and offer it to others for their own liberation. Never would I have imagined that out of my deepest sorrow and regrets such wild beauty would be fashioned and formed through the telling of my testimony. He is the One and the only responsible for covering my sin and shame.

Adam and Eve attempted to cover their shame in fig leaves, but God took the life of an innocent animal in order to fashion a new covering for their naked form. Jesus is the Lamb that was slain to cover and remove sin for us all. Now the only real shame would be refusing to accept His covering for yours.

> *Blessed is the one whose transgressions are forgiven, whose sins are covered. Blessed is the one whose sin the* LORD DOES NOT COUNT AGAINST THEM *and in whose spirit is no deceit (Psalm 32:1–2 NIV).*

Remember that God disciplines those He loves in order to correct our behavior, not to condemn us for it. He expects us to make mistakes, but He also expects us to learn from them and then take what we've learned and use it to help others. I encourage you to allow the Holy Spirit to administer His gentle correction. At the same time, I urge you to not allow Satan to administer his harsh condemnation.

Remember, there is no condemnation for those who are in Christ Jesus (Romans 8:1). God loves us even when we say or do the unthinkable. He's already aware of all of our sins, and He already has them covered, every one—for everyone. All we have to do is receive His love and salvation and we are forgiven. That's good news! We have a Father who is a merciful Judge and has given us as Christians a not-guilty verdict and the sentence of eternal life. As a friendly reminder for all of God's children, justice is our Father's business, not ours.

> *"Do not judge, or you too will be judged. For in the same way you judge others, you will be judged, and with the measure you use, it will be measured to you (Matthew 7:1–2 NIV).*

The One, The Only

Just as we should allow God to plant His seed of love and tend to our gardens, we should spread the seed of love but allow God to tend to the gardens of others.

We are not the gardener. He is, and He will tend to us all as He sees fit.

One Gardener

When my daughter was struggling, I tried my best to intervene and encourage her to bear good fruit in her secret garden. I went to work on her behalf, tossing good seed everywhere I could, hoping and praying that it would take root and grow and produce an abundant harvest of blessings in her life. My plan was to extract the harmful weeds of the enemy and sow good seeds of the Lord into her heart.

I labored endlessly, yet my exhausted efforts seemed worthless at the time. Out of my desperation to see wholesome fruits of the spirit emerge fully and instantly in her life again, I continued to throw down even more seed, over-seeding. There is nothing wrong with working to sow good seed and extract harmful weeds, and I didn't think anything was wrong with my plan.

But there was—I wasn't the Gardener. I couldn't see it until God gave me the spiritual vision and discernment to see, nor could I fix it.

It wasn't solely that she lacked good seed in her life. There was good seed mixed with bad. However, seed takes time to grow, and the disruptive weeds were choking the life from the good seed leading to a lack of spiritual maturity. Also, the soil of her heart had become hardened and wasn't ripe and fertile. Therefore, despite all of my efforts to inject goodness and extract evil, I couldn't force-feed her depleted soil. Only God could work to turn and prepare the soil for new growth. Only God could bring forth new life in His own timing and in His own plan.

Therefore, I surrendered my daughter to God, the True Gardener, and asked Him to go to work at changing her desires and turning her back to Him. I asked God to prepare and soften the hard soil of her heart with His tools by ploughing (turning the soil over) and watering the ground in ways I couldn't.

Her heart was in a season of drought. The more I had tried to give, the more she rejected my offers because of the amount of foot traffic (opposing voices to God's) trampling the ground, resulting in hard, compact soil. This dry soil enabled the birds of the air (the enemy) to come and snatch the seed away before it had a chance to take root.

Emergence

In turn, she had grown angry with me because I failed to see things from her point of view and respond according to her wishes. Anger turned to unforgiveness, unforgiveness to deception, deception to bitterness, bitterness to resentment, resentment to disrespect, disrespect to unbelief, and ultimately unbelief turned to acts of rebellion. This carried on until her heart hardened, not just toward me, but toward the truth of God's Word.

I'll never forget what my teenage daughter wrote on the chalkboard hanging on her bedroom wall after she came home from her dad's one weekend "Your opinion is invalid."

I believe she had written my husband and I off as far as our voice was concerned. In an act of rebellion, she had written these words on her angry and confused heart. She wanted to voice her own opinion and let me know where she stood, as if I didn't already know through the fruit of her rotten behavior.

See how the danger in anger often leads to sin and plays out devastatingly for all of us, giving the enemy a foothold, and turning us against one another, even those we love deeply. Sin robs us from an abundant, righteous life and blessings.

I began to pray that God would silence the lies (choke the weeds—the manipulative and deceptive voice of the disguised enemy that was turning her away). I asked Him to open my daughter's ears to hear, eyes to see, and heart to know and understand so that she could receive the seed of life and healing for her calloused heart and thirsty soul. I pleaded for the Holy Spirit to lead her into all truth and give her spiritual discernment to recognize the real enemy feeding her lies and false allegations. For a time, I couldn't understand why I couldn't get through to her and why the good seed I was throwing down was not producing good fruit.

The Meaning of the Harvest Story

"Study this story of the farmer planting seed. When anyone hears news of the kingdom and doesn't take it in, it just remains on the surface, and so the Evil One comes along and plucks it right out of that person's heart. This is the seed the farmer scatters on the road.

The One, The Only

> *"The seed cast in the gravel—this is the person who hears and instantly responds with enthusiasm. But there is no soil of character, and so when the emotions wear off and some difficulty arrives, there is nothing to show for it.*
>
> *"The seed cast in the weeds is the person who hears the kingdom news, but weeds of worry and illusions about getting more and wanting everything under the sun strangle what was heard, and nothing comes of it.*
>
> *"The seed cast on good earth is the person who hears and takes in the News, and then produces a harvest beyond his wildest dreams"* (Matthew 13:18–23 MSG).

Today I understand the reason I couldn't get through to her is because I'm not the gardener of her life. God is. Some secret gardens grow sick at times because of what or who they allow to come into their hearts. Only the Gardener has the right tools and the perfect plan to heal. He alone carries the key to turn hearts.

When I finally turned my daughter's heart over to Him, He turned her heart back to me. As I went to work praying and stopped forcing, she eventually opened back up to me. God overturned the rotten lies and distorted desires that had been planted within her. He healed her sick heart. He healed mine too as I crawled up onto His lap, followed His instructions, and allowed Him to hold me and carry me through this difficult season while I wept and waited.

When circumstances didn't go my way and I didn't get what I wanted, I could have thrown a fit and lashed out in rebellion toward God. I could have written those same words on my heart toward Him because circumstances seemed unfair. But I didn't. Even though in my past I too chose to behave this way over some circumstances, this time around, I chose not to. I trusted Him and believed that He was good and able to work all things out according to His perfect and just will.

"Your opinion is invalid" is a paraphrase of what we say every time we immaturely and rebelliously act out and play God ourselves. Isn't this what Adam and Eve ultimately said to God when they rebelled? Can you see the danger in this and how it opens us up to the enemy? They let down the spiritual guard of their heart and the enemy slithered in.

Emergence

Don't let anger, frustration, heartache, and disappointment turn you toward rebellion against God. In my season of despair, the enemy whispered lies into my ear. But I made the decision to rebuke them and turn even deeper to the Word of God for truth and discernment amidst total confusion. Rather than giving the enemy a foothold, I safeguarded my heart. As a result, my relationship with my Father grew rather than diminished.

At times, nothing will make sense, and everything will appear to be turned upside down. I won't always understand what is happening in my garden or in the garden of those I love. Some seasons of life will really stink, cause us pain, and feel so wrong. But today, I do understand that God is good regardless of how we feel.

There are times when our opinions are invalid to His purpose. What feels good to us may be evil, and what feels evil to us may actually be good. We just can't see the future goodness beyond the stench and pain in the present.

I may not be assuredly confident in my ability to discern good and evil, but I am confident in His. God is never wrong or evil, and I trust His good judgment with all of my heart.

The Lord's justice will prevail. Evil may win some battles here on Earth, but good has already won the war.

Our good Father will never turn His back on His righteous children, and He will repay evil with what evil is owed.

> *The Eternal One will never leave you; He will lead you in the way that you should go. When you feel dried up and worthless, God will nourish you and give you strength. And you will grow like a garden lovingly tended; you will be like a spring whose water never runs out (Isaiah 58:11 VOICE).*

When we run to our Daddy when wars break out, when we seek His wise counsel when put on trial, when we obey His command to forgive, love, and pray for our brothers and sisters even when they say or do the unthinkable, when we believe our God is good in the midst of our pain, when we seek after wisdom in the midst of confusion, when we trust our Judge is merciful and just in the midst of accusation, when we surrender absolute control to our Gardener when gardens grow sick, and when we remain in His vine when the enemy tempts us to turn away, we can expect a complete turnaround and full harvest of blessings in due season. Open up your eyes, your ears, and the soil of your hearts to God, and watch what seems dead spring to life as His love is planted.

My child, pay attention to what I say. Listen carefully to my words. Don't lose sight of them. Let them penetrate deep into your heart, for they bring life to those who find them, and healing to their whole body.

Guard your heart above all else, for it determines the course of your life. Avoid all perverse talk; stay away from corrupt speech.

Look straight ahead, and fix your eyes on what lies before you. Mark out a straight path for your feet; stay on the safe path.

Don't get sidetracked; keep your feet from following evil (Proverbs 4:20–27 NLT).

I hope by now you have picked up on a recurring pattern that seems to unfold every time we attempt to play God in the secret garden of our lives or in the lives of others. Our actions and behaviors interfere with God's good work and perfect plan, resulting in a sick garden and the production of a poor crop whether our intentions are good in our opinion or not.

But when we lay down and let God be God, circumstances begin to turn around as our hearts turn over to Him. Our secret gardens are miraculously healed. Only God knows what's truly good and best for us all. His opinion is absolutely valid. Only He has the ability to rightly discern good and evil. Therefore, we do best when we get out of the Gardener's way and allow Him to work His magic. God is the One and the only who is—good at being God.

One Lord

Throughout the time of grieving loss and separation, God was tending to my own garden. He strategically placed people in my life to engage and invite me into opportunities of new growth and personal development.

A small group leader from my church invited me to attend a women's Bible study she and another woman from our church led weekly at her home. Trying something new was outside my comfort zone at the time. I didn't know if I had the strength required. Regardless, I made the decision to not allow fear to keep me from walking through a door God had opened, but to trust Him to provide the strength and press forward into the journey ahead.

That decision to step out in faith paid off. Not only did God use that study to strengthen me, pour back into me, and establish beautiful encouraging friendships with like-minded believers, but He also equipped, prepared, and opened an unexpected door of opportunity that positioned me to become a small group leader. Now I'm pouring back into other women what was poured into me.

In the movie *The Lord of the Rings: The Fellowship of the Ring*, Sam and Frodo, best friends who happen to be hobbits, find themselves on a path far from home.[21] As they step onto an unfamiliar road, they remember the wise teachings of Bilbo, Frodo's uncle. They're reminded that stepping out their door can be dangerous business. That's why Bilbo cautions them that it's important to keep your footing along the path you travel. Otherwise there is no way of knowing where you could be swept off to.

This movie series is my all-time favorite. I love the battle between good and evil. I'm enamored at how the movie captures the dealings with fear, pain, sorrow, and despair, but at the same time, centers on the beauty of hope, perseverance, loyalty, friendship, fellowship, goodness, triumph, and love.

Leaving the security of what you've known to step into the unknown can be scary, but there is no greater destination than discovering the love of Jesus. Taking the step to follow Jesus promises to lead us to our true home; that's a certainty we can count on. He is the One Lord that rules over all, but unlike the evil, dark lord from *The Lord of the Rings*, God is love. He doesn't force us to follow Him, but He sets us free as we do. He doesn't seek to kill and destroy as He reigns over all; He seeks to give life to all who choose to bow down before Him.

Our enemy knows this and wants to do everything in his power to prevent us from taking that next step toward love and light. He promises us false hope and power and threatens us with fear to hold us back and keep us on the path of darkness.

In the above movie, the great Rings were forged in fire promising power and strength to govern each race of men, hobbits, elves, and

The One, The Only

dwarfs. Yet each Ring-bearer was unfortunately deceived. There was another Ring forged in secret to rule them, to find them, and to bind them. It was the weapon created by the enemy to control all inhabitants throughout the land. One by one, each race fell into darkness. The only hope was to set aside differences and unite as one people to destroy this one Ring in the fires from which it was created. Only then would good triumph over evil, restoring life and freedom.

Our enemy uses this same weapon—deception fashioned in fear—to control us. It's his ultimate source of power. One by one, he tries to seduce us into believing that his road is better, leading to knowledge and power.

In the movie, each creature who sought to oppose this evil force was faced with passing the test—would they give in to temptation and submit to the evil lord who brings only darkness, or would they resist its power and continue on their journey to destroy it?

Each of us must also face this test. Will we submit to the world, choosing to be the lord over our own lives, or will we choose to submit to the one Lord who *is* Lord over all? Will we resist the temptation of our enemy Satan to go our own way and give into fear, or will we lay down our lives, unite as one people from every tribe, tongue, and nation under God, and follow His ways in order to oppose the evil darkness in our world? Each of us must make this choice for ourselves.

> *"And to Him (the Messiah) was given dominion (supreme authority), Glory and a kingdom, that all the peoples, nations, and speakers of every language should serve and worship Him. His dominion is an everlasting dominion which will not pass away; And His kingdom is one which will not be destroyed (Daniel 7:14 AMP).*

As we step onto the road of our lives, choosing this one critical step will determine whether or not we'll keep our footing or if we will be swept away. Fortunately for us, we do know where the wrong step sweeps us off to. The Bible tells us clearly that one road leads to salvation, and one road leads to damnation. There is only one path to everlasting life, and that is through Jesus Christ, our One Lord.

He won't use His power to force us to choose Him or to carry out His good will. Instead, He uses His love, grace, and mercy to capture our hearts and guide us.

Emergence

Our Father in heaven loves us so much that He didn't leave us to wander in darkness. He created one road for us to follow. Jesus *is* the road that lights the way out of darkness. He is the golden road to follow.

Jesus Is Our:
One Lord that rules us all,
One Lord that seeks to find us,
One Lord to bring us all out of the
darkness and bind us.

Therefore God also has highly exalted Him and given Him the name which is above every name, that at the name of Jesus every knee should bow, of those in heaven, and of those on earth, and of those under the earth, and that every tongue should confess that Jesus Christ is Lord, to the glory of God the Father (Philippians 2:9–11 NKJV).

But for us, There is one God, the Father, by whom all things were created, and for whom we live. And there is one Lord, Jesus Christ, through whom all things were created, and through whom we live (1 Corinthians 8:6 NLT).

The ring of covenant is the one ring Christ followers share that binds us to Jesus, forged in the fire of His love out of blood. Our One Lord is the only One who can lead us out of darkness and into everlasting glory.

One Way

In the movie *The Wizard of Oz,* Dorothy and her friendly fellowship of helpful companions must follow a yellow brick road. It would lead the way to the Emerald City so that she might find her way home.[22] In the same way, we must choose to "follow the golden road," the One that lights the way to the Holy City, the New Jerusalem, if we want to find our eternal home.

The New Jerusalem, the Bride of the Lamb

One of the seven angels who had the seven bowls full of the seven last plagues came and said to me, "Come, I will show you the bride, the wife of the Lamb." And he carried me away

The One, The Only

in the Spirit to a mountain great and high, and showed me the Holy City, Jerusalem, coming down out of heaven from God. It shone with the glory of God, and its brilliance was like that of a very precious jewel, like a jasper, clear as crystal (Revelation 21:9–11 NIV).

The twelve gates were twelve pearls, each gate made of a single pearl. The great street of the city was of gold, as pure as transparent glass (Revelation 21:21 NIV).

We use this example as a teaching tool for our youngest daughter. It helps to visualize what it looks like to follow Jesus and how important it is to surround yourself with the right fellowship so you can stay on the golden road (the path of wisdom) and help encourage others to do the same.

Many roads and temptations want to lead us astray and into dark and dangerous territory. We work at teaching our young daughter to listen to our voice when we call her and respond by following our instructions. This is teaching her to listen and obey her parents as well as teaching her how to hear God's voice and obey His commands.

Learning how to hear God and follow Him is essential in helping us to navigate safely and victoriously through life. It's the most important life skill we could ever hope to teach our children.

When facing conflict or obstacles at school or other places where our children are alone and unable to ask us directly which way to go, we have taught them to remember what they have learned at home and apply it everywhere they go. Yet, it's up to them to choose to remember these lessons and apply them. We share this healthy fellowship with them, looking out for their best interest, having their backs, and directing and guiding them in the way.

We've encouraged them to seek out this same healthy fellowship with others outside of the home as well to help protect them and build them. We've taught them that they are never alone. God is always with them, and He is always listening. Therefore, they can stop and ask God for help and directions anywhere and anytime. All they have to do is say, "Jesus, show me the way!"

We teach our youngest to remember this lesson of remaining on the golden path by reminding her to sing this song:

The One, The Only

Follow the yellow bliss road.

Obey your mom and dad.

Follow the golden road.

Follow the way of God.

I encourage you to find your fellowship of faithful companions. Dorothy found herself in friendly company with those who lacked a brain, a heart, and courage, even though they meant well. However, we should seek those who seek wisdom from above. We all need a healthy fellowship, a group of like-minded Christian believers who think wisely, act lovingly, and follow courageously the way of God. This type of fellowship helps push us on in the fight against evil. They watch our backs, hold us accountable, and keep us on the right path so that we don't stumble, lose our way, or fall into darkness as we set out to do good. A strong fellowship of people who are in covenant with God helps to keep the way bright and shining before our feet so that we won't lose our footing and get swept away.

> *The path of the righteous is like the morning sun, shining ever brighter till the full light of day. But the way of the wicked is like deep darkness; they do not know what makes them stumble (Proverbs 4:18–19 NIV).*

Recently, one of my daughter's closest friends, a member of her fellowship was killed tragically in an act of evil. Although my daughter is grieving her loss, she is comforted in knowing that her dear friend believed in Jesus.

This precious friend had formed and led a little group of girls at school, including my daughter. I asked my daughter what the purpose and mission was behind this group.

"I don't know. We don't really have one," she replied.

"If you're going to be a member of this group, it needs to have a godly purpose," I told her.

So, I helped my daughter figure out the mission statement for their group. Together, we came up with the idea "Following the yellow bliss road; follow the way of God."

The One, The Only

Their mission was to help one another stay on the golden path that leads the way to love, safety, friendship, and Jesus. They looked for those who needed a touch of love, drawing them in, and leading them toward the path of the golden road, helping to encourage one another to stay on this path.

The next day at school, my daughter presented this idea to her dear friend, who has now passed away, and she accepted her proposal as their mission. My daughter spoke to her about God and asked if she believed in Him. She confessed, "Yes!"

I don't know how successful, dedicated, or impactful these young girls were at following their ambitious mission. However, I do know that a seed of Jesus's love was planted and accepted in this friend's life, and that seed was also shared with others. I believe that seed grew and had a great and powerful impact.

My daughter was privileged to have recently spent her friend's last birthday with her. They had a school party. My daughter allowed her friend to choose all the activities she wanted because it was her special day. She showed her love and demonstrated kindness in those last days.

None of us know when we'll experience our last days, but if we're children of God, if we've been born again and believe Jesus to be our Lord and Savior, then we can know that our future days will be experienced in heaven for all eternity.

I'm thankful that God placed my daughter in this girl's path and that she helped encourage her to "follow the golden road." I'm so proud of my daughter for taking the lessons that she has been taught and for her willingness to share them with others, to demonstrate what it means to be the Father's princess. Our daughter may have helped make the difference in this girl's eternal home.

Because of her friend's confession of faith and belief in God, we can find comfort in believing that she is now walking as a child of light in the presence of God's glory on the streets of gold in heaven, and she will live happily ever after!

We have also invited the light of God's presence to shine upon this darkness and heal our sweet girl's heart (her secret garden). We know that an amazing testimony is blooming from this seed of sorrow.

I love this sweet letter and comforting prayer taken from the book *His Little Princess: Treasured Letters from Your King* by Sheri Rose Shepherd (HISPRINCESS.com):[23]

The One, The Only

Death Is Not the End

My Chosen One,

I never want you to be afraid of death, my daughter, because death is not the end of life for my children. It is only the beginning of their forever life. All those that have loved me and have died are with me now in heaven. Remember this truth: When you leave this earth, you also will be with me forever. I know you miss the precious ones who have died, but I promise you will see them again, my love. If you will talk to me when you feel sad, I will heal your heart and remind you that someday we will all live happily ever after, together as one family in heaven.

Love, your King who is preparing a home for all my children.

Jesus told her, "I am the resurrection and the life. Those who believe in me, even though they die like everyone else, will live again" (John 11:25).

PRAYER OVER YOU

Comfort Me, Lord
Dear God,

I do feel sad when someone I love has died. Help me remember that everyone who loves you will live with you after they die. Help me remember that I will see them all in heaven one day. In Jesus' name I pray, amen.

Just as Sheri Rose so beautifully stated above in her comforting love letter and prayer, death is not the end for God's chosen ones who believe in Him and choose to follow the golden road—the One and only Way. Hallelujah!

The road of right living bypasses evil; watch your step and save your life (Proverbs 16:17 MSG).

PRAYER

Lord,

Help me to guard my heart and discern good and evil without passing judgment on others. Give me a heart that is brave and willing to step onto the road and follow You into the places You lead. Bring healthy fellowship into my life and godly companions that keep me following the golden road, the path of righteousness and the way of wisdom. I declare Your Word is a lamp to my feet and a light to my path.

In Jesus' Name. Amen.

CHAPTER NINETEEN

Snow White dreams of the day she'll be reunited with her prince, her one true love. She longs for the day they'll have a beautiful wedding ceremony. Then her prince will carry her away on his white horse to his castle in the sky where they'll live happily ever after. All of creation will sing and celebrate their union together. On that special day, all of her dreams will come true.

I had the same dream all along. Satan sought to steal my dream from me, kill the possibility of finding true love, and destroy my happy ending. His intention is and has always been to steal, kill, and destroy us all. It began with Adam and Eve in the Garden, but it will end with Jesus.

Sin interfered with God's perfect plan for my life as I bit the poison apple, leading me down a painful and difficult road. Thankfully, God intervened and has been rewriting my story ever since, extracting the poison from my heart and interjecting it with love!

God can do the same for you.

He's the most brilliant and creative writer in all of history. His works aren't boring or redundant; they're glorifying and abundant. Jesus has rewritten human history for us all, and His love story is the most beautiful ever told. He has redeemed our sins, re-established our identity, reconciled our relationship with God, and restored paradise for all who choose to enter.

Emergence

God is the love I've been dreaming about for my entire life. Jesus is my One True love. He should have always been my First Love, my Beloved. Now He is!

However, God has also blessed me with a love that mirrors my love with God—my earthly husband. Marriage is meant to be a reflection of our intimate relationship with Christ. Side by side, we help one another grow in spiritual maturity, relationship, purpose, and intimacy with God. Together we love and serve one another and God above all. This was the plan for marriage in the Garden of Eden when God formed a man and woman and united them as one before Him, and it's still His plan for marriage today. Our spouse is our helpmate, and we're theirs, designed to help us follow, obey, and know our Creator. Our Lord is a giver of good gifts.

Despite how good a gift our spouses are, or try to be, they (and we) are not perfect. No love is, save one. God's perfect love is like no other. Just as Adam and Eve ultimately let one another down, so will we all in one form or another.

But God never will. He is faithful forever. He will never leave you. He will never abandon you, and He will never stop loving you. His love has the power to transform and redeem us all from a sinner to a saint.

In His eyes, we are made new, pure, and as white as snow.

A Pure Bride

In our marriage, Jesus has been purifying our hearts individually to be one heart, one soul, and one flesh. From the beginning of our relationship, my husband has had to pull me along. He has been like a car on nitrous, furiously fast moving, while I have been the parachute on the back slowing down our progress. My hesitancy to move forward as one, has been the result of me continuously looking backwards.

In the biblical story of Lot's wife, Lot and his family were rescued and pulled out of the sinful city of Sodom in order to escape the fiery judgment. God sent angels to deliver them from death and lead them into a new place. They left their old lives behind in order to start over.

They were commanded and warned, "Hurry! Don't look back!" However, Lot's wife disobeyed. Rather than focusing her attention on what new life lay ahead for them, she looked back at what she was forced to leave behind. Consequently, she went no further. She turned into a pillar of salt and remained stuck in that place.

White as Snow

Lot and his family were hesitant to move forward because of the life and possessions they were leaving behind. They had one foot in their past and one in their future. However, it was Lot's wife who disobeyed. Therefore, she was stuck (frozen in time, dead in place), unable to move on into the promise awaiting her, while her family continued on without her.

> When Lot still hesitated, the angels seized his hand and the hands of his wife and two daughters and rushed them to safety outside the city, for the Lord was merciful. When they were safely out of the city, one of the angels ordered, "Run for your lives! And don't look back or stop anywhere in the valley! Escape to the mountains, or you will be swept away!" (Genesis 19:16–17 NLT).

> But Lot's wife, from behind him, [foolishly, longingly] looked [back toward Sodom in an act of disobedience], and she became a pillar of salt (Genesis 19:26 AMP).

God sent my husband Chris as a gift to me (my angel from heaven) to help pull me out and save me from the rebellious environment and lifestyle I once lived in. God had found favor in us as we turned our hearts back to Him in obedience as individuals. He had given us this second chance. It was our opportunity to escape the sinful place we were once in and start again, fresh and new as a godly couple.

However, I was hesitant to accept that deliverance (the hand of marriage being offered to me) and nearly turned my back on it. Thankfully, I didn't. I finally accepted his hand in marriage and left my former life behind and entered into a new covenant relationship with my new husband. I made a new agreement, contract, promise, and decision to cut the physical ties to my past relationships and tie a new one. By the way, Chris and I just happily celebrated our seventeenth wedding anniversary!

This choice may have saved my life. If I had failed to receive God's gift of deliverance and rejected the opportunity to move into the new blessed state of living being offered, I may have perished. God knew I needed someone strong beside me, a helpmate, to pull me forward and help me stand throughout the fiery trials that were ahead in my future. I'm so grateful God sent me the precious gift of my husband Chris to help rescue me out of my pit!

Emergence

However, as beautiful and near-perfect as our marriage was—and no earthly marriage is totally perfect—I began to realize down the road that something was missing. One area in our marriage—physical intimacy—felt stuck, numb, and lacking, at least for me. God revealed to me that this lack was due to my picking back up an old lie from the enemy. I took another bite of a rotten apple and believed one of Satan's lies that parts of my heart were forever lost in my past.

I picked up this apple (lie) from Satan years ago and had been holding onto it and carrying it (along with some old baggage) into our marriage. Our marriage was a gift of deliverance, redemption, and restoration from God, a glorious new covenant leading us into a promising future. We both agreed this was a new start for us and had made the decision to follow Jesus into this new land. However, I continued to look back into my past, and this action of looking backwards was slowing us down from getting there.

Why would I do this?

Satan convinced me that passion and intimate desire were a thing of the past and that I would never fully have it again in this marriage. Due to the trauma my heart had experienced throughout my life, parts of me were numb and felt dead, parts I deeply longed for and wished to revive but thought I was stuck to live this way forever.

He convinced me that I was broken, defective, and unable to feel again because of the pain and suffering I had endured. Although I had cut the physical ties to my past, the emotional ties still held me captive in my soul. I had swallowed the lie's poison, and my thoughts were now distorted, causing me to hold onto a dated treasured possession—a long lost affection—that had become another idol in my heart. It was taking the place of even greater blessings that God wanted to give me in this new season, but my hands weren't free to receive them. I had a rotten apple in one hand and an idol in the other, and both of them were completely invisible to me.

To be free to receive, we first must be willing to let go. As long as we choose to believe the enemy's lie, we're stuck in it. As long as we choose to hold on to idols, we're trapped.

Therefore, that lie and idol kept me in bondage in this one area of my heart. I continued to cry out to God in desperation, pleading for Him to revive the feelings for intimacy, yet no response. My husband was content and fully satisfied in these areas, yet I remained numb toward physical intimacy with him. My empty memories lingered as I continued to look to a dead source, a false god, an idol in my heart that had no real power to satisfy the longing in my soul. As a result, God kept looking away from the resurrection I begged for.

I loved my husband dearly and gave myself to Chris intimately, acknowledging that he was the gift given to me by God, yet inside was no real desire to demonstrate that affection. Sexual intimacy had become a chore, an obligation, a responsibility, a duty, a requirement for me, not an extension of my gift. It was a perfectly wrapped present I simply had no interest in unwrapping. The passion within me had died, and now I was just going through the motions without any emotions.

I couldn't understand it. God had delivered me out of a devastating marriage and painful past and delivered to me a new attractive husband and a marriage that beautifully reflected God's heart. Our marriage perfectly fit this description, except in this one area, the very area that led me down the wrong path of physical intimacy to begin with. I was finally allowed to freely indulge in these marital gifts but couldn't.

Passionate lovemaking was the missing piece to the beautiful picture God painted for me in our love letter that promised to fulfill and surpass our hearts' desires. I questioned its authenticity and the validity of this worldly notion that marriage is the place where sex goes to die. Was this what God intended for me all along? I finally got what I wanted, but now I can't enjoy it. Figures! This was the punishment I deserved, payback for my sins, my broken promise to God to abstain from sex until marriage. The enemy continued to hold that guilt and shame over me only because in choosing to believe it, I had chosen to allow it.

How foolish of me to consider for a second that God would give me such a mouth-watering, steamy gift, yet not allow me to fully enjoy the fruits of pleasure and heat of passion that were intended to come along with it. Sex was birthed in marriage. It's the only place it was ever intended to live. We're the ones responsible for allowing its taste to not satisfy and its spark to fizzle out due to our own folly.

God's not in the business of payback toward His children. Since when does He give us what we deserve? God's in the business of payback toward sin. He hates the sin, loves the sinner, and extends grace to those who don't deserve it.

He wasn't withholding blessings from me. The only thing God withholds from His children is eternal damnation that we deserve as punishment for the sins we commit.

No, I was the one withholding blessings from myself. I was the one standing in my own way again. Although I was devoted to our marriage and not withholding my body from my husband, I was withholding my full heart because my soul was still tied to feelings of intimacy associated with former flames. I was still tied to lies. Invisible cords had never been completely cut; therefore, outside interference were affecting our marriage bed.

So there I was now, putting along on reserves like a rubbernecking sluggard, a slow moving snail, lazy in love, with eyes looking backwards rather than forward. My old feelings had been stashed away as my backup supply of emotion and only resource of intimacy while I offered modest feelings and desires toward my husband. Consequently, I held us both back as the parachute in the relationship from the full promise God had for us.

The soul of the sluggard craves and gets nothing, while the soul of the diligent is richly supplied (Proverbs 13:4 ESV).

This heart issue had absolutely nothing to do with physical attraction for my spouse and absolutely everything to do with spiritual distraction from the enemy. Our eyes are the window to the soul. This was his window of opportunity. If he can't steal your soul, he'll attempt to steal your eyes in order to get to your soul. This distraction got my eyes temporarily off course in this one area, and my heart followed.

Once again, the enemy's sparkling temptation had caught my attention and my affection. The enemy wants us to look back so that we'll walk blindly into his trap. When we aren't watching where we're going, we're bound to stumble, lose our way, or collide carelessly with another. Once you're captured and fractured, only God can set you free and heal you. Where your treasure is, there your heart will also be (Matthew 6:21).

I was guilty of storing up lost, stolen, and dead treasures of affection that were of no real or eternal value. Believing the lie, I looked back to these empty possessions to fulfill the longing in my soul, all the while wondering why I felt unsatisfied. The enemy had placed one more obstacle in the road of our journey, a snare I stepped into rather than over, a lie that trapped me and had me stuck. He wanted to slow us down from reaching and entering into our promised land.

Although we continued to move forward physically and spiritually as a couple, pieces of my heart had fallen into an invisible treasure chest. The memory box, my "hope chest," had locked me in. Once again, only Jesus carried the key to open it up and pull my broken heart out of that empty place and make it whole.

> *The eye is the lamp of the body. You draw light into your body through your eyes, and light shines out to the world through your eyes. So if your eye is well and shows you what is true, then your whole body will be filled with light. But if your eye is clouded or evil, then your body will be filled with evil and dark clouds. And the darkness that takes over the body of a child of God who has gone astray—that is the deepest, darkest darkness there is.*
>
> *When Jesus speaks of eyes and light, He means all people should keep their eyes on God because the eyes are the windows to the soul. Eyes should not focus on trash—pornography, filth, or expensive things. And this is what He means when He says, "Where your treasure is, there your heart will be also" (Matthew 6:22–23 VOICE).*

Serving false gods is an empty experience that promises to fuel our deepest desires yet leads only to a dead end. No longer! No one can serve two masters. I choose to worship and serve the One True God wholeheartedly, an experience that's thrilling and fulfilling, that leads to destinations beyond measure. This is the cup I choose to drink from and the portion I desire.

It was high time for that long-lost connection to be cut loose and broken off once and for all. Upon receiving the revelation from God that I was not broken beyond repair, I turned away from lies, repented for holding onto idols, and looked up to God. I cried out once again for His help, acknowledging that I was trapped, and only He could set me free. I asked for His help to completely let go of former flings and move on into greater things.

Emergence

I pulled out the hidden treasure chest stashed away in my heart and brought this darkness into the light and offered it up to God. After asking Him to heal me from the inside out from these old memories, I confessed it to Him and to my husband and asked for their forgiveness.

I invited God to cut *all* soul ties to my past relationships—physically, emotionally, mentally, and spiritually—allowing Him to deliver me completely from this bondage and break me free from this captivity. Tired of being a slave to false gods and in service to dead objects, I refused to look back into ancient history or be tied to any old emotional baggage any longer. They slowed me down and wore me down long enough. I was tired of carrying it with me everywhere I went. I had better things to do with the time God has given me here on Earth, and I have better places to go that God has prepared for me down the road.

The promised land ahead requires full focus, full devotion, and total freedom. I now look away from the enemy's fake treasure and fix my eyes on Jesus, my everlasting and most valuable possession of all.

> *"No one can serve two masters; for either he will hate the one and love the other, or he will be devoted to the one and despise the other. You cannot serve God and mammon [money, possessions, fame, status, or whatever is valued more than the Lord] (Matthew 6:24 AMP).*

I repented for my disobedience to the instructions given in marriage, of "looking back" and to other objects of affection, my keepsake memories, to fill me. This behavior was an unhealthy habit created in my past, an old way of thinking and coping with disappointment. It never should have been carried over into our new covenant. I spit out the lie of the enemy and replaced it with the promise of God's Word.

My husband Chris and I prayed over our marriage and intimacy. I declared, "I'm a new creation. There is no part of me that is dead, gone, or stolen forever that God Almighty does not possess the power to resurrect. I'm alive in Christ, and my God is a redeemer of life and giver of good gifts. I am forgiven!" (Ephesians 2, Acts 17:28, Romans 8:11).

Yes, I had to let go of someone I loved dearly in my youth but was forbidden from due to the captivity of sin. I had mourned for that connection to be restored for most of my life. I also grieved over a failed marriage.

White as Snow

The one I thought was lost wasn't the one and God's best for me. He has restored that intimate love connection, but not in the way I thought He would. He restored it His way, and His way is always better. First, He reconnected me to Him (this is where I found true love and everlasting intimacy). Then He connected me to the husband He chose for me, Christopher, meaning "Christ bearer." Now He's leading us both on a well-watered path.

All along, I had those desires in me to offer to my husband.

Grace has a hold on me now. I'm not letting go of His hand. He's renewing my youth, and Chris and I are making up for lost time. Each new day together is an adventurous quest to uncover more hidden gems.

Even though I moved at a much slower pace, my husband never left my side. He has fought for me since day one and has remained faithful and patient while God has been healing my heart from my painful past and setting me free from captivity throughout our journey together. He never gave up on me. He kept pulling me forward and calling me higher. Just like my Jesus! That is a perfect picture of a *true* husband.

> *Who redeems your life from the pit, Who crowns you [lavishly] with lovingkindness and tender mercy; Who satisfies your years with good things, So that your youth is renewed like the [soaring] eagle. The Lord executes righteousness And justice for all the oppressed (Psalm 103:4–6 AMP).*

Now that my hands are free to fully receive God's blessings, He's returning what was lost, redeeming what was stolen, and resurrecting what was thought to be dead in me and in our marriage. I'm no longer stuck, numb, or dead in place like Lot's wife had been. No longer taunted and tormented in this area of my life by lies, I'm alive, free, moving forward, and looking to Jesus. I had been temporarily asleep much like Snow White after biting the apple, but Jesus awakened my heart with new passion and desire.

My eyes are now open. I'm fully conscious and emerging into a promised future where my latter days are even better than my former days. God has quenched the old flames that used to melt me. He has sparked a new furnace inside me that burns at a much greater intensity for my husband than ever before. He's doing a new thing in me and a better thing in our marriage. Now that I'm fully present, God is delivering exuberant presents addressed to us both. I too am being *fully* satisfied!

Emergence

Then, if you are pure and upright, Surely now He will awaken for you And restore your righteous place. "Though your beginning was insignificant, Yet your end will greatly increase (Job 8:6–7 AMP).

Intimacy shouldn't be a drag in marriage. That's not what God intended. Intimacy is a wedding gift from God. Don't store it away as a worshipped keepsake memory of what once was. Pull it back out. Open it up. Treasure it. Protect it. And enjoy it together! This enchanting flower is meant to arouse your senses and blossom over time, not decay.

I'm now moving forward at a healthy pace alongside my wonderful husband because I was willing to let go of an unhealthy desire. I was willing to trust and look to God to meet all my wildest needs, desires, and dreams, even those *thought* to be dead. No more sluggard syndrome. We are fully one. Our bodies now move along in unison, without hesitancy or resistance from outside forces.

Faith without works is dead, so act on the desire you hope to be fulfilled. It was our action in faith and belief that God could, would, and is resurrecting the passion in our marriage that activated the fulfillment of the promise made to me in my love letter (James 2:17-18, paraphrased).

We fix our eyes on the true prize, our greatest treasure—Jesus. There, our heart will follow. We walk in total freedom, hand in hand with Him as He leads the way forward on the golden path He has for us. Husband, God, and wife move together as three in one.

We have decided to follow Jesus. No looking back! No holding back!

My love letter from God continues to fully unfold in my life and our marriage day after day. It's happening just as He said it would. As we *both* become intimate, satisfied, fulfilled, and content in Him, He delivers on His promises time and time again. He first gave us the gift of Himself separately. Then He gave us the gift of each other. Now that we have grown as a couple and become one, rooted and established in Him alone, He's delivering to both of us His perfect plan intended for our marriage.

Sometimes due to unresolved pain or hidden hurts, the idols we create are rooted much deeper in our hearts than we even realize. It can take time to fully identify, extract, and dethrone them. However, if we're able to recognize the numbness in our hearts, acknowledge that we're holding onto something we shouldn't, seek the Holy Spirit to identify the culprit, and turn away from it, then God is able to finally release the power it holds over us. He fills that empty space with much *more* than we had before.

I encourage you to make room for Him to release the lavish love and blessings He has in store for you, your marriage, your family, and your future. Begin by making this powerful declaration over yourself: "I want You more, God!"

Watch how He begins to shift your focus and shift your desires to come into alignment with His perfect plan. Watch how intimacy in your relationship with God and your spouse explodes as the parachute is exposed and deposed. Letting go of unhealthy habits, ungodly obsessions, and hidden desires will release you and propel you into your promise.

If you or your spouse are lacking in passion, desire, and intimacy, you might be holding on to an idol. On the other hand, you could be feeding a lie or possibly both. Either way, ask God to help you identify the problem. Put your faith into action. Believe in His promises. Remember that no problem is too big for God to solve.

Look up, cry out, and ask for help. God wants to set you free and deliver you from whatever is holding you back, interfering with your marriage, and preventing you from experiencing the full satisfaction of the gifts intended for you to receive.

A New and Living Way

Therefore, believers, since we have confidence and full freedom to enter the Holy Place [the place where God dwells] by [means of] the blood of Jesus, by this new and living way which He initiated and opened for us through the veil [as in the Holy of Holies], that is, through His flesh, and since we have a great and wonderful Priest [Who rules] over the house of God, let us approach [God] with a true and sincere heart in unqualified assurance of faith, having had our hearts sprinkled clean from an evil conscience and our bodies washed with pure water (Hebrews 10:19–22 AMP).

I'm so grateful our Redeemer is fully faithful to His bride, that He's faithful to love and forgive, faithful to keep His sweet promises, and faithful to remain patient and merciful even when our behavior is unfaithful, adulteress, idolatress, disobedient, and hesitant to move into the places where He is wanting to lead us. Jesus is the perfect husband.

I'm grateful to have an earthly husband who reflects His nature. It's my heart's greatest desire as a wife to do the same.

Thank You, Lord, for the freedom to unveil my messy heart and soul before my husband and You without shame and the fear of rejection and abandonment. Thank You for Your compassion for Your bride, Your commitment to Your bride, and Your promise to purify Her heart and make Her glisten as the falling snow. Thank You for removing the veil that once separated her from seeing Your shining face and feeling Your loving grace.

Thank You, Lord, for the new covenant of marriage we have with You. What a gift!

> *"Do not fear, for you will not be put to shame, And do not feel humiliated or ashamed, for you will not be disgraced. For you will forget the shame of your youth, And you will no longer remember the disgrace of your widowhood.*
>
> *"For your husband is your Maker, The Lord of hosts is His name; And your Redeemer is the Holy One of Israel, Who is called the God of the whole earth.*
>
> *"For the Lord has called you, Like a wife who has been abandoned, grieved in spirit, And like a wife [married] in her youth when she is [later] rejected and scorned," Says your God. "For a brief moment I abandoned you, But with great compassion and mercy I will gather you [to Myself again].*
>
> *"In an outburst of wrath I hid My face from you for a moment, But with everlasting kindness I will have compassion on you," Says the Lord your Redeemer (Isaiah 54:4–8 AMP).*

A Dream is a Wish

God's promises of the perfect love in my love letter weren't just intended for me. A friend of mine delivered that hopeful message from God to me when I needed it most, so consider this book in its entirety an extension of His message of hope now being delivered as a gift to you. My friend, I pray you can hear loud and clear God's promises written especially to you in this love letter from Him. He loves you and desires greater intimacy with you. He promises to deliver greater plans for your life than you could possibly ever dream of if you let Him.

May you too believe it and be fully satisfied in Him.

Through this story of my life, I have revealed my journey with God up to now. I've shared how I received God's gift of salvation when I was a child, how He later met me at my empty well, delivered me from bondage, rescued me from oppression, protected me through storms, shielded me through battles, guided me in the wilderness, transformed my heart through circumcision, refined me through fire, commissioned me into service, and is leading me further and further into the promised land.

Jesus has been working throughout my life to change my heart and make me as white as snow. Throughout every trial and tribulation, He has been stripping away my old rags of shame, insecurity, jealousy, pride, doubt, anger, fear, idols, and much more. But He has also covered and clothed me with a new robe of righteousness that radiates grace, mercy, freedom, healing, humility, peace, love, joy and much more. He has delivered and continues to deliver special gifts, custom-made for me. He has fulfilled and continues to fulfill dreams and wishes, hopes and promises.

However, complete fulfillment and satisfaction doesn't come from getting your wish—the dream your heart desires and the vision you plan and imagine for your life. Full satisfaction and completion come when you begin to fulfill *God's* wish—the perfect dream His heart desires and the perfect plan He envisioned for your life.

A life fulfilled is more than a wish granted.

God's perfect gifts are always delivered with intention and purpose. They're not delivered in full bloom (2 Timothy 1:6–7). They begin as a seed that grows and develops over time as it is tended to properly. My husband Chris was not delivered to me just because I dreamed of having a husband and a complete family, nor was the gift of intimacy we now share delivered just because I wished for it. He didn't answer my prayers just to make me happy.

Obtaining happiness is certainly a part of God's plan for His children and for marriage, but it's not its original purpose. Each gift (seedling) I received was delivered so that together we would grow more in love with God as we remain in His vine and bear much fruit. Then one day, we can help others to climb upwards and cluster in this same way as we cling to Him.

Through His good gifts, God wishes for us to become one in marriage, one in intimacy, mission, destiny, purpose, and one with Him. He first built in us so that through us we would take the beautiful and fragrant fruit of our marriage and use that love vineyard as seed to benefit others and multiply, thus glorifying Him and serving His kingdom purpose. This is when a marriage truly blossoms.

Like all marriage, our marriage was created to reflect marriage with Christ. This is His intention for marriage and His purpose behind each—to reflect who He is and to direct others to Him.

From the beginning, it was intimacy that God desired with mankind. That was why He created Adam. Then He created a helper and companion for Adam—Eve—because it wasn't good for man to be alone. They rebelled, sinned, and lost intimacy with God. Still, God didn't abandon them. Instead, He made a way for intimacy to be restored. Just as Adam and Eve failed short to obey God, so did my husband and me. So have we all.

Just as God didn't abandon His disobedient children then, He didn't abandon my husband and me either. He took two very imperfect people who shared the same dream—the faithful wish for a godly marriage and godly spouse—and wove them together with Him so that He could put together the perfect puzzle as a whole.

That was His plan all along. He took all of our broken, scattered pieces, and one by one, combined them to make one complete picture unveiling who He is—the magnificent face of restoration, redemption, and resurrection.

In the beginning, God had a vision for marriage. From the beginning, God has had a vision for our marriage. Through our fulfilled wishes and testimony of His faithfulness and goodness, He's building a ministry to serve as a mirrored reflection of His kingdom marriage. It's the glorious picture of a redeemed relationship, restored intimacy, and a resurrected bride all made possible through the resurrected Son.

Who knew what greater purpose His intentional spiritual gifts would serve in our own lives and in His kingdom? Who knew that in fulfilling our wishes, we would one day be granting His? God knew, that's who.

White as Snow

As He restored our lives, we had no idea of the vision, the picture, and the model He was preparing through our beautiful union. We had no clue in the beginning that our marriage would one day be used to display and direct others to Him. We didn't yet understand the higher implications that our marriage has on the kingdom. We were just living life while loving God. But now we do understand because it has been revealed to us by the gift of the Holy Spirit living in us.

That is what the Scriptures mean when they say,

"No eye has seen, no ear has heard, and no mind has imagined what God has prepared for those who love him."

But it was to us that God revealed these things by his Spirit. For his Spirit searches out everything and shows us God's deep secrets. No one can know a person's thoughts except that person's own spirit, and no one can know God's thoughts except God's own Spirit. And we have received God's Spirit (not the world's spirit), so we can know the wonderful things God has freely given us (1 Corinthians 2:9–12 NLT).

God uses what the enemy abuses. God redeems time through troubling times.

Today, my husband is helping lead others to discover who they are as kingdom men. I'm helping others discover who they are as kingdom women and kingdom kids. We absolutely love it. It's the perfect marriage of the beautiful ministry He has given us. I find true joy in teaching and sharing with women, children, and couples the lessons the Father has first taught me and what it means to be the Father's princess.

I'm not talking about a pretty pink princess here either. Although she certainly has wonderful qualities similar to the princesses we're familiar with, this princess is in a class of her own. She is truly an original.

Sure, she's graceful with a servant's heart like our Snow White; she portrays beauty that lies within like Sleepy Beauty; she looks beyond appearances like Belle; she is generous and kind to all like Cinderella; she longs to follow the deep call of her heart like Moana; she's fierce and brave like Merida, and she's a warrior and fighter like Mulan and She-ra.

Emergence

However, this princess of power has a characteristic none of the others have.

She's real. She isn't an imaginary storybook character. She's genuine. She isn't a make-believe fairytale princess; she's true royalty. She isn't fashioned from mankind's imagination; she's authentic. She's fearfully and wonderfully made by the Creator of mankind and is a reflection of God's own image. She exists because her Father, her Maker exists. He has made her into who she is because she has chosen to believe in who He is.

Thank you, Lord, for first teaching me and my husband who we are so that we can take what we've received, turn it around, and use it to help teach others who You are. It's our greatest joy and honor to do so for Your kingdom marriage.

With each gift given, we're to give back to Him. They're not meant to be kept only for our personal use and satisfaction. We're not meant to hoard and store up earthly treasures; we're meant to store up treasures in heaven.

We give back sowing and planting, what has been so generously given that reflects the heart of God. Taking what we've been given and offering it up to God in sacrifice reflects an image of what our relationship with God looks like. It's a gorgeous picture of the everlasting union of beauty, perfection, and love that God promises to give and offers to us as stated in my love letter. Jesus demonstrated this perfect love on the cross.

Laying down our individual lives and our marriage, devoting both our hearts and dedicating each of our gifts to Him and His kingdom purpose are the perfect demonstration of our love offered back to Him. These acts of our service store up everlasting treasures in heaven. They bring about the fullness we all hope and wish for—to discover who we truly are and for what purpose we were originally created. We are His! We were made to love and be loved.

> "Don't hoard treasure down here where it gets eaten by moths and corroded by rust or—worse!—stolen by burglars. Stockpile treasure in heaven, where it's safe from moth and rust and burglars. It's obvious, isn't it? The place where your treasure is, is the place you will most want to be, and end up being" (Matthew 6:19–21 MSG).

White as Snow

God's gifts are meant to change lives for the better and to draw people to Himself. They're never meant to hold a greater place than He has in our treasure chests. He's a jealous husband who desires a faithful bride and intimacy with her. He's making us white as snow because He desires, dreams, and wishes to behold His pure and righteous bride on His wedding day. He wants to reap a white harvest. He wants a bride whose heart is fully devoted to Him, a marriage that's fully invested in the kingdom and whose hope and treasure is fully placed in heaven, locked safely and secure above.

Give yourself completely, totally, and unreservedly to the One who gave Himself completely for you. Give to Him—the One Gift who came into this world as a seed planted into Mary's womb, the One who was without sin, the One without stain, the One and only spot-free Lamb who was and is as white as snow, who grew, matured, and blossomed into fulfilling His destiny and purpose so that we might do the same.

Jesus has planted His seed of love into my heart. That seed has grown and is now blossoming. In my storybook, *The Father's Princess: The Story of the White Daisy*, Princess Daisy is transformed by His seed of love. She has experienced an encounter with Jesus that changed her, touched her, and moved her forever. Without even realizing it at the time I wrote it, my story and testimony mirrors the biblical story of the woman at the well.

Upon experiencing a personal encounter with Jesus, she also left changed, touched, and moved.

> *Then, leaving her water jar, the woman went back to the town and said to the people, "Come, see a man who told me everything I ever did. Could this be the Messiah?" They came out of the town and made their way toward him (John 4:28–30 NIV).*

Upon receiving a touch from Jesus, the woman was moved to go into the town and share her miraculous transformation story. Her longing changed from being centered upon her own heart and desperate desires to compelling others to come and meet the One she met at her empty well. Her longing was now centered upon Jesus and His heart and desires.

His truth and Word shed new light and revelation into her story, and she couldn't help but tell others about it. He taught her who she was and revealed who He is. Jesus's words not only teach but they save, and that salvation is extended to the world.

Her story impacted the people. It carried influence. Her words held power because they were saturated in His grace, mercy, redemption, salvation, and love.

Jesus washed over the old bitter words that had been spoken over her and poured in new ones. His sweet words changed her heart, her tune, her language, and revealed her destiny. His words brought her new life that was now bursting from her fruitful lips. They carried so much weight with the people that they were also moved to come and meet with Him. They too were touched by His words, so much so that they too believed and were changed forever. Her words were no longer borrowed words; they became personal to them.

Because of one woman's testimony, many came to meet Jesus and know Him for themselves. Never underestimate the power and potential of a single seed. An entire city experienced an encounter of their own that forever changed their hearts and souls. They were invited to drink from His well and eat at the King's table. Many believed He really was the Savior of the world. He is the Messiah!

Many Samaritans Believe

Many of the Samaritans from that town believed in him because of the woman's testimony, "He told me everything I ever did." So when the Samaritans came to him, they urged him to stay with them, and he stayed two days. And because of his words many more became believers.

They said to the woman, "We no longer believe just because of what you said; now we have heard for ourselves, and we know that this man really is the Savior of the world" (John 4:39–42 NIV).

Jesus met with the woman at the well that day because He had a plan, a bigger plan. Beginning with a single seed spoken into a single woman, He planned to reap a great harvest of souls and multiplication. He saw that the fields were ripe and white for harvest.

"Do you not say, 'It is still four months until the harvest comes?' Look, I say to you, raise your eyes and look at the fields and see, they are white for harvest'" (John 4:35 AMP).

White as Snow

> *As the crowds emerged from the village, Jesus said to his disciples, "Why would you say, 'The harvest is another four months away'? Look at all the people coming—now is harvest time! For their hearts are like vast fields of ripened grain—ready for a spiritual harvest (John 4:35 TPT).*

This is also my testimony. You're reading the story and hearing my words of *Jesus told me everything I ever did!* His powerful words washed over my life. His seed brought me fresh revelation and new life, and now, I too long to share that seed with others so that many may receive what I have been given. My once-empty bucket is now overflowing, so much that I can't hold it in. I have to give away the abundance of all that is being poured so generously into me.

I believe with all of my heart that the vision God gave me years ago of how He saw me, His radiant child, His pure and free little girl, singing, dancing, and smiling in the field of white flowers, and the mission assigned to me to fulfill the calling to write *The Father's Princess: The Story of the White Daisy* was a prophetic glimpse of the story He's telling through my life to impact the story of others. I believe it tells the story of what is to come for those who desire to meet with the King personally as a result of my encounter with Jesus, my transformation, and my testimony. And I believe that many will come to know Jesus and believe in who He is because of this grand testimony that the enemy did everything in his power to steal, kill, and destroy so that it would never be heard. But he failed because God's power is greater than our enemy.

Now, by hearing it, you play a role in this tale. You were a part of His grand plan from the beginning. God wanted you to hear how much He loves you and all that He is capable of doing in you, for you, and through you.

God was revealing to me my true identity, writing the words to my story, and painting the picture of my ministry before I had any idea of the "bigger plan" He had in motion. The joyful image He gave me that is now on the cover of the children's book He wrote through me is in celebration of the salvation and the harvest reaping in the field of white flowers. The white daisies in the field represent the harvest of souls, the people, who come to meet Him and believe in who He is because of one princess's testimony.

Emergence

As a result of that personal encounter with Jesus, lives are forever changed. New believers choose to receive the seed of life, emerge as His creation, and bloom as pure white flowers.

There is power and life in the words of our testimony, not because of who I am but because of Who I know. The words spoken from God are the seed of His Word and His Spirit.

The woman at the well and Princess Daisy from my story were nobody remarkably special, at least looking from the outside. But, just like me, each shared one special thing in common—*they believed*. Jesus could work with that. They each made time in their day and room in their hearts to sit with Jesus and hear the voice of God speak directly to them. Not only were they changed personally because of it, countless lives were changed as well.

Numerous nobodies emerged, becoming prominent children of God because of the seed that was shared. Each one is *somebody* special and unique to Him. I believe that the woman at the well was nameless in the Bible because her story wasn't about *her*. It wasn't about who *she was* or all that *she did*. Although no doubt God knew the woman at the well, and He was well aware of her name, it was about all that God did and who He is. Her story wasn't about making a name for herself. Her story was about making known *His great name*.

This is also true of my story, and I hope multitudes will come to know Jesus well, emerging as snowy white flowers because of the beauty of this testimony. The question is, "Do you believe?"

Will you be among the flowers in the field? Or will you be among the laborers that come alongside the sower to work the field and share in the joy of the reaping of this great harvest celebration? Make no mistake; the fields are white for harvest. A grand reaping and revival are on the way.

> *And everyone who reaps these souls for eternal life will receive a reward. And those who plant spiritual seeds and those who reap the harvest will celebrate together with great joy! And this confirms the saying, 'One sows the seed and another reaps the harvest.' I have sent you out to harvest a field that you haven't planted, where many others have labored long and hard before you. And now you are privileged to profit from their labors and reap the harvest"* (John 4:36–38 TPT).

White as Snow

Don't withhold your heart from God. Demonstrate your affection and devotion. Cut loose the invisible ties to this world and its old baggage. God wants to deliver you from this world and its idols and lead you into true eternal paradise. Don't stand in your own way by allowing the empty promises of this world to hold you back (as the parachute in the relationship) from the full promises and intimacy God wants to share with you. Let go! Step into the field and experience a great awakening.

Come and meet Him for yourself. Take His hand and allow Him to deliver you from the fiery trials ahead and into His promised plan. A new covenant of marriage has been arranged. You have the opportunity to become one heart, one soul, and one flesh with the One and Only Jesus! He promises to deliver the fulfilling, satisfying, complete life we all long for.

Jesus was sent to this world to fulfill the work and will of the Father who sent Him. Likewise, we're to follow His footsteps. We begin to enter into His promised plan as we begin to fulfill His calling on our lives to complete His work and to help lead others to fulfill His will. His plan is the most thrilling plan existing! Jesus said this is the work of God the Father.

Then they asked Him, "What are we to do, so that we may habitually be doing the works of God?"

Jesus answered, "This is the work of God: that you believe [adhere to, trust in, rely on, and have faith] in the One whom He has sent" (John 6:28–29 AMP).

My husband was called into ministry at the age of seventeen. Like me, he got sidetracked and veered from that path and his calling. Still, he continued to follow Jesus and eventually caught back up to Him.

God had to prepare my heart to be a part of this ministry and plan. If you would have told me twenty years ago that one day I would have a burning passion for women's ministry and lead not just one, but two Bible study groups for women, I would have said, "You're crazy! Women *never* seem to even want to give me a chance, and I'm not wild about giving them one either. I'm always misunderstood."

Also, if you would have told me that I would one day write and illustrate a book dedicated to children's ministry, coming from the girl who once said, "I'm never having kids until I'm thirty," again, I would have said, "You're out of your mind! I never even read books, much less ever think about writing them!" Now I'm reading, writing, and teaching through them. Never say never.

When I was growing up, my mom always came home from work and put on the same tired pair of old gray sweatpants. I despised those pants and swore I would never dress like that in front of my husband or my poor children.

Well, guess what. Lo and behold, I'm now notorious for wearing my own favorite comfy charcoal gray cardigan along with my favorite gray yoga pants. God help my poor husband and children! This cardigan of mine is such a necessity that it travels with me on vacation and has even been given a name. We call him "Old Trusty, the Gray." Forget about my pledge to not dress like my mother; I've gone *way* beyond that. I look like Gandalf the Gray from *The Lord of the Rings* now.

So, when your momma says, "You better watch your mouth! You may end up eating those words one day," you might want to listen to her. The woman knows what she's talking about. Inner vows always come back around to bite you in the butt. Although I'm making a funny, remember, inner vows are no joke. I'm just saying, you better all be praying, "Inner vows, *you shall not pass* thy humble lips, lest I develop my mother's hips!"

Now my poor family has to pray this silly poem I made up,

"Every day she puts on gray.

Lord, please help her change her way.

Of all the colors from the rainbow;

Yet every day, it's the same ole, same ole.

Oh Lord!

How we trust Thee.

To put to rest,

Dear Old Trusty."

White as Snow

Meanwhile, while they keep praying that prayer, I keep singing,

"I'm bringing Trusty back.

Those other mothers don't know where it's at!"

Oh Lord, please help me change my ways.

My grandma used to say, "Learn to like everything." Granted, she was referring to vegetables, but I believe there's some truth in this statement here for us to learn today. Anyone with a *teachable* spirit can learn to like anything and anyone. God has a way of changing our ways and our wishes. Then when Holy Spirit is finished with us, we won't merely like where His plan has planted us; we'll love it! One Word, a single seed, from God can change your life forever.

God knows just what we need for finding true happiness and a fulfilled life. Its secret is revealed not only through His Word and Spirit, but also in His perfect love letter. We must allow Him to give us the gifts He promises. We must learn how to open up our hearts, our minds, our eyes, and our ears so that we may receive from God.

The secret to living a full and satisfying life is found in learning to love Him first above all else and in learning to surrender to His perfect plan. It's found in learning to hear from God and receiving His instructions outlining the perfect will and work He has uniquely planned for you and your marriage. This is the secret to experiencing perfect love. This act of obedience promises abundant rewards.

Until we give ourselves completely over to God, we're incapable of giving ourselves and our gifts completely to another. Until we develop an intimate and personal relationship with God, we're incapable of experiencing a fulfilling intimate relationship with someone else.

God is love, and His ways are absolutely perfect. Until we discover that our satisfaction is found in Christ alone, there is no other way we'll be completely satisfied in this life. He is the way to experiencing the dreams that we truthfully wish would come true. Without knowing Him deeply and personally, we won't even discover what those dreams really are.

Until we and our spouses become satisfied in Him as one and the life that He has prepared for our marriage together, we won't experience His promise of perfect love. It's the divine dream and pristine portrait He wishes to reveal through our unique union that reflects the inspired image of the everlasting union He shares with His bride. This gift of experiencing perfect love is God's wedding shower gift to those who want it and should be listed first on every wedding registry.

God's divine dreams are far better than our wildest wishes.

Wishful thinking and hopeful daydreaming got me nowhere on its own. But pair my thoughts with God's, add in obedience, put faith into *action*, and suddenly we're traveling to remarkable destinations together I never imagined were possible. We need His perfect love, we need His wonderful spiritual gifts, and we need His thrilling plan. God wants to give you the *best* life possible. Will you allow Him to? Believe in His dreams, and be satisfied in His wishes.

Have faith in the dreams and visions He gives. Believe that someday His rainbow of promise will come shining through. No matter how your heart has grieved and suffered, if you have believed and trusted in Him, the dream that He wished will come true.

A life fulfilled is *His wish* granted.

Jesus said the will of the Father is to do His will. God's will is to give new life to everyone who believes in His Son, so that they will be raised from the dead by Jesus.

> *For I have come down from heaven, not to do My own will, but to do the will of Him who sent Me. This is the will of Him who sent Me, that of all that He has given Me I lose nothing, but that I [give new life and] raise it up at the last day. For this is My Father's will and purpose, that everyone who sees the Son and believes in Him [as Savior] will have eternal life, and I will raise him up [from the dead] on the last day"* (John 6:38–40 AMP).

Will you grant Him His wish? *Believe* in the One He has sent, and He will raise you up. This dream is the wish His heart makes.

PRAYER

Elohim (God of Power and Might),

Make me and my spouse as white as snow. Replace our wretched rags with righteous robes. Help me to be a pure and radiant bride. I desire greater intimacy with my spouse. I declare there is no part of me or my marriage that is too stuck, numb, or dead for Your power to resurrect. Cut all soul ties to previous partners from my past. Reveal any idols I may be holding and any lies I may be feeding so I may renounce them and turn from them. Help me to not look back into sin or ungodliness or hesitate to move when You are calling me out and leading me into higher places. I fix my eyes on You Jesus. Give me Your heart for my spouse and Your desires. Help me to obey Your instructions so I do not become stuck in place like Lot's wife. Bless our covenant union and awaken our marriage bed with heated passion and desire from above. Help us to love You first above all else, surrender to Your perfect plan, and have a teachable spirit so we may fulfill Your will and wishes through our marriage and our testimony. Thank You for rekindling our intimacy, healing our hearts, rewriting our story, and returning what the enemy has stolen.

In Jesus' Name. Amen.

PRAYER OVER YOU

Here is a Scriptural prayer you can pray over yourself to receive greater intimacy with God. I pray that Holy Spirit would come and meet you in a personal way as you call on Him to draw nearer and dearer to your heart. As you read this prayer out loud, envision His face shining on you with approval and love and His arms reaching out for you with acceptance and great joy. The King, the Messiah, the Creator wants to share His riches and secrets with you, beloved. Welcome Yahweh to light up your life. Get ready for an encounter with the Holy One!

I pray that the Father of glory, the God of our Lord Jesus Christ, would impart to you the riches of the Spirit of wisdom and the Spirit of revelation to know him through your deepening intimacy with him.

I pray that the light of God will illuminate the eyes of your imagination, flooding you with light, until you experience the full revelation of the hope of his calling—that is, the wealth of God's glorious inheritances that he finds in us, his holy ones!

I pray that you will continually experience the immeasurable greatness of God's power made available to you through faith. Then your lives will be an advertisement of this immense power as it works through you! This is the mighty power (Ephesians 1:17-19 TPT).

CHAPTER TWENTY

Someday Our Prince Will Come

Have you ever heard a child say, "I *get to* celebrate my birthday soon!"

In my household, celebrating birthdays is a huge ordeal. It takes weeks of planning and preparation to orchestrate a spectacular party, and I've always enjoyed giving my princesses the "royal treatment." With each extravagant theme, we do it upright, paying careful attention to every detail. The food, decor, games, and even costumes are coordinated to match the theme of the event. Some of my favorite themes include *The Greatest Showman*, *Frozen*, *Masquerade*, *Camping*, *Rapunzel's Royal Ball*, and *The Mad Hatter's Tea Party*.

Although it takes a lot of effort ensuring my little one's special day is just right, (note—my oldest is now in college but will always be my first little one), my children and I have always had so much fun collaborating together and dreaming of the highly anticipated moment we get to celebrate their birth. Even better is witnessing their adorable excitement and enthusiasm when it finally comes time to make a wish, blow out the candles, and open presents. As a parent, this is my favorite part. I can't wait to see the joy on their faces as they tear into each special gift that has been handpicked for them.

Emergence

A Royal Celebration

In the same manner our children eagerly anticipate celebrating their birthdays and opening up their gifts, we as God's children should do the same when it comes to celebrating God's gifts, including marriage. We should be celebrating year after year with enthusiasm and opening up our wedding gifts with appreciation, joy, satisfaction, and excitement.

I imagine that almost nothing brings God more joy than to watch two of His children celebrate the choice to become man and wife for the rest of their lives here on Earth and to unwrap the very special gift He single-handedly created as a wedding present—the gift of consummating our wedding and becoming one. How terribly sad and ungrateful of us to toss this gift aside or reject it entirely.

Not only should we accept His beautiful gift, but we should be collaborating alongside Him throughout every intimate detail of our entire lives. This collaboration is a luxury, a privilege we've been granted and can't afford to pass up in foolishness. We get to celebrate sharing this life with Jesus.

Even better, as God's children, we get to celebrate our new life in Christ. We've been born again. We should be celebrating our spiritual birthdays and eagerly anticipating the gift of everlasting life, a future spent in eternity, married to our Bridegroom. Our Father has been planning His children's royal wedding and preparing for this special day since the beginning of mankind. This highly anticipated event will be celebrated soon.

Get excited, children of God!

I also can presume that nothing will bring our Father in heaven more pleasure than to witness His sons and daughters commemorate becoming one with Christ forever in heaven. He will hand over the exceptional offering He formed as a wedding present—the gift of His Bride (the Church) to His Son Jesus.

Our Father wants to walk us down the aisle and give us away to the perfect Husband. How dreadfully disappointing and unappreciative of us to cast this (Gift) aside or dismiss (Him) entirely. Do we not know the price paid for us to receive such a gift? Do we not value its worth? This gift cost everything but was freely given.

Someday Our Prince Will Come

As I mentioned earlier, I nearly rejected and denied myself the gift of my husband Christopher who was sent to me from above, the perfect match, tailor-made and chosen for me. I had my eyes and my heart set on the image I had picked out and dreamed up for myself.

Comparison blinds us toward the gifts God designed for us and stands in the way of His gifts being delivered to us.

Oh, how I would have missed out and paid the price for my arrogance and foolishness. God had planned out our lives together. He could see into our enchanting future and knew that this marriage was meant to be. It was the key to our happily ever after as long as we would choose to accept it and open the door of our hearts.

You face this same choice. You *get to* make this choice for yourself. Jesus Christ was sent from heaven to save us all from perishing. He was sent by God to pull us out of the pit of this world and rescue us from the fiery trial ahead. Our Father in heaven loves us so much that He was willing to sacrifice everything He had in order to deliver this one Gift.

God is preparing a supreme celebration. The Creator of the universe has personally orchestrated this kingly event. Unlike myself, He has unlimited resources. He isn't restricted to staying on budget. I can't even imagine the impeccable taste, the unrivaled imagination, and the exquisite attention to detail He has put into this affair. He has access to any venue, connections with the finest caterers, and is surrounded by hosts of angelic voices and melodic instruments. He has the ability to wisp up a cascading waterfall of crystal water at the blink of an eye or a spectacular display of shooting stars at the flick of His fingers.

This is the one event we should all be waiting for.

God the Father

Requests the Honor of your Presence

at the Royal Marriage of His Children:

The Bride of Christ and Son of God, Jesus Christ.

The company of everyone's presence is requested.

Only those who have accepted the Prince's proposal to receive Him in their heart and accept His hand in marriage will be permitted to partake in this glorious Wedding Celebration.

Emergence

Speaking of celebrations, a few years ago, I attended my nephew's birthday party. He loves to play video games, so the theme chosen was *Super Mario Bros.*[24] I can't blame him. Who doesn't love Mario and Luigi? Hello, they're Italian and love their pizza just like me. I also loved playing Nintendo and even saved the princess in the first Super Mario Bros. game when I was a kid.

While serving the cake at his party, my sweet little niece spoke up and requested her chosen piece. "I want the whole *Muigi*," she announced. She had adorably confused the names of the *Super Mario Bros.* characters and combined them into one like they do to Hollywood couples (Mario and Luigi became "Muigi").

Don't we all want the whole Muigi—that perfect slice we get to choose, a little bit of everything we love packaged in one piece? Earlier, I had said that my husband was the angel sent to help rescue me. However, when God delivered my husband Christopher to me as a gift, he might have been the ideal present for me, but he wasn't the perfect package. My husband is *not* my Savior. Only Jesus is my Savior. My husband was given to be my helpmate to *help* rescue me and lead me closer to Christ, not to be my Jesus. My husband is my slice of heaven, my chosen piece of cake cut from above. But make no mistake, he's my number-two guy; Jesus Christ is my number-one Man. My husband, as tasty as he is, cannot and should not try to meet all my deepest needs nor should I expect him to and vice versa. I go to God first for that, and he should do the same.

Just like in the game *Super Mario Bros.* where Mario is player one and Luigi is player two, Mario is the head honcho and protagonist, and Luigi, his resembling brother, is like his shadow. Mario goes first into the Mushroom Kingdom and leads the way to save Princess Toadstool from captivity and the kingdom from the evil antagonist Bowser, and Luigi follows.

My husband Christopher is like Luigi, but he follows—chases after—Jesus, which is what makes him so attractive and dreamy to me. The closer he shadows Jesus, the more I fall in love with him, because he walks like Him, talks like Him, looks like Him, and his mission is to help save the princess and those in captivity and bondage to sin and the kingdom from the evil one.

Someday Our Prince Will Come

He may not be the total package, only Jesus is, but he is my "whole Muigi." He's a man, but he has God's Spirit living inside him. Just like my Jesus, my Christopher (Christ bearer) helped come to the rescue of this princess (me), his "white daisy" who was once held captive.

Did you know that oftentimes, Luigi's love interest is speculated to be Princess Daisy? How cute is that fun fact! Chris and I are a match made in heaven; no, seriously, we really *were* a match made in heaven. God put us together. Although neither of us is perfect, we are indeed perfect for one another.

You and I were made, chosen, and put here for God. But will you choose Him? Don't miss out on the gift being offered to you because you believe that in this fallen world, there's something or someone better. There's not! Nothing or no one can compare to the love of God. We're His divine match, and Jesus is the ultimate package. There's no need to fix this One up, girls; He's tailored to perfection.

Will you honor the King's wishes? Will you accept the slice of heaven that has also been cut for you? Will you choose to take the key that has been offered and use it to enter into His royal palace where the most highly anticipated event of all time is soon to take place?

You are formally invited. An entire wedding cake, ceremony, and reception party are being designed for you upstairs. Will your name be written down in the Lamb's Book of Life? His banquet table has more than enough room to seat those who will come and enter into His kingdom.

The Marriage Supper of the Lamb

Then I heard what seemed to be the voice of a great multitude, like the roar of many waters and like the sound of mighty peals of thunder, crying out, "Hallelujah! For the Lord our God the Almighty reigns. Let us rejoice and exult and give him the glory, for the marriage of the Lamb has come, and his Bride has made herself ready; it was granted her to clothe herself with fine linen, bright and pure"—for the fine linen is the righteous deeds of the saints.

And the angel said to me, "Write this: Blessed are those who are invited to the marriage supper of the Lamb." And he said to me, "These are the true words of God" (Revelation 19:6–9 ESV).

Emergence

Will you accept this invitation?

The Story of the Dinner Party

That triggered a response from one of the guests: "How fortunate the one who gets to eat dinner in God's kingdom!"

Jesus followed up. "Yes. For there was once a man who threw a great dinner party and invited many. When it was time for dinner, he sent out his servant to the invited guests, saying, 'Come on in; the food's on the table.'

"Then they all began to beg off, one after another making excuses. The first said, 'I bought a piece of property and need to look it over. Send my regrets.'

"Another said, 'I just bought five teams of oxen, and I really need to check them out. Send my regrets.'

"And yet another said, 'I just got married and need to get home to my wife.'

"The servant went back and told the master what had happened. He was outraged and told the servant, 'Quickly, get out into the city streets and alleys. Collect all who look like they need a square meal, all the misfits and homeless and wretched you can lay your hands on, and bring them here.'

"The servant reported back, 'Master, I did what you commanded—and there's still room.'

"The master said, 'Then go to the country roads. Whoever you find, drag them in. I want my house full! Let me tell you, not one of those originally invited is going to get so much as a bite at my dinner party'" (Luke 14:15–24 MSG).

Please RSVP as soon as possible. Let Him know that you'll be in attendance for this royal celebration.

There's still room. Your future happiness depends on how you respond to the Master's invitation. Make sure a place setting will have your name written on it in His love. Say yes.

Someday Our Prince Will Come

He placed me at his banquet table, for everyone to see that his banner over me declares his love (Song of Solomon 2:4 VOICE).

Happily Ever After: A Redemption and Resurrection Story

God's affectionate love is not just a fairytale. It's real, and it has been offered to us all—male and female, young and old, rich and poor. His kiss of salvation is His devoted bestowal of grace and mercy and our only hope for being revived from the Sleeping Death.

Christ's redemptive act of love demonstrated on the cross is true love's kiss. We can't do anything to deserve it or earn it. However, it's only by faith and declaration that we may receive it.

If we confess with our mouths that Jesus Christ is Lord and believe in our hearts that Jesus, the Son of God, paid the price and died for our sins, rose from the dead, and is seated in His heavenly throne as King of kings and Lord of lords, then we'll receive the gift of eternal life.

Jesus's sacrificial love offering of Himself was the greatest gift ever given. His dream is that we'll come to Him and receive this precious gift as we put these words on our lips.

In order to receive this kiss of salvation, we have to open our mouths to confess while we believe sincerely in our hearts that Jesus Christ is Lord. This one kiss is the innermost, intimate, and personal exchange between mankind and God.

Make this kiss and its love will last forever.

But what does it say? "The word is near you, in your mouth and in your heart"—that is, the word [the message, the basis] of faith which we preach—because if you acknowledge and confess with your mouth that Jesus is Lord [recognizing His power, authority, and majesty as God], and believe in your heart that God raised Him from the dead, you will be saved. For with the heart a person believes [in Christ as Savior] resulting in his justification [that is, being made righteous—being freed of the guilt of sin and made acceptable to God]; and with the mouth he acknowledges and confesses [his faith openly], resulting in and confirming [his] salvation (Romans 10:8-10 AMP).

Emergence

> *Three things will last forever—faith, hope, and love—and the greatest of these is love (1 Corinthians 13:13 NLT).*

Our Savior has already been given to us, and someday our Prince *will* come again for us. Jesus is our wonderful Counselor, mighty God, everlasting Father, and Prince of Peace.

> *For unto us a Child is born, Unto us a Son is given; And the government will be upon His shoulder. And His name will be called Wonderful, Counselor, Mighty God, Everlasting Father, Prince of Peace (Isaiah 9:6 NKJV).*

Our Prince will return for His virtuous bride, who is patiently watching and waiting to be reunited with her beloved. Those who have been sealed with the kiss of His Holy Spirit will emerge from the Sleeping Death, be caught up in the air, and carried away to His castle in heaven.

It looks like I'll be back upon those dreamy marshmallow clouds again after all. But I won't be alone. My true love, my Prince of Peace, promises to meet me there.

He is coming again!

The Coming of the Lord

> *But we do not want you to be uninformed, brothers, about those who are asleep, that you may not grieve as others do who have no hope. For since we believe that Jesus died and rose again, even so, through Jesus, God will bring with him those who have fallen asleep. For this we declare to you by a word from the Lord, that we who are alive, who are left until the coming of the Lord, will not precede those who have fallen asleep. For the Lord himself will descend from heaven with a cry of command, with the voice of an archangel, and with the sound of the trumpet of God. And the dead in Christ will rise first. Then we who are alive, who are left, will be caught up together with them in the clouds to meet the Lord in the air, and so we will always be with the Lord. Therefore encourage one another with these words (1 Thessalonians 4:13–18 ESV).*

Someday Our Prince Will Come

We will have a triumphant honoring of matrimony where the true worshipers will be crowned in perpetual beauty and rule and reign at His side as His radiant bride.

> *For I am jealous for you with the jealousy of God himself. I promised you as a pure bride to one husband—Christ (2 Corinthians 11:2 NLT).*

Our Bridegroom will come down from heaven riding on a white horse followed by the armies of the heavenly kingdom. Our enemy will be destroyed as his evil plan is turned back upon himself.

The final scene of *Snow White* has a major plot shift. The story began with the black-hearted queen's scheme to kill the innocent Snow White. She hated her because of her rare beauty, pure heart, and the intimate relationship she had with the prince. If you recall in the story, when Snow White and the prince had their first encounter at the wishing well, the Evil Queen witnessed the exchange from her castle window, and her anger and jealously stewed.

She brewed up an evil ploy to have Snow White killed. She sent her huntsman to track the princess down and bring back her heart. Luckily, Snow White's beauty and grace captured the huntsman's heart, so he allowed her to escape into the dark forest.

However, she wasn't out of the woods yet. Death continued to chase after her. Fortunately, she was led to the seven dwarfs' cottage where she found refuge and friendship among seven little men. Each man's character and nature were revealed in his name—Happy, Sneezy, Dopey, Grumpy, Bashful, Sleepy, and Doc.

These tiny men adored the endearing Snow White and sought to provide for her and to protect her from the wicked queen. Despite their greatest intentions, their ability to save the princess sadly fell short, for they were mere men. Unfortunately, evil made its way into the heart of Snow White after all when she made the choice to bite into the poisoned apple.

But, the queen's wicked recipe backfired. It wasn't Snow White who was destroyed; it was the wicked queen.

Although Snow White gave into temptation and took a bite of death, she wasn't doomed for all eternity. She merely slept, waiting for her redemption to come to her rescue.

Emergence

Meanwhile, the queen disguised as an ugly hag, fled for her life as the seven dwarfs, who weren't fooled, chased after her up a mountainside. She reached the edge of a cliff where she realized she was trapped.

In one final effort to escape, she attempted to send a large boulder tumbling down onto the dwarfs. Suddenly, a bolt of lightning struck the edge of the cliff where she stood. The villainess fell to the ground below, and the mighty rock tumbled down and crushed her.

It was finished!

Saints, just as the Evil Queen's plot to destroy Snow White backfired, likewise, Satan's evil plot to destroy God's children in the Garden of Eden has done the same. Look up, for our redemption draws near.

Our enemy is doomed, and his sentence is coming soon. He realizes he's approaching the end of his rule here on Earth. In one last desperate attempt to rip out the hearts and steal the souls of God's creation, he grows increasingly wicked and influential in his efforts.

Still, his means to destroy all will not succeed. Jesus is coming to redeem His beloved bride. He comes to avenge His children who have been deceived. We have been bought back and paid for at a great cost by our mighty High Priest. The deal is sealed.

It is finished!

We're simply waiting for our Prince to carry us home.

There will be a loud roar from the clouds of heaven. Jesus our Rock and Redeemer, along with His heavenly hosts, will come down and strike our enemy. With a crashing blow, He'll crush the head of the serpent once and for all. We'll again walk freely and live intimately with God face to face in paradise as Adam and Eve did once before.

Christ on a White Horse

Now I saw heaven opened, and behold, a white horse. And He who sat on him was called Faithful and True, and in righteousness He judges and makes war. His eyes were like a flame of fire, and on His head were many crowns. He had a name written that no one knew except Himself. He was clothed with a robe dipped in blood, and His name is called The Word of God. And the armies in heaven, clothed in fine linen, white and clean, followed Him on white horses. Now out of His mouth goes a sharp sword, that with it He should strike the nations.

Someday Our Prince Will Come

And He Himself will rule them with a rod of iron. He Himself treads the winepress of the fierceness and wrath of Almighty God. And He has on His robe and on His thigh a name written:

KING OF KINGS AND LORD OF LORDS.

(Revelation 19:11-16 NKJV).

There will be no end for those who choose life over death, who choose God. All have bitten the apple of sin that leads to death, but all have the choice to be redeemed of that sin and led to life.

We have two voices whispering in our ears. The enemy's picture of false hope is so clear, vivid, and promising in your mind, but it's not reality. It's a false impression, a lie leading to sin, planted with evil intentions. When it fails to take root and flourish as it promised, devastation always follows as it did with Adam and Eve.

No forbidden seed may ever produce righteous fruit and true life in the garden of God's creation. If the seed is ingested, then it and the one who bares the seed of sin must be cast out. Without the light of God's presence, the seed and the one who carries it dies. His garden is a sacred and holy place in which He dwells and sin may not.

Like Adam and Eve, I too have witnessed such devastation in my parents' lives. I also experienced this destruction for myself as I bought the enemy's convincing lie and ate from the forbidden treat only to discover I was tricked.

For a season, I was similar to Snow White. I sought refuge and shelter in the arms of men, hoping to one day find lasting security and love within one man's heart. I thought a man could rescue me. So just like Snow White promised to cook and clean for the seven dwarfs in exchange for a safe place to stay, I found myself working to gain the affection of men, hoping to find a permanent safe place of residence in their hearts. During my search I dated many "interesting" characters, such as—Sexy, Stinky, Dumpy, Sleezy, Unfaithful, Artsy, and Jock. Despite their noble efforts to meet my greatest needs, each character sadly fell short.

Men couldn't save me. No matter the size of their heart or the scale of their character, ultimately, salvation is not in man's nature. Only my true love was able to open my eyes with His tender kiss and save my soul. Jesus Christ is the name *above* all names. His name is Messiah, the Chosen One, the Savior of the world, and our *only* means of escaping death.

If Snow White hadn't met the prince and sealed their bond of love in spirit before she fell into the Sleeping Death, he wouldn't have returned for her. She would have missed her kiss and becoming the prince's bride. She would have missed her ride to the castle in the sky, and she would have remained asleep in that glass coffin forever. He would not have known her.

I'm so relieved that my charming Prince knows me and that I don't have to work in order to gain His affection. He is bigger than that. He has *no* character flaws. I don't have to worry that He'll grow tired of me. I don't have to fear that He'll trade me in for a newer, younger, hotter model once the new wears off or the edges get rough. I don't have to strive to meet His needs. I'm welcomed in His heart, His arms, and His home always and forever. Even better, I'm *safe* there. What a relief to know my heart is secure.

Help us, Holy Spirit, to finally put to rest our devastatingly desperate attempts to "work" for mankind's affection out of fear and insecurity. Once and for all, pull out this longing in our soul and come and fill these empty places that are void of Your love, God. Erase all traces of bitterness, brokenness, and cold-heartedness as characterized by the Evil Queen. Portray in us the beautiful, graceful, and lovable pure-heartedness of Snow White through the "work" of your Holy Spirit.

Today, I can rest in peace knowing that the Prince of Peace will return for me. I am fully known and loved by Him. There is no greater feeling on this earth.

> *But if anyone loves God [with awe-filled reverence, obedience and gratitude], he is known by Him [as His very own and is greatly loved] (1 Corinthians 8:3 AMP).*

In *knowing* Jesus, I've seen and experienced amazing grace—His very nature—that redeems and restores such devastation. His grace flips everything the enemy intended for harm around for the good of those who've received and accepted the seed of perfect love into their hearts.

Thankfully, the light has come, and the seed of new life now lives within us. Jesus is the seed that extracted sin and cast out death. He's forever faithful to produce and deliver true hope and life-giving fruit in everlasting abundance. He has created an opportunity for all to enter into a new garden—the new Jerusalem—where the light of His delightful presence will forever dwell and where we'll once again have access to the tree of life.

Amazing grace. How sweet it is indeed!

Have you received this amazing grace that saved a wretch like me? "I once was lost, but now I'm found."

Christ died in place for me!

Christ also died in place for you.

Eden Restored

Then the angel showed me the river of the water of life, as clear as crystal, flowing from the throne of God and of the Lamb down the middle of the great street of the city. On each side of the river stood the tree of life, bearing twelve crops of fruit, yielding its fruit every month. And the leaves of the tree are for the healing of the nations. No longer will there be any curse. The throne of God and of the Lamb will be in the city, and his servants will serve him. They will see his face, and his name will be on their foreheads. There will be no more night. They will not need the light of a lamp or the light of the sun, for the Lord God will give them light. And they will reign forever and ever (Revelation 22:1–5 NIV).

God can reverse every curse. Whatever the enemy meant for your demise, God can turn it around and make you rise. Resurrection is also in His nature.

This miraculous plot reversal is seen over and over again throughout Scripture. He reversed Pharaoh's curse in the Book of Exodus when He set the children of Israel free. He reversed Haman's plot to kill Mordecai and annihilate the Jewish people in the Book of Esther. In fact, the Jews were delivered, Mordecai was promoted, and Haman was hanged from the very gallows he had built to execute Mordecai.

God reversed the intended plot in the Book of Daniel when Daniel was thrown into the lion's den yet came out unharmed as his accusers took his place in death. When the enemy stole all that Job had in the

Book of Job, God restored all. In the Book of Matthew when God sent His only begotten Son to pay the penalty of death for the ransom of His children, He instead provided life to those who deserve death.

When the enemy sought to steal my dream, banish me from my love, cover my name in shame, take my life, and rob me of my health, my child, and my testimony, God gave me a better dream, introduced me to true love, dressed me in a righteous robe, wrote on me a new name, and blessed me with abundant life. He restored my health, returned my child, and used every bit of the enemy's evil work to create an even greater miraculous work—the making of this grand testimony, just as He had promised.

> *But the Lord stood at my side and gave me strength, so that through me the message might be fully proclaimed and all the Gentiles might hear it. And I was delivered from the lion's mouth. The Lord will rescue me from every evil attack and will bring me safely to his heavenly kingdom. To him be glory forever and ever. Amen (2 Timothy 4:17–18 NIV).*

> "And I will compensate you for the years That the swarming locust has eaten, The creeping locust, the stripping locust, and the gnawing locust—My great army which I sent among you.

> "You will have plenty to eat and be satisfied And praise the name of the Lord your God Who has dealt wondrously with you; And My people shall never be put to shame.

> "And you shall know [without any doubt] that I am in the midst of Israel [to protect and bless you], And that I am the Lord your God, And there is no other; My people will never be put to shame (Joel 2:25–27 AMP).

This testimony is my redemption, resurrection, and my revival story of all the miracle work God did and continues to do in my life. He has resurrected from the dead all that seemed lost, stolen, and destroyed. He does this for all those who have chosen to put their faith and trust in Him. Our enemy always has a plan that he's ready to unleash for our demolition; however, our God always has a master plan that trumps our enemy's and is unleashed for our reconstruction and resurrection.

Someday Our Prince Will Come

It's simple. Satan hates us and whispers lies offering deceptive tricks and disguised treats for our downfall. God loves us and whispers truth offering forgiveness and everlasting life for our sins.

Which voice will you listen to? What path will you follow?

Will you choose to attend the wedding supper of the Lamb?

It will be the most renowned occurrence in all of human history. I promise, you won't want to miss it! I encourage you to reserve your spot today.

Receive Jesus as your personal Lord and Savior. You don't have to be all fixed up and flawless to meet Him. He's not concerned with His bride's outer beauty; He's concerned with her heart, which is where He makes His home.

Just as a bride gets ready and prepares for her wedding day, get ready and prepare a place for Him. Get out your broom just like our beloved Snow White did and make some room for the Son of Man. Receive Jesus into your heart. Receive His love for you, and receive His gift of salvation. Open your heart, and let Him in so that He may open your eyes and awaken your spirit to beauty and new life. Whistle while the Holy Spirit works inside of you to sweep away the dead and dark ashes of your old life and clear a new golden path for you to walk into your enchanting promised land. Your beloved Prince of Peace is waiting to revive you!

Will you choose to follow Jesus?

Just as my husband and I received a home that felt like a mansion as a wedding gift from his parents, we can trust that God our Father is preparing a place for His children, His followers to live forever in His eternal Home, a mighty mansion like no other (and this one won't need any renovations). This immaculate permanent residence will be move-in ready.

When it's ready, He'll take those who have made a place for Him in their hearts to the place He has made for us in paradise. This is His promise to us because He loves us.

Jesus Comforts His Followers

"Do not let your heart be troubled. You have put your trust in God, put your trust in Me also. There are many rooms in My Father's house. If it were not so, I would have told you. I am going away to make a place for you. After I go and make a place for you, I will come back and take you with Me. Then you may be where I am (John 14:1–3 NLV).

Emergence

Will you allow Jesus to sweep you off your feet as His bride and carry you over the threshold of the Father's mansion?

I have a sweet tooth for happy beginnings, and this delightful wedding portrait so deliciously tops this royal wedding cake.

This testimony is my love letter to God.

This story is an expression of the lyrics of His heart being sung out in my life.

For true love always finds a way to express itself.

I was once lost, lonely, and broken. I cried out to God for help. Jesus, my Good Shepherd, heard my cry and came to find me. My Prince met me at the wishing well and quenched my thirst for living water. My Healer repaired my broken heart and made me new. My Deliverer turned me around and led me on a path to freedom and destiny. Together, we sang a beautiful love song. His kiss saved me from death. His Spirit led me home.

And we lived happily forever in the kingdom of everlasting glory.

This is the story of how I met my One True Love:

My beloved spoke and said to me,

"Arise, my darling,

my beautiful one, come with me.
See! The winter is past;

the rains are over and gone.
Flowers appear on the earth;

the season of singing has come,
the cooing of doves

is heard in our land.

The fig tree forms its early fruit;

the blossoming vines spread their fragrance.
Arise, come, my darling;

my beautiful one, come with me"

(Song of Solomon 2:10–13 NIV).

Someday Our Prince Will Come

Will you sing this final sweet love song with me?

I have decided to follow Jesus.

He's coming back! He's coming back!

You and I have now reached the end of our destination together. Thank you for coming alongside me. But the road doesn't have to stop here. Will you now continue on this journey alongside Him?

You can decide to follow Jesus too.

My hope and prayer in writing this book and sharing my story is that you too will discover how much you are loved by God, that you will receive His kiss of salvation, that you will emerge from the Sleeping Death, that you will be washed white as snow, that you will accept His hand in marriage and say yes to becoming the bride of Christ, that all His dreams will come true in your life, and that you will live forever in His royal kingdom . . . happily ever after!

This is how my story never ends.

May this also be the never-ending to your story.

The End

A Royal Invitation

If you've never met and accepted Jesus Christ as your personal Lord and Savior, now you can. If you're ready to follow Jesus and have an encounter of your own so that you too may live forever in His kingdom, you can pray this prayer of salvation out loud, declaring your confession in faith and belief:

> "Lord Jesus, I have sinned and rebelled against You, a holy God, and there is no excuse. I confess my sins to You now and repent of my rebellion. I ask for Your forgiveness, as I believe that You died for my sins on the cross. I receive Your forgiveness now and believe that Your blood is more powerful than my worst sins. I am now totally forgiven by You, and I forgive myself. The past is behind me. I confess You now as my Lord and Savior. I step down from the throne of my heart, and I pray that You will now sit on that throne as my Lord and King. Come into my heart and give me the gift of eternal life. I know I don't deserve it, but I receive it by faith as a gift of grace and now believe I am forgiven, born again, and on my way to heaven. I will live the rest of my life for You. Fill me with Your Holy Spirit and lead me, speak to me, and give me the power to change, make right decisions, and live for You.
>
> **In Jesus' Name, Amen."**

Emergence

This prayer was taken from the book *Ten Steps Toward Christ* by Pastor Jimmy Evans. I highly recommend this book for all and especially new believers. It's a wonderful tool that will help guide you along your journey to the heart of God.

If you made the decision to accept Christ into your heart and receive salvation for your soul, then welcome to the royal family of God!

May God bless you abundantly for making Him the Lord of your life.

Acknowledgments

Rooted in Love and Gratitude

I told you in the beginning of this journey that my country roots still exist. Those country roots taught me to care for the needs of others.

Today, I'm a city girl and no longer live in the country or on a farm. I now help tend to the farm belonging to my Daddy (my Heavenly Father's) but in a spiritual way through ministry. While He's still teaching me how to sow seed and reap a harvest, I help feed the sheep—those who hear the Shepherd's voice and follow Him—and I help feed the lambs, those who are helpless and in need of tender and loving care.

I'll always be a country girl at heart who was raised up tending to God's creation just like Eve and Snow White's early beginnings, and I'm proud of it.

I still put on music and sing, dance, worship, and have fun whistling while I work just like my beautiful and creative mommy taught me. I still put on my little karate uniform (the armor of God) and fight to defend myself and others using techniques, just like my strong and handsome daddy taught me.

I'm beyond thankful for the fun parents God assigned to me. They have helped shape me, build me, and have always loved me. Most importantly, they helped establish my roots in Christ. I'm honored and proud to call them my parents. Well done, good and faithful servants! I love you, Mom and Dad.

Thank you also to my amazing stepparents, grandparents, and siblings. I'm so grateful God brought you into my life. I love you, all.

I'm beyond thankful for my wonderful spouse Christopher, God's gift to me. Chris has helped me become the child of God I was created to be. He has helped me grow and blossom into a white daisy. Without his help, I might have withered. I'm honored and privileged to call him my husband, my number-two guy, my whole Muigi. He has brought beauty and happiness into my life and has helped me deliver the same into our children's lives, my beautiful, rare, and precious jewels. I'm so proud of my children, and I can't wait to see how God uses their gifts and talents to impact His glorious kingdom.

Emergence

To my oldest daughter, I'm beyond thankful for all that God has done in our lives. I treasure our love, our friendship, our unbreakable bond, and our miraculous story. How I have enjoyed witnessing your new growth in Him and look forward to seeing how He makes you open up and bloom even further. He has healed us both, my dear little buttercup.

To my youngest daughter, I'm so grateful for your fun spirit, your heart for God, and your love for people. Thank you for your patience while Mommy worked on her books and for filling my life with laughter and beauty, my sweet sparkling gem.

What an adornment each of you are to become to His crown, my beautiful daughters.

I love you girls, so much, and I love you, Chris. Thank you for all you've done for me and our children.

Thank you, Trinity Fellowship Church of Amarillo, Pastor Jimmy and Kim Witcher, and Pastor Jimmy Evans, for helping me to experience God, find community, and fulfill my purpose. I am beyond grateful for your ministry, leadership, and training that has played a huge role in shaping my ministry, my marriage, and my life.

Thank you, Michelle Robinson, Sherrie Clark, Rhonda Biondi, Monica Nagy, and the amazing design team from BOSS Media, for all of your help with this book project. I couldn't have pulled this off on my own. I'm so grateful God crossed our paths.

Also, thank you to Reba Russell, Lana Spencer, and my amazing Heart to Heart and Kingdom Women Bible study groups for all your support, assistance, and prayers. You are mighty women warriors, heroines of the faith. I love you, ladies.

More so, in the end of this journey, I'm honored and proud to be called a child of God, a daughter of the King, His little country girl, wildly innocent and free, the Father's princess, adopted, chosen, and loved, the bride of Christ, pure, white as snow, newly radiant, and eternally and happily bound in marriage to my one True Love—my Prince of Peace, Jesus Christ.

I'm honored and proud to call you my Father in heaven, the King of my heart, the Lord of my life, the lover of my soul, the Savior of my world, my *all*, my everything. I love you, God, wholeheartedly. Thank you for loving me the same. Thank you for rescuing me and moving me from rags to riches.

Let There Be Light

Mistie House

In the beginning

When God made all of Creation, He dispelled darkness with a spoken command.

He called out into the darkness,

"Let there be light,"

And it was so.

When the fall of man came upon us, God created a way for us.

He called His Son to dispel the power of darkness by sending the light to us,

So that in Him

Light could shine through us.

He commanded,

"Let there be light,"

And it was so.

In His Word, God has spoken the command for us to dispel the darkness in this world.

He has called us to become a new creation

Salt and light for our generation.

Emergence

He commands,

"Let there be light,"

And may it be so.

In the end

God will speak the command to dispel darkness once and for all.

He will call His Son to reappear

And on that day

Darkness

Will forever

Disappear!

For the Lord God is the light

And all will see

The glory of God

Who gives us light

And the Lamb

Who is the Lamp

Forever…forever…forevermore!

The command is coming,

"Let there be light,"

And it will be so.

About the Author

Mistie House is an everyday Christian woman who is a loving wife, creative mom, and treasured daughter of the King. She has authored and illustrated the children's book *The Father's Princess: The Story of the White Daisy*. Mistie is also the host of the Beloved Bride podcast, a women's Bible study group leader, blogger, and ambassador for Esther Calling. Her passion is to guide gals to walk with the King of kings through her testimony, teaching, and storytelling. She lives in Amarillo, Texas with her amazing husband Chris, and is a mother of two precious daughters, her shining jewels. Connect with her on a daily basis:

Blog: www.mistiehouseauthor.com

Facebook: www.Facebook.com/mistiehouse.author

Instagram:@MistieHouse

Emergence

Notes

(Endnotes)

1. ¹The Brothers Grimm, *Snow White* (Grimm's Fairy Tales, December 20, 1812).

2. ² *Snow White and the Seven Dwarfs*, Directed by David Hand, Wilfred Jackson, Ben Sharpsteen, Perce Pearce, Larry Morey, William Cottrell, (Walt Disney Productions, 1937 Film), DVD.

3. ³ Jimmy Evans, *Ten Steps Toward Christ: Journey to the Heart of God* (Gateway Press, February 15, 2018), 15, 51-52, 166. permission for excerpts given February, 27, 2020.

4. ⁴ Jimmy Evans, *Marriage on the Rock 25th Anniversary: The Comprehensive Guide to a Solid, Healthy and Lasting Marriage* (XO Publishing, August 27, 2019).

5. ⁵ Jimmy Witcher, *Kingdom Come: Living in Heaven on Earth* (Trinity Fellowship Church, July 6, 2019), 66.

6. ⁶ *Kingdom of Heaven*, Directed by Ridley Scott, (Production by Scott Free Productions, Studio Babelsberg, May 6, 2005 USA), DVD.

7. ⁷ Trinity Fellowship Church, *Zion 2015: Chuck Pierce*, https://s3.amazonaws.com/media.tfc.org/chuck-pierce-zion-2015.pdf?mtime=20160329171506

8. ⁸ MarriageToday.com, *How To Think When Life Stinks Audio Series* (Marriage Today 2015), https://marriagetoday2015.myshopify.com/collections/all/products/how-to-think-when-life-stinks-audio-series.

9. ⁹ Debbie Alsdorf, A Woman Who Trust God: Finding the Peace you Long For (Revell, November 1, 2011).

10. ¹⁰ Hannah Hurnard, *Hinds Feet on High Places* (Wilder Publications, April 19, 2012).

11 [11] Crosswalk.com, *A Prayer for Your Prodigal,* https://www.crosswalk.com/devotionals/your-daily-prayer/a-prayer-for-your-prodigal-your-daily-prayer-june-29-2016.html

12 [12] *The Hobbit: An Unexpected Journey*, Directed by Peter Jackson, (Produced by New Line Cinema, Metro-Goldwyn-Mayer, WingNut Films, December 6, 2012 USA), DVD.

13 [13] Flower Meanings, *Daisy Flower- Meaning, Symbolism and Colors*, https://flowermeanings.org/daisy-flower-meaning/

14 [14] FTDFresh, *Daisy Meaning and Symbolism* (April 13, 2016), https://www.ftd.com/blog/share/daisy-meaning-and-symbolism.

15 [15] Reference.com, *What Is the Spiritual Meaning of Sand Dollars?,* https://www.reference.com/world-view/spiritual-meaning-sand-dollars-ac79cee168384917

16 [16] Margaret C. Gallitzin, *The Legend of the Sand Dollar* (December 21, 2013), https://www.traditioninaction.org/religious/f024_SandDollar.htm

17 [17] Lisa Bevere, *Girls with Swords: How to Carry Your Cross Like a Hero* (WaterBrook, February, 18, 2014).

18 [18] *She-Ra: Princess of Power*, Directed by Gwen Wetzler, (Production by Filmation Associates, Mattel, September 9, 1985).

19 [19] *The Secret Garden*, Directed by Agnieszka Holland, (Production by American Zoetrope,

Warner Bros. Family Entertainment, August 13, 1993 USA), DVD.

20 [20] *The Shack*, Directed by Stuart Hazeldine, (Production by Gil Netter Productions

Windblown Media, March 3, 2017 USA), DVD.

21 [21] *The Lord of the Rings: The Fellowship of the Ring*, Directed by Peter Jackson, (Production by New Line Cinema, WingNut Films, December 19, 2001 USA), DVD.

22 [22] *The Wizard of Oz*, Directed by Victor Fleming, (Production by Metro-Goldwyn-Mayer, August 25, 1939), DVD.

23 [23] Sheri Rose Shepherd, *His Little Princess: Treasured Letters from Your King* (Multnomah February 3, 2006), HISPRINCESS.com, permission for excerpt given February 22, 2020.

24 [24] Nintendo, *Super Mario Bros*. (September 13, 1985), Directed and Produced by Shigeru Miyamoto.

www.ingramcontent.com/pod-product-compliance
Lightning Source LLC
Chambersburg PA
CBHW060512080526
44586CB00012B/462